FURTHER EDUCATION IN THE UNITED KINGDOM

FURTHER EDUCATION IN THE UNITED KINGDOM

SECOND EDITION

VINCE HALL

Collins Educational • The Staff College

This edition published in 1994 by

Collins Educational
An imprint of HarperCollins*Publishers*
77–85 Fulham Palace Road
Hammersmith
London
W6 8JB

and

The Staff College
Coombe Lodge
Blagdon
Bristol
BS18 6RG

First edition published in 1990 by The Staff College

British Library Cataloguing in Publication Data is available from the British Library

ISBN 0–00–322403–1

Typeset by Avonset, Midsomer Norton
Cover by David Jones
Printed in Great Britain by Butler and Tanner, Frome, Somerset.

Contents

List of figures   vi
Preface   vii

Section One: What is an FE college?
Chapter 1   The development of further education   2
Chapter 2   Further education colleges   9
Chapter 3   The legal basis of further education   18

Section Two: Who are the FE students?
Chapter 4   Further education students and curriculum   34
Chapter 5   Vocational students   47
Chapter 6   Pre-vocational students   61
Chapter 7   Academic students   69
Chapter 8   Adult and continuing students   82
Chapter 9   Special educational needs students   95

Section Three: Who makes further education work?
Chapter 10   The planning of FE   104
Chapter 11   The financing of FE   118
Chapter 12   The governance of FE   130
Chapter 13   The management of FE   139
Chapter 14   The teaching of FE   145

Section Four: Where are the boundaries of FE?
Chapter 15   Locating the boundaries   154
Chapter 16   FE and the labour market   158
Chapter 17   FE and training structures   165
Chapter 18   FE and skills training   180
Chapter 19   FE and youth training   193
Chapter 20   FE and adult training   205
Chapter 21   FE and higher education   212
Chapter 22   FE and schools   227

Appendices
Appendix 1   References   242
Appendix 2   Glossary of terms   251
Appendix 3   Abbreviations and acronyms   253
Appendix 4   The United Kingdom and its education system   259

Index   268

List of figures

Figure 1:   FEFC breakdown of mode of attendance of students   34

Figure 2:   Number of UK students in further education in 1989/90 by mode of attendance (thousands)   35

Figure 3:   Participation rates of UK students in further education in 1989/90 by mode of attendance (percentages)   35

Figure 4:   UK students enrolled in further education by type of course in 1989/90 (thousands). Inc overseas students   38

Figure 5:   United Kingdom enrolments by examining and validating body in 1989 (thousands)   39

Figure 6:   Further Education Funding Council criteria for assessing eligibility under Schedule 2 of the FHE Act   41

Figure 7:   City and Guilds Institute qualification levels   55

Figure 8:   GCSE major subject entries (1992)   72

Figure 9:   A and AS level entries (1992 provisional results) arranged according to the most popular A level subjects   77

Figure 10:   Contrast in colleges pre- and post-incorporation   140

Figure 11:   Population aged 16 and over: by occupational grouping (percentages)   160

Figure 12:   Employment in the UK (1988)   162

Figure 13:   Educational qualifications of the workforce (1991). Percentages   163

Figure 14:   Employees of working age receiving job-related training in the last four weeks by standard occupational group   184

Figure 15:   Employees of working age receiving job-related training in the last four weeks by industry and type of training   185

Figure 16:   Employees of working age receiving off-the-job training during the last four weeks by location of training   186

Figure 17:   Proportion of employees of working age receiving job-related training in the last four weeks by social class   187

Figure 18:   Training credits (issues and starts), December 1991   195

Preface

Sometimes when I have sat on an Intercity train from Leeds to London amongst a group of people who know each other but are not known to me, they often seem to speak in a kind of special code, even though they are speaking English. It is usually because they are part of some professional group off to the capital city for a meeting and they are communicating in their own shorthand. I would be the first to acknowledge that if the experience was repeated with a different person and a group of further education managers the result would be the same. Further education can be as inaccessible as a lot of other professional areas.

As the principal of a college of further education, it is easy for me to talk to a group of colleagues and quickly understand the gist of what is being said. To the outsider, further education can seem complex, jargon-ridden, inward looking and constantly changing. In writing this book I have drawn on my experiences of working in five colleges of further education over a 25 year period to present a clear explanation of further education in the United Kingdom.

I have tried to cater for a variety of readers. Some will have little or no knowledge of the United Kingdom education system. In this group I would include the many English speaking visitors who come here on study visits or exchanges. Other people may know something about the UK education system in general but not further education in particular. In this category I would include the general reader who has been educated in the UK but without attending a college of further education, or a person who has worked in education outside of FE colleges. There will be other readers, such as college governors, who have a partial knowledge of further education, arising from their experience of one college, or local councillors who know only the college or colleges within their area. Finally, many student teachers are trying to find a coherent source for their study of FE.

If any of these groups of readers were trying to find an answer to the question, What is an FE college?, they might have difficulty in knowing where to look for information in the many and varied documents that are available and would certainly not be able to lay their hands on an up-to-date guide. This book tries to give both the general reader and the specialist an insight into the world of further education. Four appendices at the end of the book provide: further sources of information; a glossary of terms; a list of abbreviations and acronyms used in further education; and a brief description of the United Kingdom's geography, system of government and education. The last appendix is aimed particularly at foreign visitors.

The first edition of this book was originally commissioned by The Staff College as an update of a pamphlet which had become out of date. The pamphlet, **The FE system of England and Wales** (Russell 1979) at the time sold more copies than any other of their publications. This second edition has been written to cover the massive changes brought about by the removal of further education colleges from local government and their funding by national councils. I hope readers will find it as useful as the first edition.

Acknowledgements

The first edition of this book was commissioned by Jean Finlayson, the former Publications Editor of The Staff College, who is now retired. I could not have written it without her unfailing support and wry humour. In its final form, it was shaped by Geoff Melling, The Staff College's Director, and Fred Flower, who both helped me with the structure and various amendments. A range of other people gave me assistance and advice, particularly colleagues in Scotland and Northern Ireland, where I rapidly came to understand the English aphorism *same but different.*

For the second edition, I have largely relied on my own files for updating. I have used extensive cuttings from the **Times Educational** and **Higher Educational Supplements**, **Education** magazine, the **Educa** digest, the Guardian Education supplement, etc. I have also gathered information from a range of bodies such as the further education funding councils, the Polytechnic and Colleges Funding Council, the Higher Education Funding Council, the Further Education Units, The Staff College, Association of Principals of Colleges, the National Association of Teachers in Further and Higher Education, the Association of College Management, the Training, Enterprise and Education Directorate, training and enterprise councils, etc.: in other words, all the paper that goes through a principal's intray. The Staff College library was very helpful in finding information for me. I have also taken up comments of reviewers of the first edition.

A major source of information has been the English Further Education Funding Council. The council has blitzed colleges with questionnaires, circulars, press releases, statistical bulletins, etc., which has been useful for an author compiling information on incorporation if not for a principal suffering from information overload.

It was not an easy period in the run up to incorporation to find the time to prepare this second edition and I would like to thank my senior colleagues at Dewsbury College for all their support while I was trying to finish the writing. I am also grateful to Pippa Toogood, my editor at The Staff College, for her support and help as well as her patience with my excuses as to why the presentation of the final manuscript was always being delayed.

Finally, I would like to thank the members of my family for their understanding during the period that I have been chained to my computer in the early hours trying to rewrite this book.

Vince Hall

Section One
What is an FE college?

Chapter 1   *The development of further education*

Chapter 2   *Further education colleges*

Chapter 3   *The legal basis of further education*

Chapter 1
The development of further education

At the start of the last decade of the 20th century, the Government decided to discontinue local government control of further education colleges, ending 90 years of history. The year 1993 marked the establishment of national systems of further education in England, Wales and Scotland. The creation of the new sectors included the former sixth form colleges as further education institutions. There are 465 colleges of further education and sixth form colleges in England which are core-funded by the English Further Education Funding Council (FEFC). Wales has 36 colleges of further education, while Scotland has 46 and Northern Ireland 24. There are also about 130 small private colleges in the United Kingdom, which are limited to a few areas of vocational provision.

Most further education colleges (unlike the sixth form colleges) are comprehensive and provide a wide range of further and adult education courses, together with some higher education. A few colleges remain vocationally specialist, mainly the 50-odd colleges of agriculture and art and design. Every city or town of any size has at least one further education college; some towns have more than one and the larger cities may have half a dozen or more, although the current trend of colleges merging has reduced the numbers. Indeed, over a 20 year period the number of further education colleges fell from 687 in 1970/71 to 375 in 1989/90.

There is great variety in the way colleges are organised but the basic courses offered are very much the same. The differences between institutions arise from the size, physical layout and the specialist courses which give a distinct flavour to each particular college. Colleges often seem unusual to the visitor with a school or higher education background because of all the different kinds of student attendance. While there is a core of full-time students, the majority of students do not study on a full-time basis. They can come on day release from work, attend for a morning, afternoon and/or evening once a week or even for part of a weekend. Other students come to college for most of the week on a short-term basis in blocks of time, or for a short course or on a sandwich of work and study.

A range of other factors can give a different feel to any individual college. For example:

- Is it a small, medium or large college?
- Is the college in the town centre or is it on a green field site?
- Is it in an urban area with good transport networks or a rural area?
- Is there one main campus or a series of split sites?

- Is the adult education mounted largely on the main site or is it mainly in outside centres in other establishments?
- Are the daytime students mainly 16 and 17 year olds?
- Are there distinctive local industries whose needs are being met?
- Is the college catering for large groups of students with disabilities?
- Is the college in an area of high ethnic minority settlement?
- Is there an extensive child care facility?

To answer the question, What is an FE college?, asked in this section of the book, this chapter contains some basic facts about the historical development of further education. Chapter 2 deals with different types of college and Chapter 3 looks at the legal basis of further education.

The comprehensive vocational nature of colleges of further education gives them an unusual character which is not normally found in other industrialised countries. This is in contrast to sixth form colleges which would be understandable to someone from mainland Europe familiar with academic pre-university institutions.

Most colleges of further education have grown from either the former mechanics institutes or the technical schools. Vocational education in the United Kingdom grew significantly after industrialisation in the late 18th century. The growth of technological development, coupled with a climate of self-help encouraged by the Industrial Revolution, led to the rapid development of evening classes in mechanics institutes where workers could improve their basic skills, learn new scientific and technological knowledge and broaden their minds. The first institute was formally constituted in 1821 in Edinburgh. By the middle of the 19th century more than 600,000 people were in membership of 610 mechanics institutes, although this was followed by a period of gradual decline.

Examining and validating boards were formed at local and national levels to establish recognised standards for the growing number of students who wanted accreditation of their study and the boards have played a major part in further education ever since. The first national examining board was formed under the auspices of the Royal Society of Arts (RSA) in 1856. The RSA handed over responsibility for technical examining to the City and Guilds of London Institute (CGLI) in 1879, while keeping its remit for courses in the business and secretarial sectors.

In the first part of this century, basic technical education was centred on the technical school. Until the 1960s the existence of a tripartite system of schools (grammar, technical and secondary modern) meant that those pupils who were not academic high flyers on their way to higher education, did not get an academic education. The vocational work in the technical school or secondary modern was considered by many to be a second class substitute.

If school leavers were bright, working class males, the best they could hope for was an apprenticeship in engineering or construction. If they were less able, or less motivated, they would end up in semi-skilled operative or unskilled labouring jobs. Many of the girls would aim to get clerical or secretarial training for an office job. The only apprenticeships for girls were associated with jobs such as hairdressing or nursing.

Most of the education and training for young people and adults before 1940 was done in evening classes at the local 'tech'. The technical college was essentially an institution for vocational education for the employed. The inter-war economic depression caused a slump in United Kingdom industry and commerce and a large number of unemployed people, including those with skills training, were available in the labour market. Many British employers saw no need to carry on their apprentice training and this ensured that there was no strong tradition of day release from work. Those workers who were motivated to improve their training and qualifications attended evening classes until they achieved what they wanted. This was particularly true of those young adults (men in the main) who wanted to get the Higher National Certificate (HNC), a sub-degree qualification which was highly valued in some sections of industry. Students would attend classes after work several nights a week to complete an Ordinary National Certificate (ONC) and then carry on to the Higher National. The attrition rate was high. Some who survived the ONC/HNC route could take up to seven years to complete it, because of the pressures of marriage and child rearing or changes of job.

A major expansion of technical education came during the Second World War. The number of workers in daytime release to technical colleges rose from 42,000 at the beginning of the war to 150,000 by the end. Intensive wartime training meant that day release from work replaced voluntary attendance at evening classes as the main mode of attendance for vocational education. The 'techs' were flexible enough to rise to this challenge. The alternative mode of provision for intensive instruction was the government training centres, which expanded quickly up to 1945, but were run down after the end of the war.

Post-war development

Day release to attend college for training carried on after the end of the war, predominantly for apprentices in manual trades, until by 1957 more than 400,000 employees were being released from work for part-time training in college. By this time the United Kingdom had recovered from wartime devastation and the economy had grown strong again. The continuation of this strength partly depended upon a sufficient pool of trained workers for employers to draw from, but the supply was beginning to dry up. There was national concern over growing skill shortages and unfilled vacancies. A government enquiry at the time decided that technical colleges should be the main vehicle in the public sector for dealing with these shortages and that possible alternative training institutions, such as the French model of apprentice training centres, should be the responsibility of industry – not government. It would be true to say that by and large, outside of the main manufacturing companies, apprentice schools did not flourish. Where they did prosper, a large part of the training was done in conjunction with the local college. These factors helped to fuel the growth of vocational further education in colleges.

Changes during the 1960s and '70s

Vocational further education in the 1960s was strongly influenced by the statutory industrial training boards which were set up to increase skills training in industry and commerce and to ensure that all employers paid towards the cost of training within their industry through the levy/grant system. The initial result was that more apprentices were released from work to go to college. In some industries, where training was intense, apprentices did their first year of training off-the-job and a large part of this was carried out in the technical college.

The growth of colleges centred on vocational education slowed down dramatically when a world economic recession began in the early 1970s. Many college engineering departments, in particular, went into decline. Most colleges compensated for this in the 1970s and '80s by offering courses for unemployed adults and young people taking part in government training and employment schemes. This led to many more jobless people coming into colleges for vocational courses. A wide range of government schemes was introduced in the 1980s, the most significant being Youth Training (YT) and Employment Training (ET) for adults. FE colleges provided much of their off-the-job training.

Another factor compensating for the decline in vocational work was the growth of academic courses. Until the 1960s when the grammar, technical and secondary modern schools began to be replaced by comprehensive schools, those who had not gone to a grammar school were deprived of the opportunity of academic study through GCE Advanced levels. Adults who wanted a second chance to improve their academic qualifications had begun to do this through the technical college. As the number of adults grew, they were joined by an increasing number of young people who did not like the school milieu and preferred to study in the more adult environment of a college. This growth of academic education in further education was helped by the failure of some comprehensive schools to build up a viable post-16 provision. Some local authorities began to think about removing sixth forms from schools and merging them to constitute sixth form colleges, or combining sixth forms with an FE college to form a tertiary college which provided both academic and vocational education for young people after leaving school at 16.

The 1980s

During the 1980s the Government showed concern about the relatively poor levels and standards of education and training in the United Kingdom. A number of studies unfavourably compared UK education and training with that of major competitor countries. The best known study, **Competence and competition** (NEDO/MSC 1984), showed that, at the time, in contrast to 28 per cent of pupils going on to higher education in West Germany, only 14 per cent did so in the United Kingdom. One-third of German children left school with the equivalent of at least grade C GCSE (the old O level pass) in the core subjects of German, mathematics and a foreign language; in England only 12 per cent did so. The number of days of release for off-the-job training for employees in the UK was only one-quarter of that in the then West German Federal Republic. These are only a few of the findings, not only in relation to Germany but also in comparison with other major industrial nations such as Japan and the United States.

Following the research reports, the Government introduced a number of changes in education and training. For example, the Technical and Vocational Education Initiative (TVEI) was phased in for the 14–18 year old age cohort in England, Wales and Scotland. This scheme was aimed at raising the status of vocational education in schools. A second example was the plan to make colleges of further education more responsive to local labour market needs. Each local education authority (LEA) had to prepare a development plan for the local office of the government-sponsored national training agency (the Manpower Services Commission, the forerunner of the current Training, Enterprise and Education Directorate of the Employment Department). In this plan, the LEA would have to show that the colleges in its area would provide vocational education related to the needs of industry and commerce. To enforce this process, up to a quarter of the central government grants provided to local education authorities to finance their colleges was put under MSC control, and these grants were only passed on to the LEA on production of a satisfactory plan for their area.

The **Education Reform Act** 1988 brought further changes by redefining the further education sector. For the previous 40 years, the 1944 **Education Act** had placed a duty on local education authorities to provide further education, but this further education was loosely defined and included what is now known as higher education. It was thought that there should not be a strict divide between further and higher education; the idea of a continuum between the two was often referred to as the 'seamless robe'. To distinguish higher and further education courses, the terms advanced and non-advanced were used. Four decades later, the 1988 Act omitted the term 'advanced further education' and instead, for the first time, legally defined public sector higher education outside of the universities. This left the use of the term 'further education' solely for non-advanced college work, so the now superfluous adjective, non-advanced, was dropped.

Further education is now delineated by the level of courses it would normally offer. (These courses are explained in later chapters.) Thus *further education is defined as those courses at (or below) the level of the General Certificate of Education Advanced level or the Scottish Certificate of Education Higher grade, or the Business and Technology Education Council National awards or the Scottish Vocational Education Council National awards*. The general title of a college at this level is college of further education (CFE), but as the names of colleges are not laid down by statute, colleges can, and do, use all kinds of different titles – which can be confusing for the visitor.

The description **maintained** was applied to further education when the 1988 Education Reform Act came into force. The word 'maintained' came from the schools sector to designate an educational institution funded by the local education authority. At that time the term distinguished local education authority further education colleges from those that provided higher education under the supervision of the former Polytechnics and Colleges Funding Council (PCFC) in England, or under the national Education Department in Scotland, or the independent colleges in the small UK private sector.

The 1990s

At the beginning of the 1990s, the climate of government opinion towards colleges changed again. Colleges began to concentrate even more on an increasing core of full-time students arising from the Government's desire to increase full-time participation rates, which was reinforced by the continuing recession and a lack of suitable jobs or apprenticeships for young people. Thus the proportion of students attending on release from industry fell considerably and further education colleges became much more like other northern European institutions providing for the post-16 age range.

In addition to the changing character of colleges, the Government altered the method of college funding. The 1992 **Further and Higher Education Acts** covering England, Wales and Scotland launched the new national further education funding councils, which took over the financing of colleges from the local education authorities, ending nearly a century of local support. Thus the use of the phrase maintained FE was shortlived as LEAs lost control. Although it was denied that the new funding councils had a planning role, it is likely that they will have great influence in shaping new national systems of further education. It cannot be said that this was done in a very positive manner by the Conservative government of the time, because it appeared to stem mainly from a desire to transfer funding from local taxation (the unpopular poll tax) to national funding.

In addition to the growing numbers of full-time students, further education, as it is constituted in the 1990s, still provides vocational training for the employed, together with training for the unemployed under government schemes. Young people who have not made firm career decisions can take vocational preparation courses. Most colleges offer a variety of academic courses and a programme of adult education not necessarily related to employment needs. Finally, a growing number of young people and adults with special educational needs are becoming students in further education.

These trends are explained further in the next two chapters. Chapter 2 describes different models of a college of further education. Chapter 3, which looks at the legal requirements on which a college is established and operated, will appeal particularly to the specialist reader or the person who is required to have an understanding of this subject.

Chapter 2
Further education colleges

Further education colleges are not standard, bureaucratically defined institutions but rather each is a product of its own history, the policies of its previous governing bodies and local education authority, and the local demand from employers and communities. A typical college might have been influenced by factors such as the following:

- strong departments have grown quickly in the past, either based on market demand or industrial training board (ITB) and local large company support;
- a range of provision for the unemployed has developed through various government schemes;
- an expanding general education portfolio of courses has reflected both a drift of students away from school sixth forms and an increase in adults returning to learning;
- tighter local and national funding has forced a reliance on an increasing mixture of funding sources;
- equal opportunities policies have helped to increase participation of women, people with disabilities and those from ethnic minorities.

The further education curriculum is discussed in Section 2 of the book, but it is important to highlight at this stage the major influence of the examining and validating bodies on the courses that colleges offer. FE institutions have, in the main, promoted the qualifications of external bodies, rather than created their own units of learning. Students thus buy into the progression routes and status of the external body on the recommendation of college staff. Indeed, the lists of qualifications under Schedule 2 of the Further and Higher Education Act 1992 that can be funded by the Further Education Funding Council, virtually rules out FE colleges offering their own home-grown courses. This is in contrast to the higher education sector, where institutions, once approved as awarding bodies, can issue their own degrees.

The progression routes through the national qualification levels have not always been clear, so the rationalisation carried out by the National Council for Vocational Qualifications (NCVQ) has had a simplifying effect on what colleges offer to their students. As colleges have improved their guidance systems and offer better facilities for the accreditation of prior learning or experience, the time taken to obtain a qualification can be reduced, or can be slowed down so that students can pick up credit for parts of a course packaged into separate modules, at a pace which they can determine depending on their personal circumstances.

Most colleges have grown to their present size as a result of a pragmatic and entrepreneurial attitude to student recruitment during the expansionary phases of further education. Heads of department and their staffs have looked for students wherever they could find them and have trawled employers in search of possible recruits. When new courses have been introduced by examining and validating bodies, or employers have needed staff training in new areas, colleges have provided the service required. Over the last 30 years the main thrust has been at departmental level leading to many colleges being a federation of strong departments. Although this effect weakened considerably during the last half of the 1980s due to stronger college management control of the overall portfolio of courses, the balance of the curriculum in any college can be distorted by the efforts of energetic heads of department or school or programme manager, depending on what form of organisation is current.

Labour market and community influence

The local labour market has strongly influenced the balance of vocational provision. The growth of engineering and construction training in the 1960s meant that these departments (particularly engineering) were the strongest and most powerful in colleges up to the mid-'70s. The decline in UK manufacturing industry in the 1980s resulted in a shift towards the service industries, which are more diffuse and unregulated in terms of training, together with a diversification into general or adult education. The growth of academic courses has turned many technical colleges into much more broadly-based colleges of further education. LEA tertiary reorganisation, particularly the establishment of tertiary colleges, has led to a large increase in the numbers of A level students in FE, many of whom would previously have been in sixth forms. In community colleges the emphasis is on bringing in more adults to reflect the age spectrum of the local community, with the side effect that these mature students dilute some of the effects of a largely teenage student body. In the sixth form colleges, which came into the FE sector in 1993, the previous academic base is being widened to offer a greater breadth of provision.

If there is a tradition in further education, it is one of responding to community demand. A major part of this demand is from industry and commerce. FE's responsiveness to market forces has led to the filling of gaps left by other, more high profile, institutions. Thus, the rapid post-war expansion of further education has been more haphazard than planned. To critics of further education, more used to a school or university ethos, it has meant that colleges have not had a strong cultural or intellectual tradition which could have provided a framework for the creation of curriculum balance within the institution. The sixth form colleges, which have been much narrower in their offering, have fitted more into this tradition.

Further education colleges have, in the main, responded pragmatically to local demand. There has been little attempt by either national or local government to force colleges to teach within any kind of plan for national needs, except in the emergency of wartime. Some local education authorities have tried to persuade their colleges to adopt a broad-based philosophy of education and training for all, not always successfully. As there has not been any enthusiasm to raise the school leaving age above the age of 16, young people have had a variety of options open to them within a range of institutions. None of these options was covered by any kind of national curriculum, as is the case for secondary schools. However, in the 1980s, with high youth unemployment, further education started to provide in a substantial way more broad-based education for those students without clear vocational or educational objectives.

The last five years have seen increasing pressures on colleges to be all things to all people, often against a background of conflicting messages from separate Departments of State for Education and Employment, and different sections of local government. The result of this lack of clear guidelines has been a complex and varied curriculum. A college's prospectus of full-time courses or free newspaper containing adult education courses offers an enormous variety.

The confusion of names

The previous lack until now of a national model for colleges of further education in terms of course provision, financing or even a standard system of names, has confused many people who come into contact with them. Up until the early 1990s, colleges were an integral part of local government. With the advent of the funding councils in 1993, the colleges are more like a series of independent, medium-sized companies going their own ways within a national funding framework. Again it was only in 1993 that colleges adopted a separate legal identity. Although the 1988 and 1992 FE Acts clarified the legal definition of further education, they did not change the many versions of the titles of further education colleges.

Many further education colleges are still called 'technical colleges' or 'technical and art colleges', titles which date from the time when they offered virtually nothing but technical education or had merged with an art college to provide art and vocational education. Colleges which have a large amount of adult education sometimes call themselves 'community colleges'.

Some further education institutions simply take the name of the local town. Others call themselves 'institutes' rather than colleges, either when they offer virtually all adult education or when they provide a lot of higher education. Finally, where a college has been formed from an amalgamation of local sixth forms and a further education college, it is often called a 'tertiary college'. These tertiary colleges only exist in England, with the exception of two in Wales.

A typical college

Although colleges vary enormously in their range of courses, a picture of a typical college of further education in England or Wales can be given for illustrative purposes from surveys by Her Majesty's Inspectorate (HMI). It would have at least 1,000 full-time students and 3,000 part-time day and evening students. The majority of full-time students would be in the 16 to 20 age group but part-time students cover a much wider range and are mainly adults. This typical college might provide the following courses:

(a) post-16 vocational preparation courses, mainly coming under the Diploma of Vocational Education or the Certificate of Pre-vocational Education;

(b) vocational courses on both a full-time and part-time basis including integrated first year training for engineering and construction apprentices and college-based youth training;

(c) full-time and part-time general education courses leading to GCSE and GCE A/AS level, or access courses giving entry to higher education;

(d) vocational courses involving some GCSE and A/AS level provision – a mixture of (b) and (c);

(e) adult education recreational and non-vocational courses, offered mainly during the evening;

(f) off-the-job vocational education and training within Youth Training and Employment Training, mainly on a part-time basis;

(g) higher education courses mainly on a part-time day and evening basis;

(h) full-cost short courses for local industry and commerce covering a wide variety of subjects and skills;

(i) courses for young people and adults with special educational needs;

(j) provision in penal institutions.

Most further education colleges serve their own local catchment areas, which typically have a radius of between 15 and 25 kilometres. The population covered might range from 50,000 to 500,000. Part-time students on specialist vocational courses connected with their employment may travel greater distances when the appropriate course is not available locally. Many colleges operate link courses for local school children to sample vocational specialisms and a few have collaborative arrangements with local sixth forms for 16–19 provision but, for the most part, colleges operate independently of local secondary schools. Where there are tertiary colleges, the secondary schools may act as feeder schools. In the past the local education authority may have occasionally requested that a college did not operate certain courses which were already being run in a neighbouring institution, and it remains to be seen if the funding councils will adopt the same attitude. In the main, however, colleges enjoy considerable autonomy in planning, marketing and implementing their courses.

Choices at 16 plus

The United Kingdom schools system has a natural break at 16, after which it is no longer a legal requirement to attend school. If students want to stay on in full-time education, they have a choice between the school sixth form, a sixth form college operated under further education regulations, or a college of further education. In some areas all three kinds of institution operate in competition; in others, sixth forms have been closed, sixth form colleges have not been established or have not survived, and all fifth year pupils who do not want to drop out of education go to the college. Such a college is technically known as a tertiary college, because it is the only local institution offering full-time education for 16–18 year olds in the area, i.e. it provides for the tertiary stage of education.

Before describing tertiary colleges further, I will briefly describe what happens where sixth forms and sixth form colleges exist. Pupils in England, Wales and Northern Ireland who want to stay on at school after the compulsory fifth year go into the sixth form. The sixth form is based around the two year GCE Advanced level course, which forms a major route to higher education, a job or professional training. Pupils can also stay on for just one year to do a vocational preparation certificate, GCSE re-sits, programmes offered by vocational examining bodies, or perhaps one year GCE Advanced Supplementary (AS) levels.

In Scotland, the Scottish Highers (which are akin to AS levels) can be taken over one year in what is called S5, or two years in S5 and S6, if better grades are needed for entry into higher education. The opportunity to study for the Certificate in Sixth Year Studies in S6, after one year spent on SCE Highers in S5, has not been widely taken up.

Most UK secondary schools still have some form of post-16 arrangement. Although the total number of sixth forms is in decline, the sixth form is still the most common form of post-16 provision in terms of numbers of pupils staying on in education beyond the compulsory school attendance age. In 1980 there were 2,487 maintained schools with sixth forms but this had dropped to 1,998 in 1991 including sixth form colleges.

15 per cent of sixth formers in state schools in January 1991 were taught in single sex schools.

The 1988 Education Reform Act distinguished sixth forms/sixth form colleges from further education institutions on the basis that they did not provide a significant amount of part-time education to senior pupils over compulsory school age or full-time or part-time education to people of 19 years or over. The 1992 Further and Higher Education Act brought sixth form colleges into the FE sector.

In the academic year 1991/92, 67 per cent of 16 year olds in the United Kingdom stayed on in full-time education (DFE 1992a). This represents an increase of 19 percentage points over the last four years (DFE 1992a). The proportion of young people who opt to go into a college environment is increasing. The government has not tried to influence the decision of pupils, despite several reports which have highlighted the drawbacks of a restricted range of subject choice in smaller sixth forms or the better atmosphere and facilities of the tertiary college, which has been shown to enhance participation rates.

In curriculum terms, the General Certificate of Education Advanced level and Scottish Higher Grade are the major common qualifications offered by both schools and colleges. Colleges in England, Wales and Northern Ireland – together with larger schools – are usually able to provide a choice from about 15 A level subjects, with up to 30 on offer in the bigger colleges. An HMI report on secondary schools in the 1980s (HMI 1988a) highlighted the effects of falling school rolls on sixth forms with small, isolated teaching groups and less choice of options. The system of schools working together – school consortia – to provide less popular subjects was not generally found to be a successful solution.

In Scotland the colleges offer SCE Highers, and some colleges also offer a smaller number of GCE A levels for those wanting a higher education course or job outside Scotland.

As both the numbers of schools in total and the proportion of schools with sixth forms declined in the 1980s, there was a corresponding growth of competing institutions – one of which being the sixth form college. At the beginning of the 1990s there were 113 sixth form colleges in England and two in Wales, but none in Scotland or Northern Ireland. This type of institution is usually formed by merging a number of sixth forms into one college, leaving the schools from which they came to provide for secondary pupils up to the age of 16. The sixth form college has been organised under the regulations governing the operation of schools and could be seen as really a very large sixth form fed by 11–16 secondary schools. Bringing sixth forms into the FE sector means that they should be become more diversified. The sixth form college can offer a large option choice and provide a more adult atmosphere without many of the petty rules that schools impose on younger children. The sixth form college should be distinguished from the tertiary college, which has always offered both sixth form and further education courses.

Tertiary colleges

As was mentioned above, the title tertiary college was usually given to an FE college which was designated by its local education authority as the major or sole provider of post-16 education in a particular area. Although this minimises competition from other institutions, it does not rule out the existence of a sixth form or sixth form college operated by a denominational body such as the Church of England or the Roman Catholic Church. Similarly, schools or colleges just across the boundary of a neighbouring local authority could provide a counter-attraction.

The first tertiary college was founded in Devon in 1970. By 1992 there were 63 tertiary colleges in England and Wales. As HMI found when they did their inspection of 10 tertiary colleges (HMI 1989b), not all tertiary colleges are called tertiary colleges. In fact only one used the word tertiary, while seven simply used the word college and two were called community college. Of the 10 colleges inspected by HMI, the oldest was established in 1973 on premises comprising four former secondary grammar schools and a technical college. The remainder were set up between 1982 and 1986; three had been sixth form colleges and after further reorganisation became tertiary colleges. None of the colleges occupied premises which had been purpose-built as tertiary institutions.

Post-16 reorganisation has increased significantly in recent years. This growth has been gradual since successive governments have been reluctant to intervene in the process; in fact, some critics believe the Conservative government at times in the 1980s showed deliberate antipathy to major schemes of tertiary reorganisation. The Government instructed civil servants to retain 'sixth forms of proven worth' in any reorganisations. There was a major expansion in the numbers of sixth form colleges in the mid-to-late 1970s, followed by a growth in tertiary colleges in the 1980s. The main factors resulting in reorganisation were demographic changes, dwindling sixth forms, the desire of many students for a more mature environment, and pressures for a broader curriculum.

In the five years up to the 1988 Education Reform Act, the trend was for an increasing switch from sixth form colleges to tertiary colleges. Of the 40 new colleges opening in the period 1983–88, 30 were tertiary and in 1988 all 10 new colleges were tertiary. Even before their incorporation in 1993, some sixth form colleges became tertiary colleges, encouraged by the more flexible format and wider mix of students such a college could offer. It looks as though the Government, while protecting sixth forms of 'proven worth', is also sympathetic to sixth form colleges, which are more efficient in terms of pupil:teacher ratios. The advocates of a break at 16 followed by entry to a college, whether tertiary or sixth form, have suggested that this will increase staying on rates. A survey in 1988 by the **Times Educational Supplement** gave examples to support this view (Nash 1988).

Community colleges

The other force at work on further education colleges was the merger of the separate LEA community education service with local colleges to form community colleges. The community or continuing education service covers around 1.5 million adults nationally and consists mainly of leisure, recreational or semi-vocational courses. Where the adult service is offered by the college, the vast majority of its student registrations will be adult – even though the day-time visitor might find the student common room full of teenagers. This mixture of adults and young people reflects the community at large and shows a maturity in the nature of the institution.

It is my view that the 1990s may well be dominated by the creation of community colleges where they do not already exist. In many senses this could be seen as the fourth stage of college development, following first the mechanics institutes, then the technical colleges, followed by the expansion of the college in a number of different directions – gap filling. The big trend in the late 1980s for tertiary reorganisation may be superseded by community colleges – which may or may not be tertiary. There is one major contrary force. Some LEAs have sought to keep their community education service separate because they did not want it to come under the new further education corporations with governing bodies dominated by employer representatives. These LEAs thought that community education would be undervalued and underfunded within a large college budget, compared to its treatment as an independent service coming under the local authority.

Independent FE institutions

In addition to the LEA colleges of further education, a number of independent further education institutions offer full-time or part-time courses broadly comparable to those offered by colleges in the maintained sector. They include establishments for art and architecture, commerce, domestic science, drama, speech training and music, wireless telegraphy, adventure training, the teaching of English to foreign students and foreign language schools.

Independent further education institutions do not come under the control of either central or local government, but many of them have applied voluntarily to the Education Departments for recognition that they are efficient. Recognition is only given after a full inspection and the institution must be open to further inspection at any time thereafter. At present about 130 independent further education establishments are recognised, a high proportion of these being concerned mainly with the teaching of English as a foreign language.

Open learning institutes

There has been a considerable growth in the delivery of college courses through flexible learning techniques, usually coming under the general heading of open learning. The Open College was set up to take advantage of distance learning techniques, tied in to television broadcasts, pioneered by the much longer established Open University. The Open College is an educational institution set up by the Government as a company. It began broadcasting daytime television programmes at the beginning of the 1987/88 academic year. The Open College was not generally successful in attracting large numbers of individuals to register but focused instead on its work with larger companies.

An institution that has used open learning techniques for much longer is the National Extension College, an educational trust established in 1963. It has been involved in all the major developments in open and distance learning in the United Kingdom and has pioneered new flexible forms of learning.

Chapter 3
The legal basis of further education

In Chapter 2, I discussed the view that further education colleges are market-led rather than statutorily-defined. Throughout their history colleges have had to adapt in order to survive government changes of policy and also to sustain the steady expansion that has continued throughout the post-war period. Colleges have had to withdraw from those vocational areas that have declined and have moved into ones that are expanding. For example, engineering has been declining while art and design have expanded, textiles courses have virtually disappeared but caring courses are booming. None of this has been directed by Government, but rather has been the response of college management and governing bodies.

Colleges have operated in an atmosphere of competition: the competition is between themselves in urban areas; with schools and universities where there are overlaps in provision; with private and public training providers; and with companies' own training facilities. It is perhaps fortunate that there has never been enough profit in education and training to support a large private sector, which has meant both that the sector has not come in for total government 'privatisation' and that competitive pressures have not been as intensive as in private industry and commerce, thus giving the colleges' sector time to adapt in a more gradual way.

During most of this century, this market-led structure of colleges has determined that they have operated within a minimal legal framework. As part of the local authority system up to the early 1990s, colleges worked within the legal constraints imposed on local councils, rather than any which would have been binding upon themselves. This all changed as a result of the further education legislation of 1992 which decreed the removal of FE colleges from the control of local councils. The move originated in the philosophy of the Conservative government that strong central powers and controls could be used to free institutions from local constraints.

During the previous decade Conservative governments had been reducing the amount of regulation in the further education sector. For example, the long-standing statutory pay framework for academic staff (the so-called Burnham system of annual negotiations, the results of which were enshrined in law) had been scrapped. Further, instead of the LEA having detailed control over every section of a college's budget, a system of student target numbers was introduced linked to colleges having a main 'one line' budget together with various earmarked items.

Every nation has its own set of legal regulations for its tertiary sector. Compared to a number of other European countries, the United Kingdom has not had a regulatory view of the further education part of the tertiary sector. Instead, government has relied on control by the local education authority.

In the United Kingdom there has never been any legal compulsion on a student to go to college – as there is for example with school attendance – but industrial and commercial companies may require their employees to attend as part of their training. Attempts in this century to ensure compulsory college attendance for young workers or young people in full-time education have all fizzled out, as in the two major examples given below.

The 1944 Education Act required LEAs to establish and maintain a new system of colleges, to be called county colleges, 'for providing for young persons who are not in full-time attendance at any school or other educational institution such further education, including physical, practical and vocational training, as will enable them to develop their various aptitudes and capacities and will prepare them for the responsibilities of citizenship'. Nonetheless, despite the fact that a County Colleges Order was issued in 1947 making it a duty of every local education authority to establish and maintain county colleges, no deadline was given and the local authorities ignored it. This failure followed on from the earlier lack of success of day continuation schools, which the 1918 **Education Act** prescribed for a national system of part time education from 14 to 18, but which were killed off by the post-war cutbacks brought about by economic depression. Thus the UK tendency has been to avoid specific commitments to provide standard forms of further education in favour of defining a general duty to make further education available.

The United Kingdom in its system of apprentice training did not develop the kind of 'dual system' familiar in many northern European countries, which would have guaranteed a major proportion of a college's students. Indeed, the system has been so *laissez faire* that up until the end of the Second World War there was not even a legal duty on local education authorities to provide further education. This was only rectified in England and Wales by the 1944 Education Act, one of the great pieces of social legislation arising from a war time political consensus. It is worth starting here to develop the ideas on which the legal framework of further education in England and Wales has been based and which is mirrored to a greater or lesser degree in Scotland and Northern Ireland.

Section 1 of the 1944 Education Act defined the general duty of the Secretary of State for Education as being to promote the education of the people of England and Wales in conjunction with local authorities under his control and direction. Section 7, which specified the primary, secondary and further stages of education, defined the extent of the duties of the local education authority by reference to the needs of the local population. Section 41 of the Act stipulated that the provision of adequate facilities for technical,

---

commercial and arts education for their area was a duty laid on LEAs and no longer a power to be exercised at their discretion. At the same time, industry and commerce were asked to review their arrangements for training and to co-operate in associating the technical colleges and art schools more fully with the industrial and commercial life of the country. Thus the legislation largely revolved around the control of colleges by the local authority and the relationship of government to the LEA.

In the four decades after the Second World War, the amount of legislation with regard to further education was minor and changes were brought about by government circulars or local authority changes of policy. It was only in the 1980s that further education was affected by the general wish of Conservative government ministers to reduce the power of the local councils (and consequently their local education authorities). It cannot be truthfully said that it was the burning ambition of government ministers to release FE colleges *per se* from LEA control, since the range of ministers that spent a brief time in the Department of Education had little or no understanding of further education. They had not attended these colleges themselves nor had they sent their children to them. Rather, FE colleges were caught up in a wave of legislation to diminish the powers of locally elected councils, to decrease the size of the locally controlled public sector and to reduce a very unpopular local tax by transferring the funding of some services from local to national taxation.

This removal of colleges from local authorities to the more general supervision of national funding councils, while at the same time making the colleges independent legal entities, took place in two stages. The first stage, encompassed in the 1988/89 legislation, gave the colleges considerable independence while still leaving them within the local authority orbit. The second stage, incorporated in the 1992 Acts of Parliament, severed the LEA connection and set up the colleges up as independent further education corporations.

The process was a carbon copy of the removal of polytechnics from the LEA sector in 1989, except that this was completed in only one step while the colleges required two. The main difference was that the polytechnics (which are now all universities) were larger institutions, which recruited the majority of their students regionally and nationally, unlike FE colleges which remain largely local institutions. They also had had a period of planning under a national advisory body (NAB) and quality control through a national validating and awarding body (the Council for National Academic Awards).

The first of the steps described above was the 1988 Education Reform Act (ERA) for England and Wales and the 1989 **Self-Governing Schools, etc. (Scotland) Act**. The changes did not apply to Northern Ireland, where colleges have been left with the education and library boards, although with increased planning mechanisms and greater financial freedom. Amongst other changes, the Education Reform Act clarified the duty to provide further education which had been placed on local education authorities by the 1944 Act. The new Act separately defined further education and higher education for the first time, since previously it had not been seen as necessary, or even desirable, to distinguish between them in a legal sense. It was quite common for many further education colleges in towns without an institution of higher education to provide courses ranging from basic adult education right up to first degrees and postgraduate professional qualifications.

The 1988 Education Reform Act stated that 'it shall be the duty of every local education authority to secure the provision for their area of adequate facilities for further education'. The word adequate has not been defined and has not been tested in the courts which is often the way that these matters have been elucidated in the past. Further education was then defined as:

(a) full- and part-time education and training for persons over compulsory school age (including vocational, social, physical and recreational training); and

(b) organised leisure-time occupation provided in connection with the provision of such education.

The reference to organised leisure-time occupation was explained as referring to 'such organised cultural training and recreative activities as are suited to their requirements for persons over compulsory school age who are able and willing to profit by facilities provided for that purpose'.

In respect of training, or as the Act called it, further education of a vocational kind, the duty on the local authority extended 'to the provision of facilities for continuing education for persons already in employment or already engaged in a vocation as well as to the provision of facilities for education with a view to entry into employment or vocation'.

As I stated earlier, up until the 1990s, the further education colleges were maintained by, and an integral part of, local education authorities and had no independent legal existence. In law they were indistinguishable from the local education authority which maintained them; their staff were employees of the local authority, and the property and funds they used belonged to the authority. The college and its governing body acted, and entered into any contracts, not in their own name but on behalf of the authority.

It is interesting to note that the legislation freeing the polytechnics from the LEAs was also part of ERA and there was some debate at the time as to whether the FE colleges would soon follow them into independence. (In Scotland, the major non-university higher education colleges already came directly under the Scottish Education Department.) The HE colleges moved out of local authority control on 1 April 1989 into a new higher education sector coming under national funding arrangements of, first the Polytechnics and Colleges Funding Council (PCFC), then subsequently the Higher Education Funding Council for England (HEFCE). The colleges were given corporate (or company) status.

This model was then applied to further education colleges by the two 1992 Further and Higher Education Acts for England/Wales and Scotland, which I will come to in a moment.

Company status allows colleges to enter into contracts directly but it brings with it a number of duties which can be quite onerous. Colleges had experimented with this idea in a limited way. The 1985 **Further Education Act** allowed LEAs in England and Wales to set up companies to conduct commercial activities, but such a company could not do anything the LEA was prevented from doing. Quite a few colleges set up trading companies in order to engage in commercial activities, an arrangement which meant that the college as a whole was not subject to the prospect of possible financial loss and could continue to operate under the local government regulations of the time. The Government, in taking similar steps in Scotland, was keen to point out that these companies should not compete unfairly with the private sector by being subsidised from local authority funds.

After the polytechnics had become independent of the LEAs, many college principals saw that corporate status for the whole institution would give colleges greater independence. In Scotland, the further education part of the Self-Governing Schools, etc. (Scotland) Act even gave education authorities the option of setting up management companies to take over the entire task of providing further education. These companies would have operated under contract to the authorities, which would transfer to their control the staff, buildings, 'rights' and 'liabilities'. The companies would become the employers and would inherit all salaries and conditions agreements, but would assume future negotiating rights. The continued influence of the education authority would have been exercised through the annual grant discussions.

Even though it was a halfway house, the 1988 legislation had a major effect on further education colleges in England and Wales at the beginning of the 1990s, as did its Scottish equivalent. It should be noted that the Acts did not introduce changes in the further education curriculum, as for example had been done in schools with the National Curriculum; nor did they suggest new methods of assessment and examination. Instead, the Government concentrated on shifting the existing balance of power and control away from the local education authorities in line with its general policy of hostility to local councils. It also established a more transparent, formula-based funding process than had been the case previously.

Not all government departments sought to diminish the powers of local authorities. The Department of Employment, which controlled the then Training Agency, thought that the reduction of power of the local authority would make control of its various programmes more difficult, since they were based on contracts with the local authority for delivery by local colleges. Under work-related further education arrangements (see Chapter 17), Training Agency area managers worked out with the LEA a development plan which committed the authority to tailoring the range of college courses to meet perceived local labour market needs. Since ERA gave governing bodies more control over their own budgets, little could be done to stop them switching money from courses the Agency wanted them to run to other courses which the governors might favour. The increased freedom could lead to competition and duplication with other colleges which the work-related FE exercise was designed to reduce. Similarly, under the Technical and Vocational Education Initiative (TVEI), the Training Agency paid for provision on the condition that a local authority's schools and colleges met the requirements of the contract. If colleges (and opted-out schools) chose to go their own way, the Agency might have no alternative but to reduce the funding available to the LEA.

The 1988/89 changes in the laws relating to further education in England, Wales and Scotland presaged a new, more mature era for further education. The relationship between the local education authority and the college became less paternalistic and more of a partnership. The Acts, both north and south of the England/Scotland border, forced education authorities to exercise their strategic role rather than becoming involved in the detail of college operation. This relationship was only just beginning to be worked out in detail in the early 1990s when the second set of changes was announced by the Government.

The legislation for England and Wales was based on the two volume White Paper **Education and training for the 21st century** (DES *et al.* 1991), and for Scotland, on the White Paper **Access and opportunity** (The Scottish Office 1991) both issued in May 1991. The actual Act of Parliament for England and Wales was the **Further and Higher Education Act** 1992 and for Scotland, the **Further and Higher Education (Scotland) Act** 1992. Both Acts were rushed through Parliament (against great opposition from the local councils in conjunction with the Labour Party) because the Conservative government of the time was coming to the end of its period of office and all unfinished parliamentary Bills fall just before a General Election when Parliament is dissolved.

The Acts finally ended nearly a century of LEA control of local colleges. The LEAs were left with residual duties including the right to mount part-time and evening courses for adults as well as providing for 16–18 year olds via schools sixth forms, responsibility for the youth service, discretionary awards for students and education maintenance allowances. A further responsibility was for the transport of students, with a requirement to ensure that students in colleges outside the control of the LEAs be treated in the same way as sixth form students in schools remaining with the authorities.

Section 10 of the Further and Higher Education Act specifies the adjusted powers of the local education authority sector. It amends Section 8 of the 1944 Act in relation to secondary education. The LEA is now responsible:

... for providing full-time education suitable to the requirements of pupils of compulsory school age, being either senior pupils or junior pupils who have attained the age of 10 years and six months and whom it is expedient to educate together with senior pupils of compulsory school age.

Furthermore:

A local education authority shall have the power to secure the provision for their area of full-time education suitable to the requirements of persons over compulsory school age who have not attained the age of 19 years, including provision for persons from other areas.

This allows the maintenance of secondary schools with sixth forms, having pupils up to the age of 19.

The LEA is given residual powers in respect of further education, particularly as it applies to adult education. Section 41 of the 1944 Act is amended to remove the duty to provide the newly defined further education, as specified in Schedule 2, for which the funding councils assume responsibility. LEAs still retain 'the duty ... to secure the provision for their area of adequate facilities for further education where these are not covered by Schedule 2 of the Act. They may also provide education as it applies in Section 3(1) – i.e. courses under Schedule 2 – applicable to part-time students and those over 19'.

LEAs and other providers of further education for adults outside FEFC-funded colleges are able to apply for funding for courses covered by Schedule 2 of the Act via the mechanism of sponsorship. This mechanism is described in Section 6(5). In the handover of responsibilities to colleges in the run up to April 1993, LEAs were invited to apply for funding based on relevant expenditure in previous years. Applications for sponsorship had to be made by the 'governing body' of the external institution seeking sponsorship. Under Section 90 of the FHE Act, 'governing body' includes any governing body formally constituted under an instrument of government, any board of governors, or any group of persons who are, in practice, responsible for the management of the institution. Where there is no such group, the LEA is the governing body for the purpose of applying for funds under Section

6(5). The Secretary of State laid an Order under Section 6(6) of the Act which specified that all institutions in the sector were eligible to act as sponsors. It was considered preferable that the LEA should co-ordinate the applications from external institutions which it maintained or assisted (such as adult education centres).

The new responsibility for funding further education in England and Wales moved over to two new funding councils (one each for England and Wales). Each funding council is a body corporate in its own right. The Further Education Funding Council (FEFC), which is responsible for funding FE in England, is based in Coventry. The actual council has to consist of not less than 12 and not more than 15 members appointed by the Secretary of State for Education. The Further Education Funding Council (FEFCW) for Wales is located in Cardiff. Its council should have between eight and 12 members. In Scotland the responsibility for funding the colleges rests with The Scottish Office Education Department.

The FHE Act lays down what the new further education sector will provide. The councils for England and Wales have a duty under Section 2(1):

> to secure the provision for the population of their area of sufficient facilities for education ... that is, full-time education suitable to the requirements of persons over compulsory school age who have not attained the age of 19 years ... that duty extends to all persons among that population who may want such education and have not attained the age of 19 years.

The councils:

> ... (3) ... shall discharge that duty so as (a) to secure that the facilities are provided at such places, are of such character and are so equipped as to be sufficient to meet the reasonable needs of all persons to whom the duty extends, and (b) to take account of the different abilities and aptitudes of such persons.

In addition, the councils '... (4) ... may secure the provision of facilities for education to which subsection (1) above applies for persons to whom that duty does not extend'. In order to make this provision the most cost effective, subsection (5) states that:

> A council shall discharge their functions under this section so as to make the most effective use of the council's resources and, in particular, to avoid provision which might give rise to disproportionate expenditure.

Subsection (6) requires the councils to have regard to the total provision in the area.

> In discharging those functions a council shall have regard to any education to which subsection (1) above applies provided by schools

maintained by local education authorities, grant-maintained schools, special schools not maintained by local education authorities, city technology colleges or city colleges for the technology of the arts.

In addition to the duty in respect of teenage full-time students, Section 3 specifies that:

It shall be the duty of each council to secure the provision for the population of their area of adequate facilities for education ... that is, (a) part-time education suitable to the requirements of persons of any age over compulsory school age, and (b) full-time education suitable to the requirements of persons who have attained the age of 19 years, where the education is provided by means of a course of a description mentioned in Schedule 2 to this Act.

Subsections 3(2) to (4) are similar to those in Section 2. The clauses are not restrictive in that '(5) In discharging those functions a council shall have regard to any education ... provided by institutions outside the further education sector or higher education sector'.

There is a third section of the Act putting a legal requirement on the councils over and above the duty to provide, first, full-time education for 16 to 18 year olds, and second, part-time education for all over 16 and full-time education for those over 19. This is specified in Section 4: 'each council shall have regard to the requirements of persons having learning difficulties', when it is considering education in the two categories above and discharging its duties under sections 2 and 3. This section of the Act resulted from a considerable lobby of Parliament to make sure that provision for those with learning difficulties was maintained after incorporation. Indeed, the council is given considerable responsibility. For example, Section 4(3):

A council shall, if they are satisfied in the case of any person among the population of their area who has a learning difficulty and is over compulsory school age but has not attained the age of 25 years, that (a) the facilities available in institutions within the further education sector or the higher education sector are not adequate for him, and (b) it is in his best interests to do so, secure provision for him at an institution outside those sectors.

A person is considered to have a learning difficulty if:

(a) he has a significantly greater difficulty in learning than the majority of persons of his age, or (b) he has a disability which either prevents or hinders him from making use of facilities of a kind generally provided by institutions within the further education sector for persons of his age.

However, 'A person is not to be taken as having a learning difficulty solely because the language (or form of language) in which he is, or will be, taught is different from a language (or form of language) which has at any time been spoken in his home'.

Schedule 2 of the Act details which ranges of courses may be funded. The nine categories in the full list are discussed further in the next chapter. The Secretary of State can amend the list as required (Section 3(6)). It does not prohibit colleges from mounting other courses, which are funded from other sources such as the higher education funding councils, local companies, individuals themselves, local training and enterprise councils, etc.

The Secretary of State for Education determines the grant to the councils. In their turn, the councils are responsible for distributing funds to the governing bodies of the corporations under Section 5 of the Further and Higher Education Act and external institutions under Section 6. This is laid out below. There are also terms and conditions about repayments and the limiting of the councils to the powers given by the Act only.

5(1) A council may give financial support to the governing body of any institution within the further education sector or the higher education sector in respect of (a) the provision of facilities for further education, or (b) the provision of facilities, and the carrying on of any activities, which the governing body of the institution consider necessary or desirable to be provided or carried on for the purpose of or in connection with the provision of facilities for further education.

(2) A council may give financial support to the governing body of any institution within the further education sector in respect of (a) the provision of facilities for higher education, or (b) the provision of facilities, and the carrying on of any activities which the governing body of the institution consider necessary or desirable to be provided or carried on for the purpose of or in connection with the provision of facilities for higher education.

(3) A council may give financial support to a further education corporation for the purposes of any educational institution to be conducted by the corporation, including the establishment of such an institution.

(4) For the purposes of section 4(3) to (5) of the Act [persons with learning difficulties], a council may give financial support to any person other than a local education authority, the governing body of a grant-maintained school or a person maintaining or carrying on a city technology college or city college for the technology of the arts.

(5) A council may give financial support to any person in respect of (a) the provision of training or advice, or (b) the carrying on of

research or other activities, relevant to the provision of facilities for further education.

(6) Financial support under this section (a) shall take the form of grants, loans or other payments, and (b) may be given on such terms and conditions as the council may think fit.

6(5) Where (a) the governing body of an institution within the further education sector to which this subsection applies ('the sponsoring body') receive from the governing body of an institution outside that sector ('the external institution') a request for the sponsoring body to apply to the council for financial support in respect of provision of facilities for part-time, or adult, further education by the external institution in any academic year, and (b) there are no arrangements for the provision in that year of any facilities of the kind specified in the application for the population of the sponsoring body's locality by any other instutiton or the arrangements for such provision for that population in that year by other institutions are inadequate, the sponsoring body shall apply to the council specified in the request for financial support to be given to the sponsoring body on terms requiring it to be applied in respect of the provision of the facilities specified in the application by the external institution in that year.

(6) In subsection (5) above (a) references to part-time, or adult, further education are to education provided by means of courses of any description mentioned in Schedule 2 to this Act, and (b) references to the provision of facilities for such education by any institution in any academic year include the provison of facilities, and the carrying on of any activities, which the governing body of the institution consider necessary or desirable to be provided or carried on for the purpose of or in connection with the provision of facilities for such education by them in that year, and that subsection applies to an institution within the further education sector if the institution is for the time being specified in an order, or for the time being falls within a description specified in an order, made by the Secretary of State.

The councils are also charged with assessing quality via their Quality Assessment Committee. Section 9 of the Act states:

Each council shall (a) ensure that provision is made for assessing the quality of education provided in institutions within the further education sector, and (b) establish a committee, to be known as the 'Quality Assessment Committee', with the function of giving them advice on the discharge of their duty under paragraph (a) above, and such other functions as may be conferred on the committee by the council.

The majority of members of the committee shall not be members of the council, but should be people who:

have experience of and have shown capacity in, the provision of further education and, in appointing such persons, the council shall have regard to the desirability of their being currently engaged in the provision of further education or in carrying out responsibility for such provision.

In Wales, the Act stipulates that:

Her Majesty's Chief Inspector of Schools in Wales shall, if asked to do so by the Further Education Funding Council for Wales, assess the quality of education provided in any institutions within the further education sector or any other institutions for which the council give, or are considering giving, financial support under this part of the Act.

The vast majority of colleges in the new FE sector became independent bodies from 1 April 1993. The voluntary-aided sixth form colleges and the 14 colleges 'designated' as part of the FEFC-funded sector were already independent corporations. The FE corporations were established by order of the Secretary of State for Education under Section 15 of the 1992 Further and Higher Education Act for the purpose of conducting the institutions which had previously been maintained by the local education authority. An institution qualified to be part of the new sector if on 1 November 1990 its enrolment numbers of full-time and part-time released further and higher education students (weighted by factors related to mode of attendance) were not less than 15 per cent of total enrolments. This limit was designed to exclude the largely adult education institutes with few full-time or employment release students. A second stipulation, to include the sixth form colleges, stated that an institution falls within the sector if on 17 January 1991 not less than 60 per cent of the pupils at the institution were receiving full-time education suitable to the requirements of persons over compulsory school age who have not attained the age of 19 years. This was designed to exclude schools with large sixth forms.

The colleges in England and Wales set up shadow further education corporations from 30 September 1992, which ran in tandem with the former colleges for the six months up until 31 March 1993. Under the law, the further education corporations are not regulated by the Companies Act, like private and publicly quoted companies. There are no shareholders to subscribe capital. Although corporations are charities, they are 'exempted' and so not subject to the control of the Charity Commissioners. Their powers are strictly limited by Parliament, unlike corporations created by Royal Charter. An FE corporation can only exercise powers conferred on it by Parliament under Sections 18 and 19 of the 1992 Act, so that a member of its governing body who participates in an act which is beyond the power of the corporation to perform will be personally liable for the consequences.

The principal powers of a further education corporation (FEC) are defined in Section 18 and the supplementary powers in Section 19 of the Further and Higher Education Act.

18(1) A further education corporation may (a) provide further and higher education, and (b) supply goods or services in connection with their provision of education, and those powers are referred to in section 19 of this Act as the corporation's principal powers.

(2) For the purposes of subsection (1) above, goods are supplied in connection with the provision of education by a further education corporation if they result from (a) their provision of education or anything done by them under this Act for the purpose of or in connection with their provision of education, (b) the use of their facilities or the expertise of persons employed by them in the fields in which they are so employed, or (c) ideas of a person employed by them, or one of their students, arising out of their provision of education.

(3) For the purposes of that subsection, services are supplied in connection with the provision of education by a further education corporation if (a) they result from their provision of education or anything done by them under this Act for the purpose of or in connection with their provision of education, (b) they are provided by making available their facilities or the expertise of persons employed by them in the fields in which they are so employed, or (c) they result from ideas of a person employed by them, or of one of their students, arising out of their provision of education.

19(1) A further education corporation may do anything (including in particular the things referred to in subsections (2) to (4) below) which appears to the corporation to be necessary or expedient for the purpose of or in connection with the exercise of any of their principal powers.

(2) A further education corporation may conduct an educational institution for the purpose of carrying on activities undertaken in the exercise of their powers to provide further or higher education and, in particular, may assume as from the operative date the conduct of the institution in respect of which the corporation is established.

(3) A further education corporation may provide facilities of any description appearing to the corporation to be necessary or desirable for the purposes of or in connection with carrying on any activities undertaken in the exercise of their principal powers (including boarding accommodation and recreational facilities for students

and staff and facilities to meet the needs of students having learning difficulties within the meaning of section 4(6) of this Act).

(4) A further education corporation may (a) acquire and dispose of land and other property, (b) enter into contracts, including in particular (i) contracts for the employment of teachers and other staff for the purposes of or in connection with carrying on any activities undertaken in the exercise of their principal powers, and (ii) contracts with respect to the carrying on by the corporation of such activities, (c) borrow such sums as the corporation think fit for the purposes of carrying on any activities they have power to carry on or meeting any liability transferred to them under sections 23 to 27 of this Act and, in connection with such borrowing, may grant any mortgage, charge or other security in respect of any land or other property of the corporation, (d) invest any sums not immediately required for the purposes of carrying on any activities they have power to carry on, (e) accept gifts of money, land or other property and apply it, or hold and administer it on trust for, any of those purposes, and (f) do anything incidental to the conduct of an educational institution providing further or higher education, including founding scholarships or exhibitions, making grants and giving prizes.

The corporations have a legal personality separate and distinct from the personality of the members of the governing body. The corporation may only borrow money with the consent of the FEFC. The method whereby it exercises its powers is by resolution of a majority of members of its governing body at a properly constituted, quorate meeting of the membership. A corporation can only be dissolved by order of the Secretary of State under Section 27 of the Act, it cannot be wound up or discontinued by resolution of the governing body.

As before, the governing body of an FE corporation has to operate under rules laid down by the government.

20(1) For every further education corporation established to conduct an educational institution there shall be (a) an instrument providing for the constitution of the corporation (to be known as the instrument of government), and (b) an instrument in accordance with which the corporation, and the institution, are to be conducted (to be known as articles of government).

Many of the sections of the Further and Higher Education Act 1992 quoted above have their counterpart in the provision of the Further and Higher Education (Scotland) Act 1992. The main differences lie in the duty for further education being placed on the Secretary of State for Scotland. There are enabling provisions to establish by Order a Scottish Further

Education Funding Council but these have not been brought into force. Funding of the colleges comes directly from the SOED, with HM Inspectorate carrying out a quality assessment role. The equivalent of governing bodies of FE corporations are called boards of management, who have similar statutory responsibilities.

Section Two
Who are the FE students?

Chapter 4   *Further education students and the curriculum*

Chapter 5   *Vocational students*

Chapter 6   *Pre-vocational students*

Chapter 7   *Academic students*

Chapter 8   *Adult and continuing students*

Chapter 9   *Special educational needs students*

Chapter 4
Further education students and the curriculum

At the beginning of the 1990s, the United Kingdom further education service was providing for 3.7 million students, of whom 2.1 million were in colleges and 1.6 million in adult education institutes and centres maintained by local education authorities. There is a common assumption that most further education students are in the 16–19 age range, but if all courses and programmes are included – not just full-time ones – 78 per cent of students were over the age of 18, while over half (57 per cent) were 25 and over in the early 1990s.

The Further Education Funding Council has suggested how students should be categorised in its first year of operation (**Figure 1**) and these modes of study give an idea about the kinds of students involved. Full-time students are the main core of college work, but are not significant in adult education centres or institutes. Full-time students are defined as those following a course of study to which they are expected to devote the whole of their time. In further education this category includes short full-time courses lasting 18 weeks or less, unbroken by any industrial training or employment. Where a period of industrial training forms an integral part of the course and the period of study averages 19 weeks or more in an academic year, it is known as a sandwich course.

Figure 1: FEFC breakdown of mode of attendance of students	
FESR Code	*Description*
01	Full-time: 30 weeks or more
02	Full-time: less than full year (at least 4 weeks but less than 30)
03	Sandwich
04	Block release
05	Part-time released
07	Part-time: non-released
09	Evening only
10	Open or distance learning
11	Short course (full-time less than four weeks)

Figure 2: Number of UK students in further education in 1989/90 by mode of attendance (thousands)

Age	16	17	18	16–18	19–20	21–24	25+	All
Full-time/sandwich	152	124	67	343	33	21	47	443
Part-time day	119	118	82	319	101	172	761	1,352
Evening only	52	45	56	152	115	307	1,285	1,860
Totals	323	287	205	814	249	500	2,093	3,655

Source: **Education statistics for the United Kingdom.** (DES 1991)

Figure 3: Participation rates of UK students in further education in 1989/90 by mode of attendance (percentages)

Age range	16–18	19–20	21–24
Full-time	14.0	2.0	0.6
Part-time	22.4	12.3	12.8
Total	36.4	14.3	13.4

Source: **Education statistics for the United Kingdom.** (DES 1991)

Participation rates by mode of attendance

Figures 2 and **3** outline the modes of attendance of home students (those from the UK). They demonstrate that 443,000 students were attending full-time courses, of whom 77 per cent were in the 16–18 age group. Only 11 per cent of students were aged 25 or over; 54 per cent of all full-time students were female.

Students on part-time day courses attend college during the day, normally for a full academic year, and include those who have been released by their employer for one or two days a week. Within this category are block release courses, where students are released from industrial training or employment for one or more periods of full-time education averaging less than 19 weeks per academic year. Additionally, there are large numbers who attend during the day for non-vocational classes. In 1989/90 there was a total 1,352,000 part-time students in this category, 76 per cent of whom were over the age of 18 and 56 per cent over 24. Females were in the majority at 61 per cent.

The largest category of students are those who attend during the evening. There were 1,860,000 evening student enrolments in 1989/90, of whom only eight per cent were in the 16–18 age group. Nearly 70 per cent of evening students were over the age of 24. Two-thirds of the evening students were women.

Gender participation

Women made up 63 per cent of the total numbers in all sectors of further education. At the beginning of the 1980s the Government's **Regional trends** (Central Statistical Office) publication showed that male students held an eight per cent lead over females in numbers studying in FE colleges. By 1986 the position had been reversed, with females nine per cent in front of their male counterparts. During this period the total number of FE students increased by 10 per cent. In 1981 male students out-numbered females in all regions except the South West of England, while in 1986 this applied only in the North of England. By 1990, the proportion of females as a percentage of all students in further and higher education was over half in England and Wales and evenly split in Scotland.

A 1988 Further Education Unit bulletin (FEU 1988), devoted to the subject of gender participation rates in work-related further education, commented that although gender participation in further education is one factor in equal opportunities, very little work has been done to monitor participation rates. Women represent over 40 per cent of the workforce, the second highest rate in Europe, so their participation in vocational further education is crucial. Yet education, training and employment patterns still show stereotyping. Mainstream engineering and construction courses are almost exclusively male, while women predominate in most courses within the training occupational categories coming under administration and clerical; creative, education and recreation; health, community and personal services; and general education.

Participation rates categorised by ethnic orgin

At the time of writing there are no available figures for the numbers of people from ethnic minority backgrounds in further education. Although many local education authorities recorded the ethnic origin of both students and teachers as part of their policy for equal opportunities for some years, this was not universal. The Department for Education began to collect these statistics in the late 1980s. The 1987 HMI report on colleges in

England and Wales (HMI 1987) found that the one-third of the colleges inspected, which were located in inner city areas, contained a high proportion of ethnic minority groups. Students from ethnic minorities comprised as much as 70 per cent of the total student population in some colleges; in others it was a small proportion. The Inspectorate found that the variation was determined by factors which included the nature of the courses offered, local demography and the ethos of the college.

In colleges where ethnic minority groups were strongly represented, they were spread across a wide range of courses, but were particularly concentrated on the lower level vocational preparation courses. Given the ethnic structure of local labour markets it is not surprising that in some instances HMI discovered that almost all the employed students on day release were white, while students from ethnic minority groups were generally found on full-time courses. Some evidence was found that there was particular ethnic concentration in certain kinds of courses. Afro-Caribbean students were more likely to be found on community care and humanities courses, while those of Asian origin were concentrated on GCE, business studies, and science and mathematics foundation courses.

Subject areas

Apart from describing further education students in terms of modes of attendance, gender and ethnic background, they can be categorised by describing the courses they attend, either in terms of subjects studied or by noting the examining or validation bodies awarding the certificates. An HMI study of English and Welsh FE colleges (HMI 1987) in the 1980s showed the trend in enrolments in subjects between 1980 and 1985. In 1980, engineering was the most popular subject in terms of total enrolments (full- and part-time) at nearly 300,000, but had fallen to under 250,000 five years later. Its first place was overtaken by business, professional and management, which rose from under 250,000 to nearly 300,000. These two were by far the biggest subject areas in the 1980s, apart from the general category of GCE which can encompass a variety of subjects. The next largest subject group in 1985 was construction, which remained around the 75,000 mark. Hotel and catering had just over 50,000 students. These were followed by science, art and design, health and community studies and agriculture, which all had 30–40,000 students. The final category was maths and computing, which is growing. The effects of recession at the end of the 1980s and beginning of the 1990s has reduced engineering and construction enrolments considerably. Vocational students are discussed further in the next chapter.

The planning of further education has traditionally been based on expected numbers in vocational areas, which have been described in different ways. Students may also be categorised by training occupation categories. The government categories in its published statistics give common subjects which are used across both further and higher education. The 1989/90 further education statistics are given in **Figure 4.**

Figure 4: UK students enrolled in further education by type of course in 1989/90 (thousands). Includes overseas students

Subject group	Full-time	Part-time	Totals
1. Medicine and dentistry	0.4	4.0	4.4
2. Allied medicine	20.4	19.0	39.4
3. Biological sciences	–	0.9	0.9
4. Agriculture	6.9	32.8	39.7
5. Physical sciences	0.2	2.3	2.5
6. Mathematical sciences	10.7	47.3	58.0
7. Engineering and technology	34.2	209.8	244.0
8. Architecture	20.7	120.6	141.3
9. Social sciences	9.5	54.1	63.6
10. Business and finance	104.5	329.8	434.3
11. Library and info. studies	0.9	3.7	4.6
12. Languages	4.1	103.2	107.3
13. Humanities	–	3.3	3.3
14. Creative arts	54.5	123.6	178.1
15. Education	4.1	56.6	60.7
16. Multi-disciplinary studies	40.3	367.5	407.8
17. GCSE, SCE and CSE	112.1	272.0	384.1
Totals	423.5	1,750.5	2,174.0

Source: **Education statistics for the United Kingdom**. (DES 1991)

Examining and validating bodies

Full-time and day release students have traditionally wanted a certificate at the end of their courses. Thus, if one looks at vocational courses taken at centres validated by the Business and Technology Education Council (BTEC) or the Scottish Vocational Education Council (SCOTVEC), or vocational examinations sat under the auspices of the Royal Society of Arts Examinations Board (RSA) or the City and Guilds of London Institute (CGLI), a good picture can be obtained of the types of student. (The distinction between these bodies is explained in Chapter 5.) For more academic courses, the General Certificate of Education A level, the General Certificate of Secondary Education (and its forerunners, the GCE O level and CSE) and Scottish Certificates of Education can be used. There are also a number of small examining and validating bodies, and their qualifications are lumped together (**Figure 5**).

Figure 5: United Kingdom enrolments by examining and validating body in 1989 (thousands)

	BTEC/ SCOTVEC	*RSA*	*CGLI*	*GCSE/GCE CSE/SCE*	*Other specified courses*	*UK totals*
Men	214.3	14.3	281.5	156.1	79.5	745.7
Women	151.5	120.3	124.5	241.1	119.2	756.6
Totals	365.8	134.6	406.0	397.2	198.7	1,502.3

Source: **Education Statistics for the United Kingdom**, 1991 edition

---

Figure 5 shows the proportion of students on the relevant groups of courses. It can be seen that men predominate on CGLI courses and to some extent on BTEC, while women are in a clear majority for the RSA and the academic courses. The total figures show that mainstream further education provides courses leading to nationally recognised qualifications, and the introduction since these figures were compiled of the new GNVQs has further increased the range of vocationally-oriented accredited courses available in FE colleges. In contrast, a large proportion of courses in adult continuing education centres and institutes are not nationally accredited.

HMI, in the report of the Senior Chief Inspector of Schools for England in 1990–91 (HMI 1992), noted that colleges continued to cater for a wide diversity of students across a broad range of subjects. There was a significant growth of BTEC First courses, replacing to some extent GCSE repeat programmes which had poor success rates in many colleges. Some colleges had developed courses in which BTEC National Diploma and GCE A level science syllabuses are taught jointly, enabling the students to aim for different types of qualification simultaneously. The introduction of modular GNVQs at three levels, the third of which is termed 'vocational A levels', is accelerating the take up of mixed vocational and academic courses of

---

study. Demand for courses in information technology remained high. Enrolments on some craft courses, however, especially in construction, had declined.

The 1992 Further and Higher Education Act actually defined the further education that would be paid for by the Funding Council in terms of qualifications. **Figure 6** lists the categories. For Scotland, the FHE (Scotland) Act Section 6 listed the programmes of learning falling within the definition of further education as:

-   prepares a person for a vocational qualification;
-   prepares a person for:

    (i) a Scottish Examination Board qualification; or

    (ii) a General Certificate of Education qualification of England and Wales or Northern Ireland;

-   provides instruction for persons who are participating in a programme of learning which falls within this section and who have a learning difficulty;
-   prepares a person for access to higher education;
-   is designed to assist persons whose first language is not English to achieve any level of competence in English language;
-   is designed predominantly to prepare a person for participation in any programme of learning which falls within this section.

Figure 6: Further Education Funding Council, criteria for assessing eligibility under Schedule 2 of the FHE Act

Type of course/course objective	Criteria for eligibility for funding by FEFC
a. Vocational qualification	Approved by the Secretary of State
b. GCSE or GCE A/AS level	Leads to an examination by one of the GCE/GCSE examining boards
c. Access course preparing students for entry to a course of HE	Approved by the Secretary of State
d. Course which prepares students for entry to courses listed in (a) to (c) above	i.Primary course objective is progression to a vocational course, GCSE, GCE A/AS level or an access course as outlined above; and
	ii. course includes assessment of students' preparedness to progress to courses (a) to (c); and
	iii. results of such assessments enable evidence of progression to be provided to the Council
e. Basic literacy in English	Provides students with basic literacy skills
f. Teaching English to students where English is not language spoken at home	Improves the knowledge of English for those for whom English is not the language spoken at home
g. Basic principles of mathematics	Course designed to teach the basic principles of mathematics
h. Proficiency or literacy in Welsh	Course for proficiency or literacy in Welsh (Wales only)
j. Independent living and communication skills for those with learning difficulties which prepare them for entry to courses listed in sections (d) to (g)	i.Primary course objective is progression to • a course which prepares students for entry to (a) to (c) above and/or a basic literacy course, • an English course for those for whom English is not the language spoken at home • a basic maths course; and
	ii. course includes assessment of students' preparedness to progress to courses (d) to (g); and
	iii. results of such assessments enable evidence of progression to be provided to the Council.

Source: **FEFC Circular 92/09** (FEFC 1992a)

The varied nature of FE institutions

Having quantified the students in further education, it is not easy to categorise them into a nicely rounded theory about the nature of the service. Although the 1992 legislation in England, Wales and Scotland and the creation of the funding councils has given further education more shape, it is not easy to portray simply the complexity of further education colleges. If I were trying to categorise a United Kingdom school, I would enquire whether it is an LEA, grant-maintained, voluntary body or a private school, which clarifies the funding and ethos; if it is deemed a primary, middle, junior or high school, which specifies the age range of the pupils who attend; and if it is comprehensive, selective or caters for those with special educational needs. With a university, I could ask about the number of students, the proportion on first degree courses and higher degrees, and the nature of those courses, and get a clear idea of the major portion of the work of that institution from the answers.

As I explained in the first section of this book, further education colleges cannot be so easily classified. HM Inspectors have described further education provision as a rich and complex tapestry, woven and modified over the years to meet the changing needs of industry, commerce, the public sector and students. Few people have a detailed understanding of the total range of course offerings. Up to the 1990s, the colleges, having grown up without a clear or firm legislative framework, did not have a common national purpose defined by Government. The local education authorities that controlled the colleges gave only general guidelines on programme areas through their strategic plan and work-related further education schemes. The college itself may well have adopted a statement of aims – commonly known as a mission statement – but this may mention only general concepts such as quality, responsiveness, efficiency and effectiveness. To get to know what kind of students the college wants to attract would require a detailed reading of the college prospectus and course leaflets.

Various government agencies have tried to push colleges in particular ways, depending on their own predilections, but the colleges are resilient institutions and seem to have been remarkably little affected by these pressures. This has led to a prevalent view by pragmatic senior managers of colleges that they run a responsive service which tries to answer a whole range of community needs. Or, alternatively, they see themselves as running a holding company, with a group of subsidiaries acting as semi-autonomous recruiting bodies. This view was in sharp contrast to the attitude of the Conservative government in the second half of the 1980s, which had pushed forward the responsibility of further education to its vocational students as its prime task. The 1984 White Paper **Training for jobs** (DE 1984) set up a system under which the Department of Employment Training Agency held back 25 per cent of the funds intended for further education, until the production of satisfactory three-year plans and annual programmes of work-related further education. This vocational philosophy of further education reappeared when the categories of membership of the new governing bodies to be formed under the provisions of the 1988 Education Reform Act required at least 50 per cent of the representatives to be from industrial, commercial and professional bodies.

It is worth examining further the notion that colleges of further education are pluralistic, pragmatic institutions, because it gives the reader an idea of the diffuse nature of the student body. In their post-war role, colleges have been ruthless fillers of gaps left by other types of provider; their expansion has been at the expense of more high profile institutions in other sectors of education and training. College students are people who want to attend for their own needs (primary customers), or whose employing organisation has arranged for them to enrol (secondary customers). In either case the college will provide an education or training package, usually coming under the auspices of an examining or validating body. Colleges will recruit anyone they have not been forbidden to enrol (such as the under-16s and those on degree and higher degree programmes), so long as it is economic to do so. The vast majority of college work is provided in the form of courses so that viable numbers can be catered for; only a small minority is currently in the form of individualised flexible learning.

Filling the gaps in provision

Section 1 outlined the historical growth of colleges and the way they have built up courses for different types of students. The reader will remember that the birth of colleges was in the mechanics institute movement, which was a result of providing self-help to working people who wanted to better themselves over and above their initial schooling or the training their employer gave. This is part of the adult education tradition and is a current thread of what colleges offer. Motivated adults have a desire to learn that cannot be satisfied by more conventional educational bodies which tend to have rules limiting what they can offer and to whom. In its gap-filling mode, further education grew in parallel with, and often overlapped, adult continuing education provided in separate institutes and centres.

The typical post-war FE student attended part-time, and the character of the technical college was built up by the day-release or evening students doing vocational courses. When I started teaching in FE at the end of the 1960s, the impression of the characteristic FE student was that he was largely male, white and teenage or in his early 20s, except in certain occupational areas such as hairdressing, catering and community care – where females predominated. The student would also be employed and would have attended on release from work or in his own time. (In other European countries this training was more often provided by a company training school, by group training associations funded by a range of companies, by vocational schools, or by private training organisations.) This training role is still an important one for further education and these students can be seen in their protective clothing in the college corridors. But colleges have widened dramatically over the last two decades.

Alongside the part-time courses offered through bodies such as the City and Guilds and RSA, there has been a strong post-war tradition of full-time broad-based vocational courses, originally coming under the arrangements for the Ordinary National Diploma and Higher National Diploma for technicians and supervisory and junior management staff. These courses in their Certificate form could also be done by part-time day release or evening study. The formation of technician and business examining councils in the early 1970s, followed by their amalgamation in 1983 as BTEC (SCOTVEC is a separate body in Scotland), consolidated this full-time vocational route which can lead to employment in the particular occupational area or in related areas, or progression through to higher education.

A logical extension of the support for adults was the movement of colleges into academic education. Adults who want a second chance at getting qualifications such as GCE A levels or Scottish Highers usually had to go to a college to study for them because of the limited role of schools (apart from the so-called community schools) in the UK in providing only for young people. As the numbers of adults who wanted to obtain these qualifications increased, they were matched by young people who did not like the restrictions of a school environment and started opting to study in college from the age of 16 rather than stay on at school. A further group were those who needed to improve their GCE or SCE qualifications and came to college to resit. This trend increased in the 1970s and 1980s, so that the FE college in any town usually has by far the biggest 'sixth form centre' within it, and many are now the sole providers of this kind of education in the tertiary colleges.

The expansion of colleges into more academic forms of education led to colleges developing higher education programmes, as is descibed in Chapter 21. It also resulted in pressure on colleges from another direction. At the beginning of 1989 the then Secretary of State for Education and Science made one of the very few ministerial policy statements about further education. He addressed the problem of the academic and vocational divide and suggested that it would be possible to build some common components into academic studies, such as A or AS levels, or vocational studies, such as a BTEC course for language study or technology. The Secretary of State also identified a possible core curriculum for the 16–19 age group in colleges of further education. While he acknowledged that there could be no single 16–19 curriculum, he thought that a number of skills and broad-based qualifications would help students to be flexible and think and act independently. Work has been done to develop the idea of the common core. The core skills specified were:

- communication, written or oral: how to explain a complicated working procedure, or deal with a tricky customer;
- numeracy: not simply adding a column of figures, but understanding orders of magnitude;
- personal relations: team working and leadership;
- familiarity with technology: especially information technology;
- familiarity with systems: office and workshop procedures, and employment hierarchies; and
- familiarity with changing working and social contexts.

Further avenues of FE growth arose through the effects of unemployment. The economic slumps in the UK after 1974 and 1981, followed by a longer and even deeper recession from 1989, coupled with the steady transfer of jobs into the service industries, meant that a lot of unskilled and semi-skilled manufacturing jobs were wiped out. This partly eliminated the previous option of many young people to leave school as early as possible and take jobs in these areas, which had no prospects and no training. The need arose to create something for youngsters who had no aspirations for an academic career or had not decided to follow a particular vocational route. As usual, further education moved into the gap (in parallel with schools) and helped to establish vocational preparation or pre-vocational courses for those wishing to stay on after 16. The colleges had an advantage over schools in the range of vocational sampling they were able to offer. The programmes have evolved through the Certificate of Pre-vocational Education (CPVE) to the Diploma for Vocational Education (DVE).

A final example of gap filling was the move of colleges to take advantage of the new climate created in the 1980s for those young people who had learning difficulties over and above the ones encountered by the average student. The 1981 **Education Act** led many colleges to put on sampling courses and then full-time courses for young people with disabilities. Provision for those with special educational needs is now a well-established feature of most colleges of further education (see Chapter 9).

Curriculum bodies

As well as a lack of clear guidance about the nature of the further education curriculum, there has until recently been no common body to impose national standards on vocational education and training. In England,

Wales and Northern Ireland, the major examining and validating bodies – BTEC, CGLI and the RSA – do not have common systems and levels of attainment. To complicate matters further, a large number of specialist, smaller awarding bodies operate on a national and international basis. There were also long-established regional examining bodies, but these have now virtually disappeared through amalgamation with national examining and validating bodies.

There have been piecemeal reforms in the past, such as the formation of BTEC from separate technician and business examining bodies to cover middle level occupations, the creation of SCOTVEC as the main vocational examining and validating body for Scotland, and the linking of CGLI with regional examining bodies through the unified system, but these developments did not go far enough. The Government became so concerned about the 'jungle' of vocational qualifications that it established a National Council for Vocational Qualifications (NCVQ) in 1986, whose work is discussed in the next chapter. The NCVQ's remit was to standardise vocational education and training units based on competence via vocational examining and validating bodies in conjunction with industry, which in turn was encouraged to contribute to a range of ILBs, based on occupational sectors, with curriculum design briefs. The new units are available for all providers of education and training, not just FE, so the NCVQ cannot claim to play a primary role as a further education national curriculum body. However, the National Vocational Qualifications (NVQs) and the National Record of Vocational Achievement (NROVA) have become an integral part of the work of further education students in the 1990s.

As an extension of NVQs, an adapted form of NVQs, called General National Vocational Qualifications (GNVQs), were piloted in 1992. GNVQs were suitable for running in education establishments as the content was not set by the industry lead bodies and did not rely on work-based assessment. GNVQs are much more broad-based vocational courses for full-time students in schools and colleges. They can also be taken with existing A and AS level subjects.

Chapter 5
Vocational students

Vocational students are at the heart of colleges of further education. They give the colleges their particular identity and differentiate them from sixth form colleges or adult education institutions. Vocational students were responsible for the main growth of further education colleges during the 20th century up to the 1980s and represent the major thread in the range of provision (see previous chapter).

The qualifications taken by vocational students have various strengths which were listed in the 1986 report of the MSC/DES **Review of vocational qualifications in England and Wales** (MSC/DES 1986). They are:

- the established examining bodies have credibility with employers, with providers of education and training and with registered students;
- their assessment procedures and testing arrangements are dependable;
- the long history of examining and validating bodies and qualifying institutions engenders respect and trust;
- there is a diversity of provision which shows the responsiveness to the market, and many qualifications have international standing.

On the other hand, a number of shortcomings were also highlighted:

- there is no clear, readily understandable pattern of provision;
- in addition to gaps in the system there are considerable areas of actual or apparent overlap;
- the arrangements for progression and transfer are not always well defined or practicable;
- access is frequently unnecessarily restrictive;
- assessment methods are usually knowledge or skill-based rather than recording competence required in employment; and
- there has not been sufficient responsiveness to all new needs and some commercial and industrial sectors, such as retail distribution, had a low course take-up.

The National Council for Vocational Qualifications

In an attempt to remedy the weaknesses identified above, the Review of Vocational Qualifications Working Group recommended the creation of the National Council for Vocational Qualifications (NCVQ). It was duly established by the Government in 1986 to undertake reforms of the system of vocational qualifications in England, Wales and Northern Ireland. It is an independent company limited by guarantee, which reports primarily to the Department of Employment. NCVQ's remit can be summarised as:

- the establishment of a National Vocational Qualification framework which is comprehensible and comprehensive, and facilitates access, progression and continued learning;
- the improvement of vocational qualifications themselves, based on standards of competence required in employment.

National Vocational Qualifications

The NCVQ requires designated lead bodies (often known as either lead industry bodies, LIBs, or industry lead bodies, ILBs) in each major sector of industry and commerce to specify in detail what standards of skills and knowledge are needed in the workforce in that sector and to embody those features in National Vocational Qualifications (NVQs). The process of establishing the new qualifications included identifying competences required by the workforce as a whole and the mixture that was relevant to various different sectors of that industry. Elements of competence and performance criteria had to be specified to spell out the standards by which competence at work could be judged. Elements of competence were combined into discrete units and the units grouped into qualifications at appropriate levels in the framework. Before proposals were put into effect there was consultation with interested parties. Assessment procedures were formulated which would measure competences achieved in a reliable and cost-effective manner.

Each lead body organised national publicity and promotion of the process of standard setting, developing qualifications and encouraging the adoption of the new qualifications. The lead bodies provided training in assessment and assessment monitoring. It may have been possible for each lead body to undertake all of these functions itself, without bringing in any examining and validating bodies, but this was discouraged by the Department of Employment. The common pattern is for partnerships between lead industry bodies and the major examining bodies. There are five levels of National Vocational Qualification.

Level I   Competence in the performance of a range of varied work activities. At a similar standard to pre-vocational certificates or semi-skilled training.

Level II   Competence in a significant range of varied work activities performed in a variety of contexts. Individual autonomy and collaboration with others may also be a requirement. At a similar standard to basic craft certificates, GCSE and BTEC First Award.

Level III Competence in a broad range of varied work activities; considerable responsibility and autonomy; control/guidance of others. At a similar standard to National Diplomas, Advanced Craft or A/AS levels.

Level IV Competence in a broad range of complex technical and professional work activities; substantial degree of personal responsibility and autonomy; responsibility for the work of others and allocation of resources. At a similar standard to Higher National Diplomas and lower professional awards.

Level V Application of a significant range of fundamental principles and complex techniques across a wide variety of contexts; substantial personal autonomy; accountability for analysis and diagnosis, design, planning, execution and evaluation. At a similar level to vocational postgraduate professional qualifications.

The levels are being used to create national education and training targets (NETTs). For example, the Government hopes that 80 per cent of 16 to 19 year olds should achieve at least NVQ Level II by 1996. This is broadly equivalent to four GCSEs in academic terms. There have been a number of criticisms of NVQs. A typical example was in the Institute of Manpower Studies' report for the construction industry. The survey of key organisations in the industry concerned with the introduction of NVQs found supply, demand and access for the qualifications were being inhibited by inadequacies in information, funding and resources. As the lead body is heavily rooted in its industry and rarely works with other LIBs, it is helping to produce NVQs which do not enhance transferable skills or development of competences between and within the industries and occupations. The employer-led competences were limited and too narrowly-defined. Contrary to expectations, assessment procedures were unlikely to take place in the workplace due to feasibility problems, cost and reliability. Only a minority of assessors and trainers at the time of the survey had received any training themselves.

The National Record of Vocational Achievement

NCVQ also launched a national system for recording vocational achievement. The system operates through the National Record of Vocational Achievement (NROVA), which provides a common method of recording credits within different qualifications. The credits are in the form of units of competence, which contribute towards National Vocational Qualifications (NVQs). The NROVA was introduced in June 1988 and is supported by all the major examining and validating bodies and the industry lead bodies. It was piloted in 38 colleges and training centres from September

---

1988. The National Record was adopted by the Training Agency within its Employment Training and Youth Training programmes from 1988 and 1989 respectively.

The system of credit accumulation and the National Record offer a number of advantages:

- easier access to qualifications;
- units can be built up over time;
- trainees are motivated by immediate recognition of their achievements;
- units from different awarding bodies can be brought together in one place;
- different types of learning are integrated;
- tutors and trainers will be able to operate within a common system;
- more flexible learning programmes can be designed;
- it provides a clear record of an individual's skills;
- it records credits from one learning programme to another through a person's career.

The first students to receive NVQs gained them for Certificates in Food Preparation and Cooking, jointly awarded by City and Guilds and the Hotel and Catering Training Board in June 1988.

NCVQ and the FE sector

The Further Education Unit highlighted some concerns about the impact of the NCVQ on the further education sector. It was worried about the effect which the NVQ credit accumulation system would have upon existing student record systems and modular course delivery. Further problems were envisaged in the move to learning and assessment in the workplace or in simulated work, although this led to a crucial role for college staff in the training and support of workplace supervisors, who have to carry the bulk of work in accrediting workplace competence. The assessment of prior learning necessitates guidance to candidates on the identification and presentation of evidence for prior achievement.

The NCVQ itself has made suggestions about the role of colleges in the new system. Lecturers can provide learning opportunities through modular training, open learning packages, computer-assisted learning and experiential learning, as well as through more traditional courses. Colleges can provide consultancy and guidance services to help design and run effective training and assessment programmes, and staff development and training for those in industry and education.

General National Vocational Qualifications

In 1992, General National Vocational Qualifications (GNVQS) were launched by the Government and were expected to be on offer for students throughout England, Wales and Northern Ireland by the mid-1990s. GNVQs offer cross-curricular themes or core skills, continuous assessment and separate study modules. The GNVQ is seen as a halfway house or 'third pathway' between academic A levels and work-related NVQs. GNVQs are not based directly on occupational competence and do not demand workplace assessment. They focus on the skills, knowledge and understanding that underpin a range of NVQs in a broad occupational area. GNVQs rely more on the traditional further education mixture of knowledge-based learning, workshop practice and simulation, together with periods of work experience. The new qualifications are broadly similar to the BTEC diplomas.

GNVQs were initially piloted in five vocational areas: leisure and tourism, manufacturing, health care, business and administration, and art and design. They became available to all colleges from September 1993. Nine further subjects were then due to be piloted, including science (in 1994) and engineering/technology (from 1995). The qualification framework is designed to cater for the first three VQ levels, designated 'Foundation' (level 1), 'Intermediate' (level 2) and 'Advanced' (level 3). Students obtaining a Level 3 GNVQ qualification over two years will have passed 12 separately assessed modules, equivalent in standard to two GCE A levels. Each module has a final written examination as well as coursework assessment. The qualifications are awarded by the main examining and validating bodies, BTEC, City and Guilds and RSA.

The GNVQs have core skills including problem-solving, communication, personal skills, numeracy and information technology. The introduction of a sixth element – competence to GCSE standard in a modern language – has been delayed owing to the shortage of qualified teachers and lecturers.

NVQs and examining/validating bodies

While the NCVQ organises the system of vocational qualifications, it is still incumbent on the major vocational examining and validating bodies to submit the revised qualifications in conjunction with the relevant lead body. During the period from 1988 to 1990 a number of qualifications were given two year conditional accreditation on the basis that the lead body and examining and validating bodies would revise them in the period up to 1992 for full accreditation. The examining and validating bodies are still strong forces in influencing the further education curriculum. The work of some of the major bodies is outlined below.

The Business and Technology Education Council

The Business and Technology Education Council (BTEC) was established in 1983 by the merger of the Business Education Council (BEC) and Technician Education Council (TEC). It is a company limited by guarantee and is a registered educational charity.

BTEC is governed by a council which has a chairperson and 25 members, all of whom are appointed by the Secretary of State for Education to serve in a personal capacity for a period of three years. BTEC operates through advisory boards to cover employment areas: the built environment; business, finance and public administration; computing and information systems; design; distributive, hotel and catering and leisure services; engineering; land and countryside management; science; and caring.

BTEC's principal activities have been to advance the quality and availability of work-related education. It operates over 11,000 programmes running in over 1,000 centres across England, Wales and Northern Ireland. Its client group is 'those in employment, or preparing to enter it, who need to develop the necessary competence for success in their careers either on their own behalf or their employers'. Over 130 professional bodies and associations recognise BTEC qualifications and the Council works closely with industry, commerce and government.

BTEC is a validating body, not an examining body like City and Guilds or the Royal Society of Arts. It approves centres to run courses or units of initial or continuing vocational education and training for which it issues certification. It does not itself run courses or set and mark nationally devised examinations, although in the light of the development of the new General National Vocational Qualifications (GNVQs) it requires approved centres to undertake and report on appropriate assessment, testing and evaluation of student or trainee performance and achievement as a basis for certification. Assessment can take into account practical work experience. BTEC's course approval system is backed by a system of quality assurance and control. This system is a combination of curricular guidance developed in close association with employers, detailed evaluation of centres and course proposals against this guidance (i.e. validation), and regular monitoring of the courses at centres (i.e. moderation). Industrially and commercially experienced moderators check closely on courses and guide and advise teaching staff. BTEC emphasises a balance between the education and training needs of students and trainees so that all approved courses have a core of transferable skills such as literacy, numeracy, problem-solving, communication, working in teams and other practical skills. The courses can be studied by different modes of attendance such as full-time, day release, evening, block release, sandwich and, where appropriate, open and distance learning. Virtually all BTEC work is organised in units comprising approximately 60 hours of study for those in employment and 90 hours for full-time courses where students need extra time to compensate for their lack of experience.

The Council has three main patterns of provision. The first is initial education and training for young people aged 16 and over. Units are grouped into courses to provide one, two or three years of full- or part-time study. These qualifications are set at three levels within the BTEC system: the First, National and Higher National Certificates and Diplomas. Certificates are normally awarded at the end of part-time study, and Diplomas after full-time study. In some areas, Certificates are in the majority because of the pattern of recruitment and release from industry, e.g. construction and engineering, while in others, the Diploma predominates, e.g. agriculture, computing and design. In 1990/91, registrations for BTEC programmes of study were:

First Certificate	16,853
First Diploma	33,456
National Certificate	53,982
National Diploma	71,305
Higher National Certificate	33,818
Higher National Diploma	31,033
Continuing Education Certificate	6,931
Continuing Education Diploma	668
Short programmes of study	868
Total	248,914

In comparison in 1987/88, there were 16,500 First level registrations, 104,000 for National level and 55,000 for Higher National.

The second pattern is continuing education for adults wishing to extend or update their work-related experience. Specially devised units may be taken in specified groups to lead to Continuing Education Certificates or Diplomas which represent progressive levels of attainment.

The third option is any pattern of individual units or groups of units which can be studied to meet particular student or trainee needs, and can lead to the award of BTEC Certificates of Achievement which record the units completed and the grades of performance achieved. Certificates of Achievement can be used as credit towards a full qualification.

Courses leading to BTEC qualifications are run in colleges and universities in England, Wales and Northern Ireland. The Highers are technically classed as higher education. The Higher Certificate falls within the remit of both the further and higher education funding councils. There has been an increase in the number of colleges of further education offering Higher Diplomas as the universities and higher education colleges respond to the increasing demand for degrees. For example, at the beginning of the 1990s, the rate of increase in HNDs was three per cent, while that for first degrees was 12 per cent, whereas demand for Certificates fell due to the recession. Some companies also conduct courses, and some schools work in association with local colleges. BTEC uses the term 'centre' for any institution that runs BTEC courses. Individual centres are not able to offer all available courses or units to order. Most educational institutions have their own strengths or specialised areas and levels of work. Before a centre can start a course it must satisfy BTEC that it has the necessary physical and staffing resources.

The City and Guilds of London Institute

The City and Guilds of London Institute (CGLI) was founded in 1878 by the City of London livery companies. According to a contemporary account its purpose was to provide and encourage education adapted to the requirements of all classes of persons engaged, or preparing to engage, in manufacturing and other industries. It also encouraged the formation of evening classes in Britain's principal industrial centres for workmen and foremen engaged in factories during the day. CGLI has grown to become the largest technical examining body in Europe. On the way it has spawned off-shoots such as the Imperial College of Science and Technology in the University of London.

The Institute today is an independent non-profit-making organisation, registered as an educational charity, and operating under a Royal Charter. It is governed by a council which still has representation from founder members such as Mercers, Goldsmiths, Dyers and Cordwainers. There are also elected and co-opted members as well as assessors from the DFE and the Training, Enterprise and Education Directorate (TEED). The council is advised by a series of national advisory committees which work through a network of examination subject committees and ad hoc development committees whose total membership approaches 8,000.

City and Guilds does not itself run courses, it operates through approved centres. Something like 1,500,000 students in schools and colleges are following CGLI courses. This produces around 500,000 candidates for a range of 850 different examinations in nearly 300 different vocational subject areas. A further 50,000 students enter for skill tests and other types of examination on demand. Virtually all City and Guilds income comes from examining and testing fees. The Institute works through over 2,500 education and training centres in the United Kingdom and overseas. All

UK further education colleges are recognised as approved centres for CGLI courses and examinations; college chief administrative officers usually act as local examination secretaries.

CGLI has been converting its courses to a competence-basis since the early 1980s and this fits in well with the work of NCVQ and the Department of Employment. All examination syllabuses were rewritten to reflect the skills candidates need in their jobs. City and Guilds has worked closely with industry to set national standards; representatives from industry, commerce and public service provide expertise in the development of syllabuses as well as in assessment and moderating standards. Some 6,000 representatives are involved as committee members, assessors, examiners, verifiers and moderators. The move over to lead industry bodies has resulted in a number of joint certification agreements.

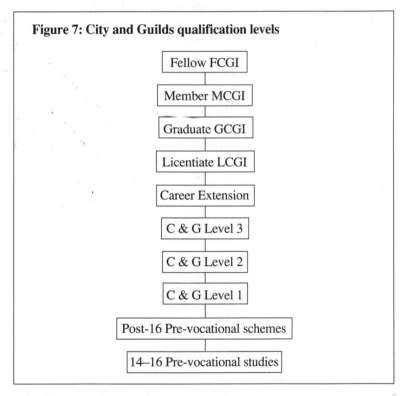

Figure 7: City and Guilds qualification levels

Fellow FCGI

Member MCGI

Graduate GCGI

Licentiate LCGI

Career Extension

C & G Level 3

C & G Level 2

C & G Level 1

Post-16 Pre-vocational schemes

14–16 Pre-vocational studies

The Institute has traditionally maintained a flexible, open system with no entry requirements for the majority of its certificates. There are no age restrictions and few stipulations about how or where the necessary learning has been acquired. It has also tended not to issue regulations on the length of courses. From 1988 CGLI allowed all its certificates to be available on the basis of credit accumulation so that candidates may enter for individual components of an examination and build up to a full certificate at whatever pace is appropriate. For success in individual components, students are awarded a record of achievement towards a full certificate. The local examination centres are based at colleges or training centres approved by City and Guilds. Centres can give credit for practical achievement at work, as if it had been done on a formal course, if they are satisfied that a candidate has met some or all of the performance criteria required for a particular component.

City and Guilds qualifications are awarded at a range of levels from awards for 14 to 16 year olds in schools right up to senior management level in industry, technology, education and commerce. Candidates can progress form one level to the next at their own pace. In addition to the three main occupational levels, there are four senior awards – the Licentiateship; Graduateship; Membership; and Fellowship of City and Guilds (see **Figure 7**). CGLI awards do not always correspond to those of National Vocational Qualifications, although adjustments are being made as industry lead bodies redefine their needs.

The Royal Society of Arts Examinations Board

The Royal Society of Arts Examinations Board (RSA) originated commercial and technological examinations in England in 1856. It has since helped to set up other organisations which deal with technical examinations, while itself concentrating on those concerned with information, business and communication. In 1987 the Examinations Board effected a formal separation from the Royal Society of Arts by establishing itself as a company limited by guarantee with charitable status. It is independent and self-financing, with most of its income coming from candidates' fees. The RSA is governed by a board which has ultimate responsibility. Its members are well-known people in industry, commerce and education, some of whom are nominated by national organisations associated with the work of vocational examining. The DFE and the Department of Employment appoint assessors to the board. The detailed work is supervised by a series of committees made up of representatives of employers, employees, professional organisations, teachers and trainers and other relevant bodies.

The RSA employs a full-time staff of some 150 which handles more than 625,000 entries each year; 40,000 of which are from overseas. Candidates for RSA certificates are examined and assessed by several thousand part-time staff, all with current (or very recent) practical experience in the relevant area. Open meetings are arranged at which representatives of those preparing candidates for the schemes can discuss every aspect with committee members and RSA assessors.

The activities of the RSA Examinations Board cover a wide range of vocational and pre-vocational education and training. RSA has tried to identify the major role to be performed in specific occupational areas, and to assess whether individuals have acquired the skills and abilities necessary to carry out that role. RSA schemes are used widely within Youth Training and the Technical Vocational Education Initiative. The RSA worked with the Southern Examining Group for the General Certificate of Secondary Education so that pupils' achievements could be recognised both for GCSE and vocational qualifications, to facilitate progression to employment and further education. The Board has endeavoured to relate its pattern of awards to the NVQ framework. In the meantime, it is best known for its single subject examinations based on three levels as below:

– Stage I indicates that a basic course in the subject has been completed and the successful candidate has sufficient knowledge or skill to begin employment, although further study would be beneficial.

– Stage II indicates a sound understanding and competence in the subject and a recommendation for employment. It also suggests that someone who holds such a certificate may well benefit from advanced studies.

– Stage III indicates an all-round knowledge and understanding of the subject and in the practical skills a very high degree of proficiency.

The RSA is the largest United Kingdom provider of certification for those who wish to enter office-based occupations. It is one of the leaders in the field of testing the effectiveness of communication and from this has developed a series of internationally-known schemes in the Teaching of English as a Second or Foreign Language (ESL/EFL). The RSA has collaborated with the University of Cambridge Local Examinations Syndicate to extend its EFL and ESL provision. The RSA's schemes run in all colleges of further education and most evening institutes. Its advanced certificate courses are offered in the higher education sector and many secondary schools enter pupils for the pre-vocational programmes. Entry to RSA courses is usually through approved centres based on institutions which cover both the public and private sectors. Many of these centres are represented on the RSA's advisory and scheme committees. Committees concerned with syllabus preparation and revision and question paper moderation always have a majority of teachers and lecturers directly concerned with the schemes.

The Scottish Vocational Education Council

The Scottish Vocational Education Council (SCOTVEC) was established in 1985 by the Secretary of State for Scotland from the merger of the Scottish Business Education Council (SCOTBEC) and the Scottish Technician Education Council (SCOTEC). SCOTVEC is responsible for developing, awarding and accrediting vocational qualifications. The Council works closely with industry, commerce and education to ensure that its qualifications are relevant to the needs of employment, flexible, responsive to change and recognised both nationally and internationally.

SCOTVEC's qualifications are based on a system of free-standing units which can be built up to group awards. The provision extends from individual National Certificate modules through to Higher National Certificates and Diplomas and postgraduate awards. SCOTVEC's qualifications cover the whole range of vocational education and training, including areas such as accounting, computing, engineering, secretarial, agriculture, construction, hotel and catering and many others. SCOTVEC units are blocks of study. Each unit incorporates a number of outcomes or goals which have to be achieved. When all of these outcomes have been successfully completed, the unit is awarded. The different types of unit include the National Certificate modules, higher national units, workplace-assessed units and industry units.

The Scottish National Certificate is a single vocational certificate listing modules successfully completed by any student, regardless of whether the modules have been taken in colleges, schools, as part of a training scheme such as YT or a recognised apprenticeship. The Certificate also offers an alternative for pupils in the fifth and sixth years of secondary schools who do not follow a full timetable of Higher grades of the Scottish Certificate of Education (SCE) or the Certificate of Sixth Year Studies (CSYS). A close relationship with certification for YT has developed through matching less specialised modules for the Certificate with the objectives of YT.

The National Certificate, which arose from the 1983 Scottish Action Plan, is based upon a collection of modules, usually of 40 hours' study, with a range of points of entry and exit. The Certificate allows opportunities to change areas of study with recognition given for earlier achievement. Full-time courses in further education are assembled from up to 20 modules taken each year, while day-release courses have about six modules. Modules can be combined to provide general education and training for pre-vocational courses or to meet specific vocational needs. In the earlier stages, appropriate modules may be common to several courses. The majority of the 100,000 enrolments are in further education colleges but two-thirds of Scottish secondary schools now present pupils for the National Certificate.

The Council recognises groupings of modules within the National Certificate as group awards. The group awards arrangements allow for joint certification with other bodies such as industrial training boards, non-statutory training organisations and other examining and validating bodies. SCOTVEC is also working on the recognition of prior learning as a contribution to a National Certificate. SCOTVEC assures the quality of the National Certificate by careful design and writing of the module descriptors, thereby defining the knowledge, skills and behaviour to be acquired, and specifying the standards to be achieved. Centres are validated in a similar way to BTEC to ensure that they have appropriate staff and resources. Subject assessors are appointed on a part-time basis from industry, commerce and education to monitor the assessment arrangements for modules.

SCOTVEC has moved away from a system of externally devised and examined courses to the use of the validation mechanism for its higher awards. The Council accepted a unit-based system which incorporated group awards as its favoured option for the future of the Higher National awards. The group award is either a Certificate or a Diploma depending on the grouping of units, each of which would be separately accredited. The unit credits are recognised by the award of a Certificate in Higher Vocational Studies. The awards are built up from blocks of 40-hour Higher National units, which attract a credit. It is possible to accumulate and transfer units smaller than one credit between and within institutions, even though national accreditation will only be available for one credit. A Higher National Certificate will need at least 12 credits and a Diploma will require a minimum of 20 credits. Units will be graded at pass or merit levels but the overall award will not carry any kind of grade. SCOTVEC has adopted a competency approach with an emphasis on outcomes rather than processes of learning. The units can either be college-devised or centrally designed.

SCOTVEC has introduced the Record of Education and Training (RET) to certify and record achievement in vocational education and training. The RET is a cumulative certificate, which is updated automatically each time success in a SCOTVEC unit or group award is achieved. It can also record recognition of a qualification by industry, professional bodies or others. The RET is computerised and has been designed to document life-long achievement. In addition, SCOTVEC operates SAMI, the System for Accessing Modular Information. SAMI is a computerised guidance information system comprising a set of software units which can be used to access information and provide guidance with the general framework of the SCOTVEC modular system.

Scottish Vocational Qualifications

Scottish Vocational Qualifications, like NVQs, are based on explicit standards of required performance defined by industry lead bodies. Assessment is on the basis of evidence of demonstrated performance in a work role and is independent of the learning programme, so that it could be achieved on the basis of prior achievement. Awards are categorised in 11 occupational areas. SCOTVEC was expected to have accredited 460 SVQs by the end of 1992. Unlike NVQs, as SCOTVEC National Awards, SVQs have an additional dimension with criteria which include breadth of application and range of activities beyond immediate technological and market conditions.

SVQs are commonly acquired through programmes of learning and training, but they can also be gained on the basis of evidence of prior learning and achievement. This makes them accessible to experienced employees, avoiding discouragement at having to undertake periods of extended training to cover already familiar ground. SVQs can be assessed at least partly by systematic production and assessment of evidence produced during the course of normal work. Credit can be accumulated unit by unit to build up a whole qualification over a period of time and by a combination of assessment of prior learning and learning based on a programme tailored to needs.

General Scottish Vocational Qualifications

Scotland also has an equivalent to GNVQs in its GSVQs. The General Scottish Vocational Qualifications were laid out in **Access and opportunity**, (SO 1991) the 1991 Scottish FE White Paper. They are based on the need to have broad-based qualifications for students who want to keep their options open. GSVQs will prepare students for employment in an occupational sector and will give grounding for more specific training leading to a SVQ. They will also enable students to progress up the educational ladder and into higher education. The GSVQ does have similarities to the SCOTCERT which was proposed by the Howie Committee in its report (Howie 1992).

GSVQs will build in guaranteed levels of attainment in communication, numeracy, information technology, problem-solving, and personal and interpersonal skills. Although core skills like these were originally envisaged in the Action Plan document (SED 1983a), which led the way to the introduction to the National Certificate, they were not introduced in a systematic way. The HMI survey, **Six years on** (HMI 1991a), pointed out that students were no more likely to have developed these skills than before the Action Plan. Unlike in the National Certificate, it is possible for students to gain a merit award based on very good performance in an additional integrative assignment. This new approach differentiates students' achievements on the basis of their ability to use their knowledge and skills in an integrated and rounded way.

Chapter 6
Pre-vocational students

Background

Until the 1970s further education was largely for students who had clear views about what they wanted to do. If they were in employment they could attend a part-time vocational course to secure training or qualifications, or if they wanted to prepare for employment they would enrol for a full-time vocational course. If they felt that academic study was best for them, they could join the growing numbers of young people and adults trying to secure GCE or SCE qualifications for entry into higher education or as a route into a middle range or professional post. If they were concerned with self-improvement, they could go to an adult continuing education course, usually in the evening.

The above groups did not cover all sections of young people, let alone adults. A major group that was missing was the large numbers of people who left school at the earliest opportunity in order to get a job. Young people of average ability were not encouraged to stay on at school, nor were they encouraged to attend college unless they were vocationally committed. This situation ended with the first UK post-war recession in the early 1970s, mainly induced by sharp rises in international oil prices. One of the consequences was that many companies shed labour, particularly unskilled labour. This caused unemployment to rise and those leaving school without qualifications joined the growing numbers of unemployed. Previously they would have taken an unskilled, semi-skilled or apprentice place with a company, and only some of them would have received training.

The dramatic effect on youth unemployment of a decade of recession can be seen from a Careers Office survey. At the beginning of 1974 the number of notified job vacancies for young people totalled 92,000, or 2,000 vacancies for every 100 unemployed school leavers. By January 1983 the number of unemployed school leavers was 133,400, and this excluded the 300,000 on government training and employment schemes. The number of unfilled vacancies at this time was 4,900, or about 3.6 vacancies per 100 unemployed school leavers.

A basis for choice

The Government reaction to youth employment was two-fold. The first was to use the newly created Manpower Services Commission to set up training and employment schemes. (These are described in Section 4.) The second was to look at ways in which more young people could be persuaded to stay on at school or college for further study. Further education colleges had to look at the design of schemes which would cater for this new group of potential students. In 1978 the Further Education Unit commissioned a study on post-16 pre-employment courses in which it found a variety of courses on offer. They are listed in the 1979 report, **A basis for choice** (FEU 1979).

First, there were extended general education courses, which were characterised by the influence of traditional subjects and the pursuit of nationally recognised accreditation as a well-established means of gaining entry to certain types of employment and/or to further study. The second category was transition courses distinguished by the priority given to assisting personal development, improving basic skills, preparing young people for entry into the world of work and enabling them to make a realistic choice of occupation. The final category was foundation courses identified by the grouping of subjects or by the integration of content to provide appropriate foundation or pre-vocational studies for entry to a group of closely related occupations or to clearly identified further vocational studies.

The authors of the survey concluded that the provision of courses was so tangled as to confound the investigator, let alone the undecided 16 year old. They argued for a rationalisation of provision in order to make available a chance of countering the dominant influence of the GCE O level (the forerunner to GCSE). An FEU study group recommended a unifying curriculum structure to promote the rationalisation and effectiveness of the range of available programmes. The target group was seen as school leavers with a wide spread of ability and attainment, who were intending to enter employment in the reasonably short-term and probably had a disinclination to embark on a full-time course of more than a year's duration. The young people were assumed to have a mixture of motivation, which might include:

- a genuine aspiration to continue in broad-based general education, with a vocational bias;
- a desire to defer vocational choice for another year, and/or provide themselves with a better basis for such choice;
- a feeling that a further year of full-time education would enhance the range and level of jobs available to them, either by improving their basic skills or by giving them some vocational preparation;
- a wish to commence a vocational education, though allied only to a generalised job preference;
- a need to postpone entry to the labour market for the time being;
- a hope to avoid unemployment.

The ideas in **A basis for choice** (ABC, FEU 1979) were piloted over the following two years in a series of college schemes validated by the City and Guilds of London Institute. A report, **ABC in action**, was published by the FEU in 1981. The Government, in its consultation paper **Examinations 16–18** (DES/WO 1980), considered that the right course was to secure the development of a pre-vocational examination, broadly along the lines recommended in ABC, which could be taken by young people attending either schools or colleges. At the same time the Employment Department's Manpower Services Commission was operating two youth employment and training schemes: the Youth Opportunities Programme (YOP) for the unemployed, and the Unified Vocational Programme (UVP) for the employed.

The Certificate of Pre-vocational Education

The Certificate of Pre-vocational Education (CPVE) was originally proposed by the Department of Education and Science and the Welsh Office to fill the gap in the range of qualifications available to young people. In its 1982 statement, **17+: a new qualification** (DES/WO 1982), the DES focused on school leavers who had not decided on the kind of occupation they wanted to enter and so were not in a position to pursue a vocational course in further education. These youngsters covered a wide range of abilities but the statement specifically excluded those who had the potential to take two or more GCE Advanced level examinations or who might be advised to concentrate on improving their GCE results. The new full-time programmes in education were to be seen as a parallel to Youth Training for those who wished to stay in full-time education. CPVE was to give a vocational bias to a continued general education programme and also to rationalise the qualifications within the pre-vocational area.

At the outset, the DES hoped that about 80,000 young people would eventually enrol on CPVE every year. This was roughly half the total number of young people thought to be potential candidates. It was recognised that it would take several years before CPVE was sufficiently well established to attract everyone who could benefit. However, 1987/88 entries were only about 40,000 and fell further in 1988/89. In 1991, the Department for Education estimated that CPVE was available in 60 per cent of sixth forms, and was taken by 22,000 pupils. The low numbers resulted from: competition from the new BTEC First Diploma offered in schools from 1991; the problems with sorting out progression routes; and the concentration of students within the lower ability range.

The 1986 White Paper (**Working together: education and training**, DES/DE 1986) which approved the establishment of the new National Vocational Qualification framework made specific reference to the place of CPVE. It suggested that appropriate combinations of CPVE preparatory modules might equate with, or contribute to, Level I NVQ and could constitute an important route to attainment at that level, in full- or part-time education or within YT. In 1987 the NCVQ agreed that the preparatory units could make a contribution towards a National Vocational Qualification in the foundation part of Level I.

An HM Inspectors' report on CPVE (**A survey of courses leading to the CPVE**, HMI 1988c), published in 1988, said that CPVE work had strengthened the links between schools and FE colleges. Enrolments had levelled out in school sixth form schemes but had fallen in further education, largely due to the counter-attraction of BTEC First Awards. The fact that First Award units can now be offered as CPVE preparatory modules should increase its attractiveness. The fall in CPVE numbers in further education would have been greater if some colleges had not begun to provide CPVE for students with special education needs or with language difficulties.

Diploma of Vocational Education

At the beginning of the 1990s, City and Guilds was given the remit to give CPVE 'more rigour'. After preparatory work in 1991, it launched the Diploma of Vocational Education (DVE). The Diploma will take over both CPVE and the CGLI foundation programmes, with a single title qualification covering a range of vocational needs for students aged 14 to 19. The Diploma of Vocational Education operates at three levels: Foundation; Intermediate; and National.

The Foundation level is for pupils aged 14 to 16 and uses a similar format to City and Guilds foundation programmes. Students are offered a very broad-based approach to vocational education in contexts including manufacturing and technical services, providing business services, and providing goods and services. City and Guilds aim to use the Diploma across the whole ability range, rather than focusing on either a narrow range of students or a limited range of vocational skills. A list of required experiences and components is being produced for each area to ensure national comparability and easier progression.

After 16, the Diploma operates at the Intermediate and National levels. The Intermediate is for one year and the National for two. It is intended to link with GNVQs at Levels II and III. It is hoped to establish the Diploma within the GNVQ framework. City and Guilds had approved over 200 centres to start the Diploma of Vocational Education, and over 1,000 separate programmes started in 1992.

Technical and Vocational Education Initiative

Alongside the initial development of CPVE was another scheme, which came under the Department of Employment rather than the DES. At the beginning of this chapter I reported that while the forerunner of CPVE, the ABC scheme, was developing, it was matched mainly by the training schemes of the former Manpower Services Commission, an arm of the Employment Department. Thus there was the Youth Opportunities Programme and the Unified Vocational Preparation scheme, which eventually combined to form the Youth Training Scheme (YTS, now YT). (These issues are discussed in Section 4.) A different kind of scheme, which was to operate in schools and colleges, was announced in 1982. This was the Technical and Vocational Education Initiative (TVEI). Its start in 1982 was not proclaimed by the Secretary of State for Education, as one might expect, but by the Prime Minister.

The Technical and Vocational Education Initiative (TVEI) is not an examination or a qualification but a learning framework for the 14 to 18 year old age group. The initiative was originally created and administered by a special TVEI Unit inside the Manpower Services Commission; it is now administered by the Training, Enterprise and Education Directorate (TEED) of the Employment Department along with the training and enterprise councils (TECs). TEED works closely with the Department for Education, HM Inspectorate, the Welsh Office and the Scottish Education Department.

TVEI's concerns are with the education of young people in the 14 to 18 age range. It aims to improve their preparation for the world of work; accustom them to using their skills and knowledge to solve real problems; emphasise the development of personal qualities such as initiative, motivation, enterprise and problem-solving skills; and establish industry's confidence in the curriculum.

TVEI started off as a large experimental scheme. The first round of TVEI operated through local authority pilot programmes which tried to explore and test ways of organising and managing readily replicated programmes of technical and vocational education for young people across the ability range.

Some local authorities were opposed to bidding for money for the early schemes because they thought the TVEI curriculum would be too narrow for comprehensive secondary schools and would introduce an unwelcome early specialisation. Nonetheless, in the end, all the authorities in Great Britain put in bids. The first round of TVEI approvals covered 14 pilot projects starting in September 1983. The projects in the first two years included 19 sixth form colleges, eight tertiary colleges, 75 colleges of further education and 19 other FE institutions.

Although the review of the pilot projects was declared a success by the Government without proper evaluation, it was generally thought that the scheme had provided valuable experience in identifying effective ways in which the education of 14 to 18 year olds could be made more relevant to the demands of adult life. The Government announced in its 1986 White Paper, **Working together: education and training** (DES/DE 1986), that TVEI would be extended into a national scheme. The intention was that students of all abilities in the age range 14 to 16 would eventually be covered by the scheme. The extension has now been implemented across all local authorities.

Local authorities were required to submit development plans to the Employment Department to show how they would provide programmes of full-time studies drawing on the experience of the TVEI pilot projects for all the 14 to 18 age range. The statement of curricular criteria submitted had to be consistent with the Government's policies for the curriculum as expressed in the White Paper, **Better schools** (DES/WO 1985) for England and Wales, and the **Munn Report** (SED 1982) and **16s–18s in Scotland: an action plan** (SED 1983a) for Scotland. TVEI was not introduced into Northern Ireland because it was considered that the existing pre-vocational schemes were already achieving the same results.

The Employment Department has stipulated that the common cores and option choices made available to TVEI students should be broad and balanced. Students should be able to acquire a proper balance of knowledge, understanding, attitudes and skills including practical applications. Programmes should include English, mathematics, science, humanities and the arts, practical and technological work, and access to modern languages (or, in Scotland, the modes of study set out in the Munn Report). There should also be provision for individual and social development, including personal counselling and guidance. Relevance may be improved by pre-vocational studies in appropriate cases and by relating what is taught in a broad sense to potential career opportunities locally and nationally, linked to good careers education and guidance.

There should be planned work experience from the age of 15 onwards. Differentiation should be built into programmes to cater for a range of abilities and aptitudes so that all students are stretched but are not put off by tasks that are beyond them. Wherever possible, the course of full- or part-time education and training should lead to nationally recognised qualifications approved by the Schools Examination and Assessment Council or the National Council for Vocational Qualifications or, in Scotland, the qualifications of SCOTVEC and/or the Scottish Examination Board. The qualifications will include GCSE, A and AS levels, BTEC, RSA, CGLI and CPVE or, in Scotland, SCE Standard, Ordinary, Higher and Certificate of Sixth Year Studies and National Certificate modules.

The DFE advice to authorities throughout the life of TVEI has stressed that colleges should not just become involved with TVEI after the age of 16, but that they should be part of the planning process from the outset. Programmes have had to show how students joining a TVEI programme at 16 in a college are to be integrated into the scheme. Authorities have also been asked to take note of the extended use of AS levels to broaden the sixth form curriculum and the role of CPVE and DVE. NCVQ accreditation in particular occupational sectors should be used where available. Progression through appropriate pathways should be highlighted to give maximum vocational and personal development.

The announcement of the National Curriculum for schools by the Secretary of State for Education caused some consternation for those operating TVEI. They feared that the new styles of learning introduced by TVEI could be affected because the pressure to cover the National Curriculum would lead to the teaching of mandatory subjects within the TVEI modules. The TVEI approach relies heavily on experiential learning and practical work delivering the curriculum in a modular form, rather than a reliance on subject teaching within a conventional school timetable.

The National Curriculum has increased the influence of the Department for Education not only for 14 to 16 year olds but also for the 16 to 19s. The National Curriculum Council had overall responsibility for all teaching and learning up to the age of 19 in school until 1993; its recommendations could overrule any parts of TVEI contracts. The DFE now has control over examinations and qualifications used by schools and colleges. This conflict between the two government departments during the 1980s and '90s generated instability in colleges and schools. In 1993 the NCC was replaced by a new body – the Schools Curriculum and Assessment Authority.

An evaluation of TVEI by HM Inspectorate, covering 1990–1, claimed that the pilot projects had done little to present a more balanced and coherent education to students. They said that in the first two phases, many students received a less balanced curriculum, such as less involvement in science, humanities and the arts. On the credit side, TVEI aimed to introduce and develop new courses with a more practical or vocational bent, and to link the subject matter taught in classrooms with applications and illustrations drawn from the outside world.

Although TVEI has tried to promote equal opportunities by avoiding gender stereotyping, it has been difficult to achieve, although modern business studies courses attract more boys than the traditional typing and commerce courses, where girls continue to dominate. Information technology proved more attractive to girls than computer studies. Gender stereotyping has been more persistent among the 16 to 19s. It was reflected in choices of vocationally oriented courses and of some A level subjects. There was clear sex differentiation in the type of work experience undertaken by the students.

Compacts

Another idea for improving the experiences of young people is the notion of 'compacts', based on initiatives developed in the United States. It involves a partnership between employers, schools and colleges, parents and young people, the careers service and community organisations. Compacts are concerned with all students between the ages of 14 and 18. Once an agreement has been established, employers and education partners determine that all students who reach the agreed goals will be offered training and jobs.

Employers' involvement is not limited to offering jobs and training. Representatives of the companies concerned are encouraged to influence the design of the curriculum and its relevance to employer needs. Company employees may be seconded to schools and colleges, and young people and teachers may work alongside company staff – the system known as work shadowing. Companies have been asked to contribute in cash or kind to support innovative programmes or activities and may donate material and equipment. They can sponsor young people during their education and training.

A compact should provide a framework for building on existing activities between schools and employers and should not ignore programmes such as TVEI, YT and other national and local initiatives. Most compacts cover a group of schools and colleges, which must be within an Urban Programme Area, but employers from outside may be involved. The schemes should be concerned with all students between the ages of 14 and 18, although the employer commitment to recruit and train young people will only apply to 16, 17 and 18 year old school and college leavers. The compact has to be based on a signed agreement between the local authority, schools and employers in which all parties commit themselves to measurable goals. The original intention was for employers to agree to provide jobs with training, or training with the assurance of a job at a later date, for all young people covered by the compact who meet agreed standards. The standards not only cover a specified level of educational performance but encompass factors such as attendance, punctuality and motivation. The continuing recession has led to a more modest scheme.

The Department of Employment provides help for the development of compacts to groups of employers in the inner cities who, in association with their local education authority, submit satisfactory outline proposals. The Department initially contributed towards 12 compact proposals in England, with separate arrangements for Wales and Scotland. Most of the local authorities with deprived inner city areas applied for development funds to bid for the 12 compacts, which were funded at £100,000 per year for four years. The first compacts started in 1989.

Chapter 7
Academic students

Participation

A steadily rising proportion – currently 18 per cent – of the 16 year olds in the United Kingdom study full-time at a further education college. Another 19 per cent of the same age group attend on a part-time day basis and five per cent during the evening. These figures represent 42 per cent of 16 year olds. For the whole of the 16 to 18 age group, the participation rate for all modes of study is 34 per cent. There are also large numbers over the age of 19 who go to make up the 1.8 million participants in CFE classes. Many of these students are working towards qualifications which can be described as academic, rather than the vocational ones that were described in Chapter 5. Most colleges in England, Wales and Northern Ireland offer a wide range of subjects at GCE Advanced level, as well as at Advanced Supplementary and General Certificate of Secondary Education levels. In Scotland, Ordinary, Standard and Higher levels are available, as well as some A levels. At the start of the 1990s, 112,000 people of all ages were studying for full-time academic courses (GCSE, GCE, CSE, SCE) in United Kingdom further education colleges as opposed to 162,000 following BTEC/ SCOTVEC programmes and 63,000 for CGLI. As well as the full-time students, 64,000 attended part-time and 221,000 during the evening, giving a total enrolment of 397,000.

In a significant proportion of English and Welsh LEAs there has been post-16 institutional reorganisation which has resulted in the abolition of sixth forms, the traditional place where academic qualifications have been taught for those students beyond the compulsory school leaving age. Within a number of local authorities, the sixth forms of various schools have merged to form a sixth form college, technically part of the school system up to 1993, but now comes under the FE Funding Council. Sixth form colleges have traditionally concentrated on academic subjects. This replicated the type of institution in many countries in mainland Europe, where the top quarter to one-third of the ability range would concentrate on essentially preparing for higher education.

In other authorities where sixth forms were abolished, all the post-16 work was concentrated in one establishment, a tertiary college. Thus in a steadily growing number of local areas, the further education institution is the sole public sector provider of academic qualifications for the 16 to 18 age group. This kind of institution is peculiar to Britain. Although considerable interest is being shown in the tertiary college by countries such as Holland and Denmark, where the post-school sector is being rationalised, each country is moving towards its own particular solution.

Academic qualifications in the post-compulsory public sector can thus be taken by young people in school, in a sixth form college or an FE college and by adults in further education colleges, adult education centres or by some kind of distance learning. As the number of sixth forms has declined, the percentage of students studying for academic qualifications in FE colleges has increased. This has been give impetus in the 1990s by the Government's desire to increase the proportion of young people participating in full-time education after 16, as opposed to entering a YT programme or obtaining a job. At the beginning of the decade the Secretary of State for Education called for an increase in the 50+ per cent of the age group staying on in schools and colleges post-16. This has led to an increase in the number of students in colleges. The Secretary of State for Education pointed out that colleges were not far behind schools in equipping people with qualifications sufficient for entry into higher education. For example, 41 per cent of all GCE Advanced level entries were from the further education sector.

Examinations at 16 plus

In the last two years of schooling in the United Kingdom, young people study for examinations taken at the compulsory school leaving age. In England, Wales and Northern Ireland, where secondary schools normally start at the age of 11, the last two years are known as years 10 and 11 (formerly known the fourth and fifth years of secondary study). In Scotland, where 12 is the common age of transfer from primary to secondary school, the last two years are known as S3 and S4. Pupils at the end of S3 and S4 are entered for the Scottish Certificate of Education at either Ordinary or Standard level.

There is a significant number of students in the United Kingdom, who, having done badly in school, want to improve their GCSE or SCE qualifications. These students divide into two groups. The first group is those who leave school but go straight to college at 16 or 17. They can either repeat a full programme of subjects for GCSE or SCE or mix resits with a vocational course, under what is often called a mixed-economy programme. Results for those who do a straight programme of resits are usually not very good. The second group is those older students who want to improve their qualifications after a period of work, unemployment or child care. They usually return to college on a part-time basis to see if they can get some GCSE or SCE subjects at the higher grades. If they are successful this often leads either to progression to an A level or Scottish Higher programme, or entry into vocational courses – including the lower levels of professional qualifications. The two main school leaving examination systems are discussed below, followed by the post-16 qualifications.

General Certificate of Secondary Education

From 1987 the GCSE replaced the two former secondary examinations in England and Wales, which were known as the GCE Ordinary (or O) level and the Certificate of Secondary Education (CSE). GCSEs are awarded on a seven point scale from A to G. Grades A to C correspond to the former O level or CSE Grade 1 pass. Grades D to G are comparable with the achievement recorded in CSE grades 2 to 5. The GCSE is a single system of examinations – not a single examination. It is administered by six boards: the four in England are London Examinations, the Midland Examining Group, the Northern Examining and Assessment Board and the Southern Examining Group. The Welsh Joint Education Committee covers Wales; and the Northern Ireland Schools Examinations Council caters for Northern Ireland. All GCSE syllabuses, assessment and grading procedures which were, until 1993, vetted by the School Examinations and Assessment Council (SEAC) to ensure that they conformed to national criteria, now come under the auspices of SCAA. The GCSE aims to measure what pupils can actually achieve, rather than comparing their performance with other pupils as in the old GCE O level system.

To give an indication of subject popularity, the major subject entries in 1992 are shown in **Figure 8**.

There was considerable criticism of GCSE at the end of the first examination series in 1988. These criticisms centred on three issues: the rushed implementation timetable; differences between the examining groups with regard to administrative procedures; and the operation of the Joint Council for GCSE. Nevertheless, an HMI report (HMI 1988a) on the first two years of operation took the view that the introduction of GCSE had been largely successful. The Government said that the effective introduction of GCSE should be a model for the development of the National Curriculum, leading to changed teaching styles and curriculum processes. It was suggested that the introduction of GCSE had given encouragement to more students to stay on for further education at school or college. Over the first four years of the GCSE, the percentage of success in the higher grades has slowly risen, giving rise to criticism from more traditional quarters that GCSE is not a good test of the abilities of young people, particularly the more academic ones.

Figure 8: GCSE major subject entries (1992)

Subject	Number
Mathematics	661,655
English	654,742
English literature	394,260
Geography	295,163
Biology	293,949
Physics	245,218
History	242,760
French	238,132
Art and design	221,438
Chemistry	214,818
Home economics	187,543
Craft design	157,021
Science	113,091
Religious studies	104,009
Computer studies	97,028
German	68,675
Economics	32,449

The National Curriculum

The introduction of the National Curriculum means that young people sitting examinations at the compulsory school leaving age will be assessed at the various National Curriculum levels on a scale of 1 to 10. The National Curriculum requires all pupils aged 11 to 16 in England to study 10 foundation subjects (11 in Wales). All pupils are expected to take the core subjects at GCSE and most will take several of the remaining subjects to GCSE. At Key Stage 4 at 16, the average pupil should be able to achieve a level of 6 to 7. The GCSE A to C range corresponds with National Curriculum levels 7 to 10. (See Chapter 22 for more detail.)

The Scottish Certificate of Education

Scotland had no counterpart to the former CSE examinations which were offered in England and Wales from 1967 to 1987. The equivalent to the old GCE O level is the Scottish Certificate of Education (SCE). The

SCE Ordinary O grade course leads to an examination at the end of the fourth year (S4) of secondary school. The new Standard Grade examination caters for a wide range of academic ability, including the CSE equivalent, and covers the same range as GCSE.

Unlike in England, where there is a range of examining bodies for academic qualifications, there is only one for Scotland – the Scottish Examination Board (SEB). This is a statutory body, which operates secondary examinations and awards and provides advice to the Secretary of State for Scotland on secondary examinations. The Consultative Committee on the Curriculum (CCC), a non-statutory body, advises the Secretary of State on the school curriculum, the running of a programme of curriculum development and the issuing of guidance to schools. At the beginning of the decade, the SEB powers were widened to enable it to play a part in preparing material for testing in primary schools and ensuring the Secretary of State's reserve power to require such testing. It was also given a reserve power to require appraisal of teachers in line with regulations made by the Secretary of State.

A levels

The General Certificate of Education Advanced Level (GCE A level) was designed in the late 1940s; the first examinations were taken in 1951. The Advanced level is a single subject examination, unlike the Higher School Certificate which it replaced, and candidates may enter for one subject, or a combination of subjects, on as many occasions as they wish.

In the 1950s it was traditional to study for three A levels over a period of two years in the sixth form of a grammar school or an independent school. The 75 per cent of children who did not get into grammar schools, because they had failed the selection tests (usually called the 11 plus), attended secondary modern schools, most of which did not have a sixth form. During the 1960s many local authorities started to reorganise their schools under comprehensive principles. Separate grammar and secondary modern schools were merged to form comprehensive schools which catered for children with a wide range of ability. By the start of the 1970s in England, 34 per cent of pupils went to a comprehensive school. The comprehensives built up sixth form provision to give more pupils access to A levels. During this period more colleges of further education started offering A levels to young people who did not want to stay in school or to adults who wanted to return to education. These changes resulted in a reduction in the proportion of candidates who sat for examinations in three or four Advanced level subjects. This trend accelerated with the increase in the numbers of both full-time and part-time students attending colleges of further education to study A levels in the 1970s and 1980s.

The Advanced levels are administered by seven GCE boards in England and one in Wales. The boards are independent bodies which have considerable freedom in deciding what A levels they will offer, although all the syllabuses are subject to approval by the Schools Curriculum and Assessment Authority. The Associated Examining Board attracts a large proportion of further education candidates, while the Oxford and Cambridge board is favoured by the private schools. The Northern Ireland Board mainly takes students from Ulster. There has been growing criticism of the differing pass rates in the same subjects across the five general English boards and some people would favour a Scottish style system of one board, although this would be resisted by those institutions that shop around boards to get the syllabus which most meets their requirements.

The market for GCE Advanced levels in the education service has changed since their inception. In 1951, the first year pupils sat for A levels, 37,000 candidates took a total of 104,000 subject entries. Over the next two decades the numbers taking A levels grew tenfold. By 1985 there were 380,000 candidates who entered for nearly 635,000 individual A levels. The steadily increasing trend for young people to stay in education beyond the age of 16, partly influenced by the recession at the end of the 1980s and into the 1990s, meant that the number of subject entries had reached 730,000 by 1992. A further factor was the increase in mature students, shown by the fact that one-third of these entries were over the age of 18.

Only a small proportion of school leavers achieve any A level passes at all. A breakdown of the examination results of the 614,000 school leavers in 1990 in England and Wales shows that only 14 per cent achieved three or more passes at A level, 20 per cent obtained two or more passes; and nearly 24 per cent gained at least one A level pass. Thus less than a quarter of school leavers, confined largely to the most academically able, achieved any success at A levels. There is also a planned failure rate in that, on average, nearly one-third of those who take the examination in any subject do not receive an A level pass grade in that subject. The A level examination is not based on the achievement of specified competences, as in many vocational examinations. Rather, students are competing against others to get into the 70 per cent of entrants who will be passed. An important use of GCE A level has been to act as a filter mechanism for entry into higher education.

In the past, A level results have been used as a predictor of success at first degree level. This assumption has been increasingly questioned, with maturity and motivation now being included in the factors bearing on degree-level achievement – especially for the growing numbers of older students. The importance of the A level as a selection device for higher education is declining since only about half of those who leave school with two or more A level passes enrol on degree courses. Many more young people and adults are now entering higher education institutions on the basis of success either in vocational programmes, such as the National level courses of the Business and Technology Education Council and the Scottish Vocational Education Council, or access courses.

Passes at GCE A level are awarded at five grades. Grade A is the top grade, descending to E as the lowest pass grade. Those falling under the borderline for a pass are given an N grade for what is called a narrow failure, or a U grade which means that the candidate is unclassified. There has been some controversy in recent years about where the success point for the middle grades is fixed. Candidates with only a few marks difference in their papers could find that one is put at the bottom of Grade B and the other at the top of grade D. Revisions were made in 1987 to the A level grading system to try to solve the problem of the narrow mark range at grade C. The result was that grades C to E were more evenly distributed.

There have been a number of attempts to broaden academic post-16 curricula for England, Wales and Northern Ireland by offering something wider than the usual three A level GCEs, but all have been rejected by Conservative governments. A comprehensive review was undertaken by a committee chaired by Dr Gordon Higginson (DES 1988a). The Higginson Committee recommended in 1988 that the normal academic menu should be widened from three to five A level subjects as a norm, by creating leaner syllabuses, combined with at least one GCE Advanced Supplementary (AS) level subject. The committee felt that in the four decades since they were introduced, the syllabuses had expanded too much with the result that candidates were over-burdened with having to memorise too large an amount of information. The final report of the Higginson Committee (DES 1988a) recommended a compulsory common core for each subject to give greater comparability between examination boards and to help employers understand the value of A level courses. A further recommendation was for a reduction of the 400 separate syllabuses.

The Higginson Committee said that A level programmes of study were too narrow and encouraged a premature specialisation not found among young people in many other industrialised countries (including Scotland). The committee thought that the ability of a student to think, act and apply information should be as important as a mere understanding of knowledge and facts. They did not go so far as insisting that all full-time A level students should study a mixture of science and humanities, together with at least one modern language, as students in many other Western European countries do.

Models from other countries

Our industrial competitor countries provide more educational breadth for their 16 to 19 age group; this has resulted in national economic benefits arising from a more broadly educated and adaptable workforce. The French Baccalaureate, for example, is a multi-subject examination and is studied for over a three year period. The German Abitur consists of four subjects with written examinations in two main subjects and an optional subject, and an oral examination in a second option. Candidates must include study of German, a modern foreign language and mathematics or natural science. The grading system takes account of course work as well as the final examination. In the United States of America the high school diploma requires that, of the subjects studied, seven are compulsory: English, social studies, mathematics, science, a foreign language, health and physical education.

Despite the limited nature of the reforms proposed, the then Secretary of State for Education rejected the main thrust of the Higginson Report in favour of a reliance on the use of Advanced Supplementary (AS) levels to give more breadth when taken with A levels. The DES put forward the reasons that, with GCSE changes, the school system was in danger of becoming overloaded and Ministers were not convinced that A level course content could be made leaner without diluting rigour and high academic standards.

Figure 9 shows the number of A level entries for the subjects accounting for at least one per cent of the total entries for the English boards in the summer of 1992. The large range of A level subjects sometimes makes subject groupings difficult, but I have used the nationally published figures. The Advanced Supplementary results are shown alongside for comparison.

The figure does not show the gender differences. Males dominate in mathematics, physics, chemistry and economics. Females have the clear majority in English, biology, art/music and general studies. The last few years have seen a slow decline in the numbers taking science subjects, with the exception of biology. The increase in arts subjects has led to more entries to already oversubscribed courses in these areas in higher education, while there is a growing national shortage of scientists and engineers.

Most sixth forms have provided general studies programmes in an attempt to give breadth and balance. Particular criticism has been made for some years of arts students who lack numeracy skills and science students who need help with communication skills. The introduction of AS levels has only gone a small way towards achieving the broadening the Government wishes.

Figure 9: A and AS level entries (1992 provisional results) arranged according to the most popular A level subjects

Subject	A level	Percentage	AS level	Percentage
English	86,685	12.0	2,758	5.2
Mathematics	72,357	9.9	10,588	20.0
Social sciences	70,321	9.6	5,716	10.8
General studies	53,651	7.3	9,314	17.7
Biology	48,707	6.7	2,362	4.5
History	46,680	6.4	1,088	2.1
Geography	45,603	6.2	872	1.7
Chemistry	42,695	5.8	951	1.8
Physics	41,273	5.7	1,556	3.0
Economics	40,194	5.5	1,349	2.6
Art and design	33,644	4.6	1,460	2.8
French	31,254	4.3	3,163	6.0
Business studies	19,134	2.6	2,075	3.9
German	11,328	1.6	1,273	2.3
Computing	9,158	1.3	1,837	3.5
Technology	9,213	1.3	425	0.8
Classical subjects	8,341	1.1	623	1.2
Religious studies	7,550	1.0	1,213	2.3
All other subjects	52,424	7.2	4120	7.8
TOTAL	730,212	100.0	52,743	100.0

GCE Advanced Supplementary levels

The role of GCE Advanced Supplementary levels (AS) was outlined in the 1985 White Paper, **Better schools** (DES/WO 1985). It stated that AS levels should be intellectually demanding and coherent, with a practical emphasis where appropriate, requiring two and a half hours of teaching per week and half the time taken for studying an A level. They would be related where possible to A levels and would introduce more breadth and balance. The Government hoped that arts-based students would study mathematics, and science-based students would take up a modern language. The Secretary of State's initial aim was that 95 per cent of the secondary schools which provided A levels would be offering at least two AS levels by 1990: this was not achieved. **Figure 9** shows how the entries for AS levels compare with the most popular A levels. It can be seen that the order of popularity is not the same. This is because some AS levels are more popular than others in being tagged on to a one, two or three A level programme.

When the scheme was set up it was expected that those students taking two A levels and two AS levels should have as many demands on them as those taking three A levels. AS level syllabuses should be as intellectually demanding as A levels but would take account of the shorter teaching and studying time available. The achievement of each grade would demand the same quality of work as comparable grades in A level examinations although, inevitably, less ground would be covered. The expectation was that young people would study subjects which contrast with, as well as complement, their main field of study. For instance, if a student intends to study economics, geography and history at A level, he or she might take one of these at AS level rather than at A level and, in addition, an AS level in a foreign language or mathematics or statistics. The introduction of Advanced Supplementary levels has been generally welcomed by higher education, employers and professional bodies. Colleges, with their larger programme of A levels, have found it easier to mount AS levels than many small school sixth forms.

A DES survey of schools and colleges in England and Wales looked at the two years of operation of AS levels in 1987/89 (HMI 1989a). In 1987, in schools which offered AS levels, one in five A level students was taking them, although this represented only four per cent of the total first year A level population. The five most popular subjects were general studies, mathematics, computing, English and French. Nearly 7,000 students began AS courses in 1987; by 1992, entries were over the 50,000 mark. One disappointing fact indicated by the survey was that the vast majority of students taking Advanced Supplementary levels were taking only one subject at that level with two or more Advanced levels. Only seven per cent were taking two Advanced Supplementary levels with two Advanced levels, which the Department of Education and Science had described as the norm. The take-up of AS levels tends to be concentrated in the larger sixth forms and sixth form colleges. It can be seen from **Figure 9** that AS level entries are still only running at seven per cent of those for A level. Some smaller institutions expressed reservations about offering AS levels due to continuing lack of staff and resources, as well as dissatisfaction with what the examination boards had to offer. Like A levels, AS levels have a high built in failure rate, in this case 32 per cent, although this is reducing.

The 1992 AS Chief Examiners' Conference highlighted continuing difficulties. Some teachers still did not appreciate what AS had been designed for and were using it variously as a screening for A level entry, a half-way house or practice run for A level – all at the end of a one year course. There was a clear view that for AS examinations to be more successful, it was necessary for A and AS syllabuses to be co-teachable. The relatively weak currency of the AS qualification still acted as a deterrent to some institutions, candidates and parents. Employers appeared not to understand AS examinations and the acceptability of AS to higher education as a general requirement was still too low. There appeared to be more scientists taking AS arts subjects than arts students following AS science courses. While it was accepted in principle that a common standard across A level and AS was expected, the equivalence was proving difficult to realise in practice.

Scottish Higher Grade

In Scotland, there is an entirely different system of academic qualifications, reflecting a broad range of study. Over a century ago – in 1888 – a school leaving examination was introduced in Scotland to give a national standard on which to base entry to universities and the professions. This was the origin of the Scottish Higher Grade. Scottish pupils in the fifth and sixth years of secondary school (S5 and S6), which correspond with the two years of the sixth form in the rest of the United Kingdom, are entered for the Scottish Certificate of Education Higher grade. When Highers are taken over two years, more subjects are taken at Higher Grade than at A level. For the better H grade candidates, the range of subjects covered may be almost as wide as for the O grade. It is not unusual for candidates to study five or six subjects spanning both arts and sciences. This kind of breadth of study for Higher Grades allows a cross-fertilisation between arts and science subjects which is not seen under the A level system. It also allows young people to delay specialisation. Pass rates are also better: 36 per cent of Scottish pupils are successful in at least one subject, compared to 24 per cent in England who obtain one or more A levels while 30 per cent of the age group pass two or more Highers, in contrast to only 20 per cent in England who obtain the corresponding two A levels.

A breakdown of young people leaving during the 1988/89 academic year with SCE Higher Grades showed that a total of 26,000 achieved at least one pass; of these 17,000 obtained at least three or more passes; nearly 13,000 of the group got four passes. The percentage of leavers with three or more highers rose from 17 per cent in the mid-1970s to nearly 25 per cent at the end of the 1980s. Four passes at Higher Grade is used by three-quarters of successful candidates as the basis for entry to further education, professional training or higher education. Most degrees in Scotland take four years rather than the three years prevalent in the rest of the United Kingdom. Those pupils who have obtained the desired number of Higher passes in S5 and who wish to continue their studies in particular subjects may take the Certificate of Sixth Year Studies.

The academic/vocational divide

During the 1980s, the Government became increasingly concerned about the continuing divide between academic and vocational qualifications. In 1991, the first volume of the White Paper **Education and training for the 21st century** (DES *et al.* 1991a) tackled the subject by suggesting the creation of new diplomas – the Ordinary and Advanced Diplomas. Section 4 was headed: Equal status for academic and vocational qualifications. I quote below several paragraphs to outline government thinking.

> 4.3 Academic and vocational qualifications deserve equal recognition. All young people need to be aware of the opportunities offered by vocational qualifications. The Government believes that young people should be encouraged to choose a blend of qualifications to suit their individual needs and talents. After 16 they should have a free choice between A level, AS qualifications, NVQs and combinations of them.

> 4.4 In order to meet these objectives, the Government intends to establish a new system of Ordinary and Advanced Diplomas. We will consult widely on this proposal. The Ordinary Diploma might be awarded to those gaining four or five GCSEs at National Curriculum levels 7 to 10, equivalent vocational qualifications, or any combination of these. The Advanced Diploma might be awarded to those gaining two A levels at grades C or above, an equivalent combination of A and AS, equivalent vocational qualifications, or a combination of A level, AS and vocational qualifications.

> 4.5 The progressive accreditation of vocational qualifications by the NCVQ will provide a basis for specifying the qualifications and combinations of qualifications which will comprise the Advanced Diploma. As general NVQs come on stream, the breadth that it is envisaged they will offer should provide a particularly sound basis for award of Diplomas.

The most recent initiative in the academic/vocational area is the Technological Baccalaureate, launched by City and Guilds in 1991. The 'Tech Bac' will offer students the choice of studying for either A levels or vocational qualifications within an overall technological curriculum. Whether aiming for A levels or a vocational qualification such as BTEC National, students have to follow a core of technological and personal skills studies related to a broad occupational area. Assessment will be a combination of an external examination and other methods, but City and Guilds will accept A level and BTEC results as part of it.

It has not yet been decided how it will fit in with the new Advanced Diploma. The new qualification has no links with the International Baccalaureate. The International Baccalaureate (IB) has been taken up by some schools and colleges which have a proportion of pupils whose parents want them to have qualifications which are more widely recognised than the UK ones. This is often because the parents may be in jobs with international mobility, which will increase following the introduction of the single market in the European Community.

Chapter 8
Adult and continuing students

Adults in further education split relatively easily into two groups: adult education students and those registered for adult training. This chapter concentrates on those in adult education; adult training is dealt with in Section 4. While the boundaries between education and training are not totally delineated, they are sufficiently clear for the two groups to be separated. In adult continuing education the name of the course will usually identify the type of student involved. With adult training it is the occupational/vocational group and the category of training scheme that distinguishes students, although there can be considerable overlap. For example, in adult recreational studies, learning a language can be a leisure course taken for pleasure and interest, while for an export manager it is a vocational requirement.

Historical development of adult education

The idea of adult education started at the beginning of the 19th century. In the first half of that century it relied on the support of religious and philanthropic organisations, fuelled by an interest in the discoveries in the physical sciences. The mechanics institutes started up in the 1820s and 30 years later had a membership of over 600,000. By the 1860s there was a general decline in the fortunes of the institutes as working men dropped out and were replaced by the educated middle classes. Later, working class social and political pressure groups gave ordinary people a motive for improving self-expression. After 1850 the growth of elementary education was reducing general adult illiteracy and the people's colleges, many of which were to develop into higher education institutions, played an important role in educating the brighter blue collar workers.

Adult education developed considerably under the University Extension Movement. The original idea was to make the universities of Oxford and Cambridge endow a system of local professors; the first university extension lectures began in the 1870s. Initially the lectures were given to large audiences of intelligent working men and women but because the classes had to be self-supporting, costs forced many to drop out. In a number of areas they were replaced by middle class people wanting a more formal education, as happened with the mechanics institutes. Several provincial universities later developed from these extension centres.

At the beginning of the 20th century the creation of local education authorities meant that many of them chose to subsidise adult education, particularly the Workers' Education Association (WEA). Public money was granted after the First World War and was followed in 1924 by Regulations for Adult Education Classes which outlined the conditions under which grants could be made. These regulations were later expanded and modified several times, particularly after the 1944 Education Act.

The Russell Committee Report (**Adult education: a plan for development**, DES 1973) gave a picture of what adult education should be in England and Wales:

Our view is of a comprehensive and flexible service of adult education, broad enough to meet the whole range of educational needs of the adult in our society. It must, therefore, be integrated with all the other sectors of the educational system but at the same time firmly rooted in the active life of local communities; and it must be readily accessible to all who need it, whatever their means or circumstances.

The Russell Committee, whose terms of reference were to assess the need for and to review the provision of non-vocational adult education, saw adult education as meeting the needs of three kinds of people. First there were those who wished to continue with a formal education. The second group were those wishing to pursue creative study. Finally, adult education ought to enable citizens to play a more active part in some of the many roles they find themselves in, such as consumer, voluntary worker, shop steward and magistrate.

Even though the Russell Report said that 'permanent education is a long-term concept and we do not have time to wait for it,' progress has been patchy since 1973. Economic pressures have often meant a retrenchment in the service because of the lack of a statutory requirement upon various adult education agencies to provide a reasonable level of service. Most adult education has remained within the second Russell category – evening classes geared mainly to art, languages and hobbies.

Current provision and participation

There is a wide range of provision for the education of adults in the United Kingdom, with a large reliance on voluntary organisations reflecting the historical nature of its development. An FEU study of provision and participation in adult education and training in England and Wales (**Provision and participation in adult education**, FEU 1987) recorded that 2.5 million adults attended further education courses in public sector educational institutions in 1984/85. Further education colleges catered for 32 per cent of the adults, but the majority (59 per cent) went to a local education authority adult education centre. The minor providers nationally were the community schools, institutes of higher education, university departments of extra-mural studies, the Workers' Education Association, long- and short-term residential colleges and a range of voluntary organisations. Some courses are specifically provided for adults, but adults also attend the vocational and academic courses discussed in previous chapters.

The picture for the whole of the United Kingdom can be estimated from the figures given in the 1991 edition of **Education statistics in the UK** (DES). The total number of United Kingdom students in further education in 1989/90 is recorded as 3,655,000. If the 619,000 who are in voluntary institutions, which do not record details of the students (such as age), are ignored, along with the 1,502,000 who are enrolled on courses leading to specified vocational and academic qualifications, then the remaining 1,534,000 are probably on public sector general adult education courses. Of the total 3.6 million students, 1.86 million attend in the evening. A detailed survey in 1990/91 for England, showed 1,309,394 adult education students aged 19 and over in further education colleges and a further 1,266,216 in adult education centres. Where the age of students has been recorded, 67 per cent of those attending evening classes were aged 25 and over, while less than 10 per cent were in the 16 to 18 age group. Three-quarters were women.

In its survey of further education published in 1987 (HMI 1987), the Inspectorate described adult education within FE colleges. HMI found that the range of college provision was influenced by geographical, organisational and resource factors. Generally included in the adult education element were languages and arts and crafts, GCE and GCSE subjects, physical education and access courses leading into higher education. Training would normally include professional, industrial and commercial updating courses for the employed (PICKUP) and training for the unemployed (under REPLAN at the time). Some colleges provided opportunities for adults with literacy and numeracy problems to improve their basic skills. A number of colleges, especially in inner city areas with substantial numbers of people from ethnic minority groups, offered English as a second language.

A 1991 HMI Review, **Education for adults** (HMI 1991b), was of the view that adult education had a long tradition of responding to needs and enabling access by establishing provision in convenient locations. Its strengths lay in consistently good quality provision, a dedicated teaching force, highly motivated students, a rich and varied tradition, an ability to respond quickly to identified needs, a wide variety of provision at many different levels and a range of local delivery points. However, weaknesses were identified, including management deficiencies resulting from the ratio of full- to part-time staff, a predominance of barely adequate accommodation and equipment, inadequate machinery to plan, monitor and evaluate provision and the wide variation in the amount of provision made by different LEAs.

The review concluded that adult education was no longer always clearly distinguishable from the mainstream work of further education. Perhaps, partly because of this, the Government moved to transfer most adult education to beneath the banner of the FE colleges.

Adult education within FE colleges

Up to 1993, when colleges became independent, incorporated institutions, each of the local education authorities decided whether their further education college(s) should be the main provider for adults within their area. The involvement of FE colleges with adult continuing education has increased as they have broadened their range of programmes to move away from their previous role as narrower vocational colleges. Many FE institutions now see themselves as community colleges providing the whole range of post-18 FE courses. This concept of the community college also encompasses the tertiary community colleges providing all post-16 further education. Some LEAs, however, kept the role of their colleges to a minimum because their perception was that most college staff were not at their best in delivering adult education in small centres away from the college. These LEAs usually maintained a separate system of adult education centres within a separate community education service. In some cities and large towns, the community education service had a wide remit which included the idea of community development in conjunction with youth and community officers.

HMI found that in the colleges which were seen by their LEAs as the major providers of adult education in their catchment areas, the majority had local adult education centres associated with them. In these colleges, adult learning opportunities were usually co-ordinated by a separate department of adult and continuing education, or of adult and community studies. College departments with the title of 'community education' frequently included adult education and general education, often alongside other areas such as community development, social work, health and welfare. The Inspectors found little regular or systematic co-operation between colleges and other providers of adult education or, in certain cases, between adult education and other departments in the same college. Where a college did not have a separate department for adult education, the cross-college adult education co-ordinators (where they existed) often had insufficient status to develop their role and make demands for staff and resources from mainstream departments.

About 70 per cent of the provision for adults takes place during the evenings and not all colleges offer any substantial daytime provision in courses not leading to examination, despite the fact that many adults, including those who are unemployed, would prefer this. HMI found that

GCE courses attracted about 20 per cent of the total numbers of adults, including many from ethnic minorities.

Most colleges have developed provision under Employment Training in a variety of vocational areas, although some LEAs prevented their colleges becoming more than minimally involved prior to their independence in 1993 because of objections to the nature of the scheme. In some areas of high unemployment a range of adult vocational provision is supported by the European Social Fund.

Where adult education is college-based it is more likely to be built on the range of existing skills of the college staff than on community demand. Most of the courses are taught by part-time teachers who are not permanent members of the college staff. In specialised vocational work students are taught almost entirely by full-time staff because of the problems of recruiting part-time staff during the day. In adult education it is more usual for a small group of full-time permanent staff to co-ordinate the work of a lot of part-time staff. Many of these teachers are well-qualified and experienced in their subject areas and bring a rich and varied background to their classes. Many of these part-time teachers have taught their subjects for a number of years and are highly enthusiastic and motivated; qualities they pass on to their students.

Open and distance learning are increasingly being used for adults who do not want to attend on a regular basis and would like to study at their own pace. They can study at home with access to college staff for tutorials and seminars and help with course packs.

Adult education students range in age from those who are 16 to a not insignificant number over the age of 80. Reasons for attending are various. Some, who are settled in their jobs and family relationships, attend out of general interest. Others see a chance for career progression, especially in the wide range of professional courses. An increasing number are looking for qualifications to enable them to progress to higher education. Most of these students are well motivated, committed and involved. Drop-out can be high in general interest courses as winter weather sets in, but adult students often return the following year or, increasingly, change to open learning.

A major problem with many main college sites is the teenage culture which prevails during the day, especially in the recreational and eating areas. More colleges now have creche facilities, and most have at least some kind of limited child care arrangements. Colleges have increased their counselling and guidance systems, both in response to general demand but also to meet the particular problems of adults. Women on full-time or part-time access courses may encounter pressures from their partners, children or general family because their personal growth through successful study changes the nature of former relationships.

Adult education courses in the 1980s survived despite major cut-backs by local education authorities who had their funding reduced by central government. LEAs tended to protect courses for young people and in the vocational areas at the expense of what are seen as more voluntary activities such as adult education. The result was either a cut in the range of adult continuing education or the raising of course fees dramatically to cover costs.

Adult education after April 1993

In the 1990s, adult education was disturbed by the breaking away of the further education colleges from the local authorities. The Government divided responsibility for adults between the colleges who would provide vocational and academic courses under the direction of the national funding councils, and the LEAs who would be mainly limited to leisure and recreational classes. Large areas of the adult education curriculum were transferred to FE, but the Government, after considerable pressure from adult education interest groups, agreed that the local education authorities would still be able to supply non-leisure courses and the 700 free-standing adult education institutes and centres would be able to mount a bid for these courses through a neighbouring FE college. Section 6 of the FHE Act describes the legislative framework for sponsorship by an FE sector institution of 'Schedule 2' provision in an institution outside the sector.

The Further and Higher Education Acts of 1992 laid down the range of courses for which the funding councils would pay (see Chapter 4). Section 3 of the Act for England and Wales describes the duty on the funding councils to secure adequate facilities for certain further education programmes, something which was removed from local education authorities as a primary duty and added back as a kind of secondary duty.

The types of courses or course objectives for adults that the funding council will support are:

- vocational qualifications;
- GCSE or GCE A/AS levels;
- access courses preparing students for entry to a course of higher education;
- courses which prepare students for the previous three categories;
- basic literacy in English;
- teaching English to students where English is not the language spoken at home;
- basic principles of mathematics;
- independent living and communication skills.

LEAs and other providers of further education for adults outside the FEFC sector were invited to consider the provision for which they intended to seek funding from the Council from 1993/94 onwards against the criteria. This funding can only be provided for the recognised courses. On the other hand, offering courses that meet the criteria is not a guarantee of funding. Other courses not coming under the umbrella of the funding councils are expected to be self-financing through low cost fees, although LEAs are not barred from subsidising fees in deprived areas or for low income students.

Provision varies in different parts of the country. Rural areas have a predominance of leisure classes, often provided by colleges at an increased fee to offset costs. In major towns and cities many colleges have concentrated on providing at no or low fee levels for those who are disadvantaged or need a second chance in the education system. A survey at the end of the 1980s found that in the North of England nearly 20 per cent of enrolled students were unemployed, double the rate for the more prosperous south, although this may have altered with the effects of recession in the 1990s. The highest level of provision per head of the local population was in Inner London where almost one in 10 of the adult population was regularly participating – nearly twice that of the other areas in the South of England. Since the abolition of the Inner London Education Authority, the participation rates in individual London boroughs in the former ILEA area have fallen.

A NIACE survey, **Learning and leisure** (Sargant 1991), covering 4000 adult students in 1990 in England, Wales and Scotland found that one-quarter of all adults are involved in some kind of study and nearly one-third of the adult population had been involved in learning over the previous three years. While vocational subjects, foreign languages and computer studies topped the list of student subject choices there was a wide variety of motives for undertaking such courses. Many adults preferred the informal and uncertificated type of courses, especially women who tended to go for classes to the nearby centre located in a primary or secondary school.

Less than one half of one per cent of the education budget is spent on adult education. It is only where there have been national initiatives, such as basic literacy tuition, work with the unemployed or professional updating, that the full potential of adult education and training has been fulfilled.

Access courses

The sharp decline in the number of 18 year olds has given the education of adults a higher profile. The need to expand higher education and to update the workforce were both widely discussed in the 1980s. When the Government wanted to expand higher education by a further 50,000 students at the end of the 1980s, the extra numbers came from the adult sector rather than from the declining number of 18 year olds. This trend for the expansion of higher education to be based on students from non-traditional routes can be illustrated by the fact that at the beginning of the decade the adult education institute in the London borough of Tower Hamlets sent more students into higher education than all the borough's sixth forms added together.

Research has shown that higher education students who come via an adult education route tend to be more reliable, more enterprising and better motivated. Most further education colleges have developed access courses for adults to enter higher education, as well as into their own mainstream FE. The role of such courses is becoming more important. Higher education institutions can decide which students they admit. In the past, when sufficient numbers of applicants came through traditional routes, good GCE Advanced level grades or Scottish Highers were the principal criteria used for judging the suitability of candidates. Falling demographic trends in the 1980s and the wish to have a greater proportion of the population educated to degree level led the Government to invite all those with relevant responsibilities to consider carefully the steps necessary to secure increased participation from both young and older people. The 1987 White Paper, **Higher education: meeting the challenge** (DES 1987), emphasised the need to broaden access and to accommodate students with a wider range of academic and practical experience, many of whom do not have the traditional qualifications for entry. The White Paper stressed that it would not be enough to change entry requirements and procedures: the institutions of higher education would have to adapt their teaching methods and the design of their courses to accommodate new types of student. The institutions in the former Polytechnics and Colleges Funding Council (PCFC) sector were more successful at this than the older universities.

The three main routes into higher education are usually recognised as:

- traditional academic post-16 qualifications such as GCE Advanced and Advanced Supplementary levels and Scottish Highers, which are offered in schools and colleges;
- vocational qualifications obtained in colleges and some schools such as the BTEC National Diploma or the SCOTVEC National Certificate;
- access courses, which can be offered by a range of institutions, including colleges of further education, adult institutes, colleges of higher education, or universities.

Access courses prepare older students without traditional qualifications for entry to degree courses. They are essentially bridging courses which substitute for the GCE Advanced/SCE Highers or full-time vocational qualifications taken by teenagers to enter university. Access students gain alternative credits which are recognised by higher education institutions and allow entry to a diploma or degree programme. Access courses have attracted those adults who are having a second or third chance in the education system and who may have benefited least from previous education experiences, but can offer a range of other experiences not open to the usual teenage entrant.

The number of access courses has grown rapidly since their start at the end of the 1970s. There were 570 such courses in England, Wales and Scotland in 1989, compared to 130 in 1985. Although early courses tended to be centred on teaching and social work, the former Council for National Academic Awards (CNAA) found that 30 per cent of access programmes in 1988 offered a chance to study engineering, science and technology in higher education. The Government has asked validating and planning bodies to monitor progress in the admission of non-GCE/SCE students with vocational or access qualifications. Institutions offering access programmes were asked to ensure that the content and method of the access courses were properly aligned to those of the higher education courses to which they would lead.

The great majority of access students proceeded through single outlet courses to local or nearby higher education institutions where close ties offered an assured place on a degree or diploma course. Open outlet courses meant that some students gained places at institutions well away from their home. A number of HE institutions had taken a policy decision not to establish in-house access studies, preferring to work with a particular college, or, increasingly, groups of colleges. Considerable guidance and collaboration is usually given to the FE institution to help them plan studies and select students. Most access courses were provided by further education colleges; of the 11 per cent provided in the HE sector, most were offered by the former polytechnics, now the new universities.

The receiving institutions were asked to select access students responsibly, taking advantage of the predictive value of their performance at access level and weighing the evidence of their commitment to learn. All the institutions were told to put more effort into counselling and support for access students.

An HMI report on access to further education for adults in 1992 (DES 1992) looked at the range, quality and effectiveness of learning opportunities. They found that because access strategies in FE colleges are primarily concerned with widening participation for traditionally under-represented groups, students who are seeking access to mainstream FE are consequently found in a wide range of learning opportunities and the programmes they pursue do not fall within a simple or narrow categorisation. The students will typically have had little successful previous educational experience and include many from minority ethnic groups, women, disabled and unemployed people. Although they attend courses for a variety of reasons, most seek to boost self-confidence as well as gaining a qualification. A range of factors is significant to the participation of adult students including timing, location, duration, cost, learning support, guidance and childcare. Most of this provision is relatively costly and it relies on external funding.

Two-thirds of access courses are part-time. Students attending part-time usually depend on income support, available under the Department of Social Security rule which allows up to 21 hours of study without loss of benefit so long as the student is still available for work. There has been a tightening of the interpretation of the availability for work criteria, especially since the Employment Training programme started in September 1988. JobCentres, Restart programmes or approved training agents may regard ET (and it successor – Training For Work) as the only training for unemployed adults which fits the availability for work criteria necessary for income support.

Adult basic education

Adult basic education (ABE) students are at the other end of the education spectrum from access students. These students are among the two million or so in the UK who have problems with basic literacy and numeracy. Adult basic education makes available a service for those people least likely to approach existing formal education.

An adult basic education service has developed since the mid-1970s, helped by the fact that Department of Employment training agents found that low levels of literacy and numeracy were a major barrier to training for many adults. These are precisely the people who have found it most difficult to enter traditional courses.

Much adult basic education has been delivered in non-traditional ways, although this is changing as there is more pressure for cost effective programmes. A lot of the teaching was done by voluntary tutors on a one-to-one basis in the person's home or in local community centres. Some took place in drop-in workshops where materials and tutors are available. Much of the earlier work was undervalued, but the role of ABE is now a more regular part of mainstream provision, although it can still be marginal. The informality of the learning has enabled adult education agencies to collaborate with social workers, health education, the prison and probation services and some major employers in a way that would have been more restrictive through formal courses. People who are resident in prisons or mental hospitals are often easily accessed by education units or outreach workers.

Adults with major literacy or numeracy problems are usually very reticent about revealing their difficulties. They are not the kind of students who will just roll up to a 'course' for literacy work. A flexible system had to be created in colleges which allowed easy access and re-entry, provided a variety of counselling and guidance services, offered a spread of programmes and used all kinds of sensitive publicity, including word of mouth.

Prison education

There is considerable experience in colleges of operating prison education departments. Within each establishment there is usually a head of the education department and a deputy with perhaps a small number of full-time staff, together with a dedicated group of part-time lecturers. Convicted prisoners are seen by the education department as soon as they arrive in custody. Education is voluntary for prisoners over school leaving age. The range of programmes offered includes basic literacy and numeracy, social and life skills, English as a foreign language, recreational and leisure courses and some mainstream further education. Inmates often have access to vocational qualifications via catering, horticulture, construction and related trades through work in the prison workshops or grounds. The vocational qualifications are delivered by civilian instructors and education department staff.

From April 1993, in the wake of incorporation, colleges now have to bid for contracts in competition with private sector providers to provide education in prisons.

English for speakers of other languages

A further group of adults that colleges deal with are those who need to learn English. A large chunk of the provision of English for speakers of other languages (ESOL) is funded under a Home Office scheme designed to teach English to immigrants from Commonwealth countries. It is usually called Section 11 funding after the part of government legislation under which it was introduced. The students studying under ESOL programmes are very varied and can include a range from recent immigrants who have had little formal education in their country of origin to adults who are well-educated but need to improve their fluency in English. Many of those seeking help want to improve their English for work-related reasons.

The Workers' Education Association

There is a variety of bodies connected with the delivery of adult continuing education. Outside the local authorities, courses are provided by university extra-mural departments, the Workers' Education Association and voluntary institutes. The Workers' Education Association (WEA) is an interesting example of the kind of voluntary body that became involved in the provision of adult education. It was founded in 1903 and is registered as a charity. It is a nationwide, democratic voluntary body which aims to interest men and women in their own continued education and in education generally. The constitution of the WEA is based on the objectives of stimulating and satisfying the demands of adults, particularly the members of workers' movements, for education.

The Workers' Education Association has tried in the past to stimulate and co-ordinate the educational activities of working class bodies. It provides classes and other educational facilities, either directly or in conjunction with other education bodies and trades union and labour organisations. In recent years it has been controlled mainly by educated middle class people keen on the education of adults, with the organised labour movement playing only a minor role.

From the First World War up to 1989, the government provided around 75 per cent of the WEA's teaching costs. From 1989, the WEA has been part funded by government, and part by the local education authorities. The pressures of cuts in LEA spending led many LEAs to cut their adult education spending considerably, including funding for the WEA. From 1993, the FEFC took over the government's role in funding the Association.

The National Institute of Adult Continuing Education

One of the main national centres which co-ordinates the organisations involved in adult continuing education is the National Institute of Adult Continuing Education (NIACE). It is a national centre for co-operation, enquiry, information and consultation in the continuing education of adults. NIACE is given a grant by the Department for Education and is supported and financed by local education authorities, universities and voluntary organisations. The Institute advises on courses, conferences and study visits, both to professionals working in the field and to the general public. It has extensive international links and stores comparative information on adult continuing education. Membership of NIACE is open to all organisations directly concerned with the provision of adult education which meet the requirements of its constitution.

The Unit for the Development of Adult Continuing Education

The Unit for the Development of Adult Continuing Education (UDACE) was created by the Department of Education and Science in 1984 and originally operated within NIACE with a remit to cover England and

Wales. During its eight year life, the Unit worked on the education of adults across a wide range of sectors and agencies. It recommended strategies for new developments and sponsored projects which would work towards these ends. Priority was given to development work which would either improve access to learning opportunities for adults, contribute to the creation of a more coherent service of education for adults or improve the quality of learning opportunities available to adults. During the 1980s, the Unit was well known for its work on educational guidance, leading to the creation of a National Education Guidance Initiative, located in the Further Education Unit but supported both by the DES and the Department of Employment. In April 1992, UDACE merged with Further Education Unit to form a new expanded curriculum unit for further and adult education.

The Adult Literacy and Basic Skills Unit

The Adult Literacy and Basic Skills Unit, usually known by the acronym ALBSU, was established by the Department of Education and Science and the Welsh Office in 1980 as the central focus for adult literacy and related basic skills work in England and Wales. The unit operates as an agency of NIACE and administers grants for 'developing within the general education service in England and Wales provision designed to improve the standards of proficiency for adults, whose first or second language is English, in the areas of communication and coping skills without which progress in and towards education, training and employment is impeded'.

As well as acting as a national focus for adult literacy and related basic skills, ALBSU:
- offers a consultancy and advisory service to LEAs and other bodies;
- sponsors a range of development projects throughout England and Wales;
- publishes teaching and learning materials;
- sponsors and organises staff training, both regionally and nationally;
- gives grants to voluntary organisations;
- organises the conducting of research.

Adult education in Scotland

In Scotland, the Community Education Council is the major body for community education. It provides services and promotes development for both local authority and voluntary group sectors. The Council survived a financial crisis in 1991 to win half a million pounds in grant support from the Government so long as it concentrated on a limited number of objectives.

Chapter 9
Special educational needs students

The broad term 'special educational needs' covers a wide range of students in further education with a mix of abilities. Special educational needs arise from physical and sensory impairment, or learning, emotional and behaviourial difficulties, which can be experienced as a single handicap or in any combination. Many colleges have a commitment to try to accommodate students with special educational needs as part of their equal opportunities policies. These policies are based on the view that people with disabilities should have the same rights as others to take advantage of opportunities to continue their education and training. Evidence has shown that appropriate provision can remove or reduce handicapping situations for people with disabilities.

Most further education colleges now provide for students with special educational needs as part of their widening community role. When HM Inspectorate completed their major survey of colleges in the mid-1980s, they found that all the colleges inspected had a small number of students with physical disabilities or sensory impairment. Some colleges had specialised facilities for special needs students and a number were approved training organisations for Youth Training trainees who were eligible for extra funding because of their special needs.

Many colleges have tried to help students wishing to join mainstream courses but few, if any, guarantee physical access to all courses or parts of the buildings. This is because many college buildings were constructed in the 1960–80 period of expansion, when few disabled students attended, and so their needs were not incorporated. All recent new buildings, extensions and major improvements will have physical access arrangements for the disabled and wheelchairs.

In most colleges, co-ordinators have been appointed at senior lecturer level to deal with enquiries, to be responsible for assessing needs and to monitor the progress of students with disabilities. The co-ordinators also work with senior management and buildings managers to generate a rolling programme of work to improve access for the physically disabled.

HMI found that many college buildings have no lifts, inappropriately designed and inconveniently sited toilets, inaccessible student facilities such as the refectory, library or students' union office, insufficient ramps and unwieldy doors. A number of colleges have built ramps or lifts for the physically disabled, some from their own resources or aided by the LEA or particular charities. Others have introduced audio loops into lecture rooms for the hearing impaired and several local education authorities employ peripatetic teachers of the deaf who visit colleges regularly. This opening up of access is, however, very patchy and is dependent on the attitude of individual college managers or local authorities.

Studies of provision for students with special educational needs have been completed by HMI, the Further Education Unit, the National Foundation for Educational Research and the National Bureau for Students with Disabilities. A survey commissioned in 1985 by the then Department of Education and Science with the former National Bureau for Handicapped Students found that there were around 10,000 students on full-time courses and 8,400 on school/college links out of a total of 30,000 people with special educational needs in further and higher education.

In those colleges running full-time courses for students with learning difficulties, the emphasis is usually on personal care and on such social and life skills as independent travelling, shopping and using the telephone as well as on literacy and numeracy. Students are given opportunities for creative and semi-vocational activities such as art, drama, horticulture and woodwork, and for physical and recreational pursuits. Many courses for students with moderate learning difficulties, and a few with severe learning difficulties, have a work experience component. In the last couple of years there have been attempts to get special needs students to attempt Level I NVQs. Residential experience is commonly provided on full-time programmes. School link and other part-time courses offer a selection of such activities, sometimes as a series of tasters of further education provision.

HMI has criticised some of the teaching of people with disabilities in further education. Few of the 100 colleges surveyed by the Inspectorate in the period 1983–88 provided staff with training to enable them to understand and recognise the special needs of students. Even fewer identified the most appropriate teaching methods for meeting these needs. Although newly appointed teachers usually had experience and qualifications in special education, some required induction in the nature and scope of FE work generally. A further difficulty was found by FE lecturers in differentiating between the individual needs of students with different ability levels. Many teachers underestimated the abilities of students with special needs, particularly in relation to practical work. Matters were improved where there was regular liaison between staff and parents. HMI also found a lack of systematic monitoring and review of courses. However, the Inspectorate reported that there were a number of models of good practice which colleges with little experience could emulate. The HMI reviews in 1990/91 found some improvement in the quality of work of those students with special educational needs in further education but overall it remained variable. Good standards were closely associated with thorough initial assessment, clear objectives, varied teaching styles and close evaluation of outcomes. There was a continuing increase in provision for students with more severe learning difficulties but this tended to be in separate classes, so leaving scope for further integration. As in previous years, there were fewer opportunities for students with emotional and behaviourial difficulties than for other groups.

The major examining and validating bodies will make special arrangements to meet the needs of students with special educational needs. It is usually expected that requests for special arrangements to compensate for a candidate's handicap will be supported by a medical certificate, or, in the case of dyslexic students, a report from an educational psychologist.

NCVQ provision

The National Council for Vocational Qualifications looked at the issues relating to candidates with special needs within the context of assessment and certification of National Vocational Qualifications. The Council recognised that this student group potentially stands to gain by the introduction of NVQs because the framework covers a wider range of occupational roles and at more levels than the vocational qualification system it replaced. Further, if it is recognised that NVQs are awarded when candidates have demonstrated that they have met the performance criteria for each element of competence specified and that there is the opportunity for credit accumulation, then there is a chance for early recognition of achievement for slow learners and those with physical and sensory disabilities.

There is some concern that the competences set at Level I NVQ will exclude many people with special educational needs from ever obtaining a qualification. NCVQ's criteria and procedures document stated that 'people with special needs include those with physical or sensory disabilities who may require special help to undertake assessment. Such help could include physical or mechanical aids, extra time for assessment (except where a prescribed period of time is required under all circumstances by performance criteria), or special methods of assessment'. The Council specifically warns against creating 'special needs NVQs' but sees the need to guard against covert discrimination when specifying competences or excluding groups from NVQs unknowingly without fully exploring the consequences and possible alternative standards.

As might be expected, it is frequently difficult for students with learning difficulties to gain employment after their period in further education. Students with moderate learning difficulties can often gain employment in industries where there is a high demand for unskilled or semi-skilled workers. Students with severe learning difficulties will often go on to adult training centres (ATCs) where they can work in a sheltered environment, while some stay on in further education.

TVEI and special needs

A lot of attention was given under the TVEI scheme to developing courses and teaching styles in schools and colleges for those with special educational needs. Since an important aim of TVEI was to promote equal opportunities and to avoid stereotyping, it has been helpful in changing attitudes. An HMI report on TVEI in England and Wales (HMI 1991c), suggested that shifting established social norms had been a slow and difficult business.

Legislation

The change in climate towards recruiting and developing people with special educational needs during the 1980s, was reflected in the fact that the 1988 Education Reform Act singled out students with special needs as a category to be protected. The duty to provide 'adequate further education' laid, at that time, on local education authorities, included a requirement to have regard to the needs of persons over compulsory school age who have learning difficulties. The Act suggested that at least one employment interest governor should represent those with special needs. The consequent DES guidance on programme provision suggested that, in addition to the subject-based classifications, a further category of work needing extra resources could be used for the provision of those with special educational needs. This was taken up by most local education authorities in their schemes of delegation and special educational needs students were usually given the highest weighting in attracting funding.

Following the passage of the 1992 Further and Higher Education Act covering England and Wales, and the corresponding Act in Scotland, there was considerable concern that the needs of those people with learning difficulties and disabilities would lose out when colleges became independent from their local education authorities. The Further Education Funding Council took over the duties from the LEAs for post-16 special needs students. The Act was designed to ensure that the range of further education provision existing in 1992 for students with learning difficulties and disabilities was maintained under incorporation.

Legally the Further and Higher Education Act gave the FEFC the duty to secure sufficient educational facilities for 16 to 18 year old students in full-time education (Section 2). Section 3 established the duty to secure adequate facilties in respect of full-time students aged 19 or over and part-time students over 16 attending courses designated by Schedule 2 of the Act. In fulfilling these duties, Section 4 of the Act required the Council to have regard to the requirements of students with learning difficulties, including those with disabilities. Students with a learning difficulty are defined as those:

for the handicapped. This is out of an estimated nearly one million children who are reckoned to have some kind of special learning need.

A major debate has continued over the last 20 years about whether individual children fare better if they are segregated in special schools, which was the main form of education in the past, or if they are integrated into mainstream schools. The 1981 Education Act committed the Government to the integration of young people with special educational needs into ordinary schools wherever possible – as outlined in the proposals of the Warnock Committee in its report on special educational needs (Warnock 1978). The main feature of the Warnock philosophy is focusing on pupils and students as individuals, identifying their special needs and making appropriate arrangements to meet them. Warnock had little to say about further education as such but did recommend at the time that FE colleges consider the modification of their ordinary courses and the provision of special courses, either as links between school and college or as bridging courses to prepare young people with special needs for ordinary courses of work. The term 'special educational needs' was defined flexibly in terms of learning difficulty requiring special educational provision. This must be different from, and additional to, that usually made available to children of the same age in an authority's schools.

Most children with special educational needs are educated within the resources of an ordinary school and will not require the LEA to determine how best to meet their needs. For a small percentage of children who have severe or complex learning difficulties, it is necessary for authorities themselves to determine appropriate provision. Generally, LEAs must issue an individual 'statement' for each child who has a severe or complex learning difficulty which requires extra resources in terms of staffing or equipment. The statement lists the pupil's special educational needs and the special educational provision which the authority considers appropriate to meet them. The appropriate school (or other arrangements) must be specified together with any additional non-educational provision. The LEA must take into consideration any representations, evidence and advice from the various interested groups concerned. There must be an annual review of the pupil who is statemented. While the statement procedure requires that a child's needs are identified regardless of whether the necessary provision is available, there is no claim that provision can be offered in an open-ended way.

In applying the National Curriculum to children with special educational needs, changes were made to meet the particular needs and circumstances of the individual child. Under the statementing procedures each child should have any changes specified on his/her statement. Alterations will also be made to attainment targets, programmes of study and assessment arrangements, where appropriate, while trying to maintain maximum opportunities for the child. The Government has recognised that LEAs can find it difficult to devise a resource allocation formula to include appropriate weightings for the full range of special needs pupils and has exempted them from schemes of financial delegation.

Problems have arisen in providing for those with special educational needs in that some of the range of facilities available comes from other social services – such as the district health authority. Speech therapy is one aspect of this provision which has caused problems. Many local authorities have said they were unable to make speech therapy available because the district health authorities trained and employed the speech therapists. A High Court ruling at the end of 1988 forced Lancashire County Council to make speech therapy available to a child with a congenital speech defect, despite the council's claim that speech therapy was a non-educational need. The judge declared that if it was decided that a child's need was educational, then the local education authority had to make speech therapy available.

Section Three
Who makes further education work?

Chapter 10   The planning of FE

Chapter 11   The financing of FE

Chapter 12   The governance of FE

Chapter 13   The management of FE

Chapter 14   The teaching of FE

Chapter 10
The planning of FE

For the first seven decades of this century, further education colleges and their forerunners had grown and developed with the minimum of formal planning by any national or local body. Although colleges have been part of local education authorities since early in the century, the relationship has usually been one conducted, at least in planning terms if not perhaps in terms of detailed regulations, at arm's length. The level of intervention, which some may have termed interference, depended on the make up of the local education authority and its education committee, and particularly the style of the local councillors represented on the governing body of the institution.

Local authorities had a range of styles, including positively supportive, benignly neglectful, laissez faire or malign interference. The very supportive may have arisen because particular councillors fought for and won very good funding and facilities. The benign neglect was common where colleges were given the minimum of funding and allowed to get on with life, while major investment went into the schools sector or elsewhere in the council. Laissez faire attitudes were common in some Conservative-controlled areas where councillors did not want to intervene. Malign interference occurred across a range of local authorities where education officers and councillors intervened in every aspect of college life and did not allow the principal and his/her senior team to actually manage the institution.

As colleges have always been essentially local institutions they have not come under the kind of national planning constraints that the institutions in the higher education sector have been used to: neither have they had the detailed local regulation to which schools have been subjected, largely because colleges relate in their planning to a greater number of bodies such as industrial training organisations, local companies, governmental employment organisations, examining and validating bodies, professional institutions and other educational organisations.

In many ways, the need to plan and be self-sufficient arose as a by-product of the hostility to local councils of successive Conservative governments from their election to national government in 1979 to the passage of the Further and Higher Education Act in 1992. The gradual stripping away of the powers and range of options of local authorities impacted on the education authority and its colleges. The removal of colleges from local education authorities in England, Wales and Scotland in 1993 marked the culmination of this process. The new national funding councils, although not having a primary planning function, do impact considerably on colleges due to their decisions on what to fund and what not to fund. Before going into the role of colleges under the funding councils, it is worthwhile tracing how colleges developed a more devolved planning role during the 1980s.

FE planning pre-1980

Up to the 1980s colleges usually fitted in with other organisations' initiatives. Whether it was the massive expansion of training during the Second World War or the changes to first year off-the-job apprentice instruction brought in by the industrial training boards in the 1960s, the colleges essentially responded. They were not expected to have their own plans and to see if the requests of other organisations fitted in with the college's priorities. In essence, the college formed and reformed on the waves of governmental and other initiatives. It was expected that there would be regular base funding and a job for life for most of the staff.

The incentive to innovate came through ambitious heads of department and their staff. The role of principal, apart from the obvious managerial and honorary functions, was to pull together the efforts of the various departments. Departments waxed and waned depending on the changing nature of local industry or the growth of general education. For example, textiles was once a major factor in the life of West Yorkshire colleges and is now virtually dead; coal mining in Lancashire, Yorkshire, the East Midlands, South Wales and Scotland played a major part in colleges but has disappeared from whole areas with pit closures; engineering, from being dominant in the 1960s, is in major decline; information technology was once seen just as an expensive toy but is now central to the work of all colleges; business studies has grown over 30 years into being a major section in most institutions.

Developments during the 1980s

It was only in the 1980s that systematic planning mechanisms were introduced for further education. In its first attempt at planning, the Government used the training arm of the Department of Employment (the then Manpower Services Commission) as the instrument for bringing about changes in work-related further education. The arrangements were established by the 1984 White Paper, **Training for jobs** (DE 1984). It was significant that the Department of Employment rather than the Department for Education instigated the process. The Conservative government wanted to push local education authorities and their colleges into a greater responsiveness to central government initiatives and the needs of employers, and it was felt that the education wing of government was too protective of its charges. The intention was to reduce the influence of the local education authority by using the Manpower Services Commission as a direct instrument to get quick results, which would not be subject to the normal local democratic procedures of a council.

An incentive and penalty system was built into the plan for work-related further education (WRFE) by the shift of a quarter of government funding from LEAs to the MSC. After much controversy, a system was devised from 1986 whereby education authorities in England and Wales would prepare three year development plans, the first plan covering the period 1986–89. The three year plans included a rolling one year programme (starting from 1986/87) which was used as the benchmark for annual funding. If the Commission agreed that the authority had prepared a satisfactory three year plan and was delivering the annual programme satisfactorily, the bulk of the WRFE moneys held by the local office of the Commission would be returned in monthly instalments to the local education authority. The Commission held back some of the money due to each authority in order to form a central fund against which local authorities could bid for projects under nationally determined priorities.

In 1988 the Secretary of State for Education fought back and took up the running from the Department of Employment, using the further education sections of the 1988 Education Reform Act (ERA), which applied to England and Wales only, and the later 1989 legislation in Scotland. The WRFE exercise was pushed into a very much secondary role under the auspices first of the Department of Employment and then the local training and enterprise councils (TECs). Colleges are, however, still dependent upon their TECs for a proportion of their funding. They need to heed local TEC policy objectives and initiatives, which vary significantly between TECs, and they are directly accountable to their TECs for that expenditure. The TECs themselves are invited by the Employment Department to bid for additional funds, in line with the National Development Prospectus and the 'TEC Challenge' competition, and many TECs have involved their local colleges in these bids.

The thrust of the ERA was to require LEAs to move towards the strategic planning of local further education provision through a process which also covered the preparation of budgets delegated to colleges. The planning role arose from the legal duty placed on every local authority by ERA to secure the provision of adequate facilities for further education in their area. The Act also gave the local education authority the power to secure the provision of further education for persons living outside their area.

ERA removed the duty on LEAs to secure provision for their area of facilities for higher education after the polytechnics and higher education colleges split away into the so-called PCFC sector in 1989. The Act did require LEAs to plan any relevant higher education over which they still had an influence, i.e. that remaining in the FE colleges. The LEAs were empowered to make available facilities for higher education for people living outside the authority's boundaries. So, for example, a college which had historically offered BTEC Higher National Diplomas would continue to do so and could recruit students on a national basis.

The Government saw the proper planning and co-ordination of further education (either between colleges or between a college and neighbouring schools, institutions of higher education and other providers) as important in avoiding gaps or wasteful duplication. The Act at the same time reduced local education authority powers to intervene in the day-to-day running of the local colleges. Each LEA prepared a scheme for the DES, which contained a statement of the principles and procedures it intended to use in planning further and higher education for the colleges it maintained or substantially assisted. Authorities were encouraged to combine the WRFE plan in the same cycle as the longer term planning for further education generally. Most of the schemes of planning were approved by the Department early in 1990 and came into effect from 1 April that year.

The Department for Education saw the purpose of the planning process as the determination of the changes that were needed to the existing broad pattern of courses in order to meet more effectively the changing needs of the local population. The whole exercise threw up the need to ensure proper co-ordination between provision in further education colleges for 16–19 year olds and that which was being offered in schools and sixth form colleges. Education and training provided by the private sector had also to be taken into consideration. Education authorities were also expected to collaborate with neighbouring authorities to ensure proper co-ordination on a regional basis. This regional dimension was incorporated into the funding council system several years later. A review of the process by HMI in 1990 said that ERA had been a major factor in prompting some LEAs to determine a post-16 education policy, covering both schools and FE, but that, even when such a policy had been established, it had not always been put into practice.

The Secretary of State for Education had listed the factors which a local education authority had to take into account in planning provision. Projected student demand had to be included, taking into consideration demographic trends, participation rates, relative preferences for school versus further education, students coming into or going out of the authority to study, reorganisation proposals and the increasing access to further and higher education. As in the WRFE exercise before it, the Department of Education also expected information on changing labour market needs.

The plans had to outline examples of the development of new forms of provision and the authority had to say where and how future national initiatives could best be accommodated. Authorities were required to secure an appropriate range of education and training opportunities for those over compulsory school age who had special educational needs.

The annual review system required the authority to determine annual allocations of student numbers between colleges, after discussion with the governing bodies. These allocations were usually based on an individual college's contribution to planned student number allocation for each broad subject area in which the college was involved. DES **Circular 9/88** (DES 1988c) made it clear that the Secretary of State expected the general approach to be for each governing body to submit to the LEA annual proposals for what its college should make available to students in the short- to medium-term. Colleges had to keep the LEA informed of any changes in circumstances which would cause a significant departure from the desired allocations, since this could have had considerable knock-on effect where other institutions interlinked with the college.

After discussion with the colleges covered by the scheme, the authority determined annually how the work in each college would contribute to achieving the overall pattern in the area. The planning of student numbers went hand in hand with budget setting arrangements. Since governing bodies were responsible for the general direction of colleges, the Government saw it as vital that colleges should be involved in the strategic planning. Governing bodies, on advice from the principal, determined the exact pattern of courses to be provided by their colleges within the planning framework set by the authority. When the college had submitted its annual proposals to the LEA for the courses that it wanted to run in the year ahead and in the longer term, local authority officers had to reconcile the different proposals they had received bearing in mind the alternative range of provision on offer outside the colleges. The Department of Education and Science was not strongly directive but suggested that any gaps should be identified and filled to meet the developing needs of the local area and that unnecessary duplication with alternative providers should be removed.

The planning role of the LEA also involved the generation of student number allocations for the vocational programme areas, often based on subject groupings. Subject-based programme areas were generally derived from the Training Occupation Classification (TOC) for further education in categories such as: administration and clerical; scientific, construction and civil engineering; and general education. Non-subject programme areas could be identified as special educational needs, adult basic education or pre-vocational courses.

The process of planning was expected to become more sophisticated. After the first round, involving the submission of the schemes for planning, funding and delegation to the Secretary of State, each LEA was free to vary the scheme it originally submitted if colleges developed something new or local circumstances changed. Any alterations were not expected to be significant. Where a change would either wholly replace the existing scheme or make a significant variation to it, the LEA first had to consult the affected colleges and then submit the proposed variation to the Secretary of State for approval. Minor changes included those which would extend delegation, reduce the complexity of the budgeting formula or make minor consequential modifications. Any proposed changes which restricted the scope of delegation or added to the complexity of the funding formulae would normally be considered significant.

Not everyone was happy with this process. HMI reported that senior staff in some colleges considered that control by the LEA over post-16 provision inhibited them from being responsive and entrepreneurial. Other commentators were asking why, if polytechnics had been 'set free' from local authorities in 1989, colleges of further education could not go along the same path. It was felt that with experience of planning and financial delegation the colleges were reaching a new level of maturity. There was also increasing pressure on national government to reduce the burden of local taxation under the highly unpopular poll tax and transfer expenditure to the national level.

Developments during the early 1990s

Thus it was that colleges (except those on Inner London) had had five years' experience of planning, first via work-related further education and then one year of planning with the LEA under the ERA arrangements linked to delegated budgets, when the Government signalled the next stage in the process. This was marked by the publication in May 1991 of the White Papers **Education and training for the 21st century** for England and Wales (DES *et al*. 1991a) and **Access and opportunity** in Scotland (SO 1991). The White Papers were followed by the 1992 Acts, translating their contents into law. The very quick creation of the funding councils in the same year to plan funding for colleges removed from the LEAs in 1993 led to a rapid transition to the next stage in college planning. The changes did not apply to Northern Ireland where the colleges stayed with the education and library boards.

The word planning was not pre-eminent in either of the White Papers, unlike the word funding. However, the funding councils need clear information about the intentions of colleges in order to discharge their legal responsibilities. They have, therefore, asked colleges to submit strategic plans, and have specified the formats in which these should be provided.

Colleges were separated from LEAs in 1993, which then lost their FE planning role for everything under Schedule 2 of the FHE Act. The mantle of guiding the system of colleges was passed to the national funding councils, advised by their regional committees. The further education funding councils have a duty to ensure sufficient and adequate provision of further education and training facilities for young people and adults in England and Wales (as does the Scottish Office in Scotland) and assess the quality of education provided.

The Further Education Funding Council, which represents England, consists of 14 members appointed by the Secretary of State. A representative of the Secretary of State also attends Council meetings. The FEFC for Wales is smaller, having 12. The legislation provides that the members should 'have experience of, and to have shown capacity in, the provision of education or to have held, and to have shown capacity in, any position carrying responsibility for the provision of education and, in appointing such persons, he shall have regard to the desirability of their being currently engaged in the provision of further education or in carrying responsibility for such provision' and 'such persons who appear to him to have experience of, and to have shown capacity in, industrial, commercial or financial matters or the practice of any profession'.

The FHE Acts gave a duty to each funding council to secure the provision for the population of their area (England, Wales and Scotland) of sufficient facilities for full-time education for: 16 to 18 year olds; adequate facilities for full-time education for those over 18; and for part-time education for the over 16s. The councils also have a specific duty to have regard to the requirements of people with learning difficulties up to the age of 25. The councils have to ensure that educational facilities are provided 'at such places, are of such character and are so equipped as to be sufficient to meet the reasonable needs of all persons to whom the duty extends, and to take account of the different abilities and aptitudes of such persons'. The English and Welsh councils have to have regard to any full-time education provided 'by schools maintained by local education authorities, grant-maintained schools, special schools not maintained by local education authorities, city technology colleges or city colleges for the technology of the arts'.

In establishing the English FEFC, the Secretary of State set out what he thought were the key aims. In respect of aims related to longer term planning, he wanted the council:

- to provide a direct incentive to colleges to expand participation by relating an element of colleges' funding to actual student enrolments; the Government, for its part, has undertaken that the total resources available to the Council and hence to colleges will be determined in part by the actual numbers of students recruited in the year in question;
- to encourage the further development of flexible and part-time modes of delivery, including distance learning;

– to maintain the diversity of missions which currently exists among institutions which will enter the new sector.

The FEFC also has a regional dimension. The English council has set up nine regional offices which between them relate to the whole of the further education sector of tertiary, further education and sixth form colleges. In each regional office, there is a small team of staff who work with colleges, local education authorities, TECs and other local groups.

Each region has a committee with around 12 members drawn from industry and education which is responsible for advising the FEFC in Coventry on the adequacy of the further education facilities in the area. The Act states 'there shall be established for each region of England determined by the Secretary of State a committee of the Further Education Funding Council to advise the council on such matters relating to the facilities for the population of the region (a) for further education, or (b) for full-time education (other than further education) suitable to the requirements of persons over compulsory school age who have not attained the age of 19 years, as the council may from time to time require'. The committees look at any measures which may affect the availability of provision. They also have a responsibility for advising on provision for students with special educational needs.

In 1993, the Secretary of State advised the newly formed funding councils that he would not be looking for initiatives in the short-term to bring about significant changes in the pattern of further education provision. In 1992 the **Times Higher Education Supplement** found that a third of FE institutions expected to be involved in some kind of merger following incorporation. By March 1993, a THES/FEU survey of colleges showed that only seven per cent of colleges had merged, six per cent expected to merge and 65 per cent had no merger prospects. Of the rest that commented, 18 per cent had no plans for merger but expected something to emerge at a later date. The FEFC laid down six criteria that would be used in assessing any merger proposals:

a) the benefits to the education provision in the area;

b) the benefits to existing and future students in terms of access and choice;

c) retaining and improving the cost efficiency of provision, particularly with respect to council funds;

d) the advantages to the institutions concerned;

e) the realism of achieving the merger in managerial terms, including the provision of satisfactory arrangements for assuring financial accountability;

f) the extent and results of local consultation, including consultation with other providers and users of further education in the area and with those responsible for schools which have links with the colleges affected;

g) the steps taken to reflect in the governing body the changed nature of the institution in terms of the area and interests served.

In Northern Ireland, a Government-appointed review group recommended in 1992 that the 24 colleges in the Province should be reorganised down to 13. This has caused considerable controversy and opposition.

At college level, the further education corporations in England are asked to develop strategic plans. In England the initial planning framework specified by FEFC comprised the college mission, a needs analysis, a three-year strategic overview and a sensitivity analysis (FEFC **Circulars 92/11** and **92/18**, FEFC 1992c, 1992d).There should also be an operating statement including the financial forecast, backed by numerical information. The Welsh funding council required a similar framework (**Bulletin XIII**, FEFCW 1993a). It was stressed by the FEFC that plans should take into account the college's local community and its educational needs. In the period up to incorporation, the colleges were asked to focus first on the 16 month period from April 1993. In this first stage, colleges were invited to provide information about themselves, decide their mission and begin looking at their longer-term development. Forecasts were requested of planned student numbers and financial projections, using numerical data, and an analysis of the college's physical resources, particularly their ability to cope with future plans. Other factors which the council suggested might be included in their planning were: provision for those with learning difficulties and disabilities; plans for work-related further education provision; and collaborative arrangements being developed with other institutions for courses to be funded by the FEFC.

An annual planning framework is now evolving. The 1994 requirements are for information about college plans, including their accommodation strategy, in February, with more detailed plans in July. Welsh colleges are asked to provide planning information in June or July (Welsh funding council bulletin **B23/93**, FEFCW 1993b). The Staff College/FEU **Strategic planning handbook** (FEU 1994) provides clear advice as to the planning processes whereby colleges can satisfy both external requirements and their internal planning needs.

The process is likely to be most difficult for the sixth form colleges which did not go through the planning experiences the FE colleges experienced in the 1980s, since they were technically in the schools sector. There are currently over 100 sixth form colleges with over 80,000 students between them. Many are considering diversifying from the straight diet of academic qualifications that was their original strength.

In terms of trends in the shape of the sector, a DFE news release in 1992 (DFE 1992b) showed the following, using 1990/91 as the base year:

- there has been an estimated increase from 12 per cent to 23 per cent in full-time participation by 16 and 17 year olds in FE between 1980/81 and 1991/92, but a four per cent decrease in part-time participation;
- women accounted for 56 per cent of all enrolments, but the proportion varied from 63 per cent on courses under one year to 39 per cent on courses lasting three years or more;
- FE enrolments were more than twice those in 1975/76;
- there were 2.5 million enrolments in FE, including 0.6 million on short vocational and academic courses;
- in the previous year, the number of full-time and sandwich students in FE increased by seven per cent, while part-time enrolments fell by three per cent;
- about 35 per cent of 16 year olds and 33 per cent of 17 year olds were enrolled in FE, 40 per cent of them part-time;
- the proportion of 17 year old students had risen from 33 per cent in 1987/88 to 49 per cent, while in the same period the 18 year olds had gone from 18 per cent to 28 per cent.

Indications of Government support for the new further education sector came in the 1992 Autumn Statement, when the Chancellor of the Exchequer announced that FE colleges had been given priority over the universities in terms of funding growth. The DFE had won funding to support a 25 per cent increase over the three years from 1993 in the number of students attending FE and sixth form colleges. The rationale was that expansion in the new FE sector was vital to achievement of the national education and training targets. In contrast, the massive growth in funding for higher education was slowed to 13 per cent over the same 1993–96 period. The rise in the number of students would not be matched by major spending on building programmes with the capital spending only planned to rise from £192 million to £196 million in 1995/96. The first priority is health and safety and bringing buildings in the sector up to standard, with little room left for new projects.

The discussions in the remainder of the decade will be very much about how the new further education corporations will adapt to recruiting new students and whether the Government will make it economically viable for them to do so. This is the topic of the next chapter.

The Further Education Unit

The Further Education Unit (FEU), the one curriculum organisation which covers further education in England and Wales, is largely a curriculum review and dissemination body and has no parallel with the former National Curriculum Council in schools or the former Council for National Academic Awards in the higher education sector. The Further Education Unit mounts research projects which examine developments in various aspects of further education, and has reacted to curriculum innovations such as Youth Training and the Technical and Vocational Education Initiative or the Certificate of Pre-vocational Education.

The FEU was set up in 1977 within the then Department of Education and Science, under the cumbersome title of the Further Education Curriculum Review and Development Unit. It adopted its present title in 1983 when it was given some autonomy from the Department as a limited company, although it is still funded by the DFE. The Further Education Unit's board of management is made up of representatives of employers, examining bodies, the Department for Education, the Department of Employment, HM Inspectorate and college principals, who are the largest group.

The objects of the Further Education Unit are to promote, encourage and develop the efficient provision of further education in the United Kingdom. In particular, it has been asked:

- to review and evaluate the range of existing further education curricula and to identify overlap, duplication, deficiencies and inconsistencies therein;
- to determine priorities for action to improve the provision of further education and to make recommendations as to how such improvement can be effected;
- to carry out studies in further education and to support investigations of and experimentation in, and the development of, further education curricula and to contribute to, and assist in the evaluation of, initiatives in further education;
- to disseminate and publish information and to assist in the dissemination and publication of information about recommendations for, and experiments and developments in, further education.

The four aims have the common objective of promoting the process of curriculum development which the Unit sees as including not only subject content but also student-centred and work-related teaching and learning, assessment of students and evaluation of provision in the light of overall aims and values.

The Further Education Unit sees itself as being both proactive and reactive. It seeks to produce original curricular thinking in important areas of further education, supports the college system in these areas and, where possible, assists local education authorities and their institutions in developing their own curricular experiences.

The FEU maintains a voluntary network of more than 55 local information centres and publishes newsletters, guidance notes and bulletins to keep colleges informed of recent developments in the further education system and FEU responses. Its range of activities has expanded enormously, spanning not only the work of PICKUP (professional, industrial and commercial updating) and the former REPLAN schemes, but also the results of hundreds of projects. The breadth of curriculum covered now includes mainstream vocational further education, adult education and training, special educational needs, curriculum development for a multi-cultural society, further education college management and marketing, curriculum evaluation, innovation and change and new technology.

After its merger with UDACE in 1992, the FEU refocused its programme into four areas: guidance and participation; provision and quality; developing competence; and accrediting achievement. It has six cross-area themes: learners 16–19; adult learners; equity; staff and institutional development; resourcing; and Europe and the international dimension.

The funding councils conducted a review of the future role and funding of the FEU, together with The Staff College, in 1993.

The Staff College

The Staff College is the national management training centre for the post-compulsory education sector. It is funded, in part, by the Further Education Funding Council, although until 1992 it was resourced by funds top-sliced by central government from local education authorities throughout the United Kingdom. The college provides courses, conferences and consultancy services for each of the different further education systems within the countries of the UK.

The main activity of The Staff College is its management development programme for senior college staff. It also provides a number of other courses on new or specialised subjects which bring together specialists from various bodies and a range of college staff. Up to 1993 course fees had not covered the whole cost and the balance had been met by grants from local education authorities in England, Wales and Scotland and from the Department of Education, Northern Ireland. From 1993, the Department for Education and the funding councils will fulfil the former role of the LEAs, but colleges may increasingly have to bear the full cost.

The Staff College was founded in 1960, assisted by a grant of £100,000 from industry, and courses began in 1963. The college is based at Coombe Lodge, Blagdon, near Bristol. It expanded its provision by purchasing a nearby hotel in 1985. The college also provides courses throughout the United Kingdom. The Staff College provides a valuable information service for people working in further and higher education. It publishes regular reports on topics of interest to the further education service, which are available on subscription or by individual purchase.

The Staff College is an independent charitable trust, with the chair and governors being appointed by the Secretary of State for Education. In the past, the governors have been drawn from the local authority associations of England and Wales; nominated representatives of staff from colleges; universities; representatives of industry; the professions; the Trades Union Congress; and members of the staff of The Staff College itself.

The Scottish Further Education Unit

The Further Education Unit does not have a remit to operate in Scotland. There was no Scottish equivalent until April 1991. Between 1985 and 1991, the Curriculum Advice and Support Team (CAST), based at the School of Further Education, Jordanhill College of Education, had developed some of the same themes in Scotland as the FEU has in England and Wales. The founding mission of the Scottish Further Education Unit (SFEU) was to support key developments in vocational education and training in Scotland, by working closely with the providers, with particular emphasis on SCOTVEC provision. The purpose was to identify key developments, interpret the implications for providers and provide support services and products. In its development plan for 1992–95, the SFEU priority areas for support were: organisation and management development; staff development and appraisal; quality assurance; programme design and delivery; marketing; and Europe.

The National Foundation for Educational Research

Some research work on further education is also undertaken by the National Foundation for Educational Research in England and Wales (NFER). The Foundation, established in 1946, is Britain's leading educational research institution. It is an independent body undertaking research and development projects on issues of current interest in all sectors of the public education system. Its membership includes all local education authorities in England and Wales, the main teachers' associations, and a large number of other major organisations with educational interests.

The NFER approach is scientific, apolitical and non-partisan. By means of research projects and extensive field surveys, it has provided objective evidence on important educational issues for the use of teachers, administrators, parents and the research community. The Foundation undertakes a large number of specially sponsored projects at the request of government departments and other agencies, as well as its own work. The major part of the research programme relates to primary, secondary and further education. A further significant element has to do specifically with local education authorities, teacher training institutions and other agencies concerned with education and training. NFER is also the national agency for a number of international research and information exchange networks.

The Scottish Council for Research in Education

In Scotland, the Scottish Council for Research in Education (SCRE) predated NFER. It was founded in 1928 by an alliance of teachers and directors of education with the support of the SED. Its aim was to aid, organise and publish educational research and to act as a reference point for those involved with research. The SCRE is controlled by a board of management, whose chair and two members are appointed by the Secretary of State for Scotland. The other members are nominated by a range of professional bodies concerned with education. The core funding of SCRE comes from the Scottish Education Department, with further grants from the Scottish local authorities. Most of the research is conducted through contracts.

Chapter 11
The financing of FE

The funding councils

A further education or sixth form college is funded from a number of sources, but the major one by far is its funding council. The funding councils for England and Wales took over the role of financing FE from 1 April 1993. From the beginning of this century up to 1993, the local education authorities had been the owners and funding agents of FE colleges. In Northern Ireland, there is no funding council and most of the money for education has traditionally come from the Department of Education for Northern Ireland, owing to the political situation.

This model of a national funding body replacing a local one imitated the arrangements for the English polytechnics and colleges of higher education when they were removed from the LEAs four years previously in 1989. The higher education institutions moved first to the Polytechnics and Colleges Funding Council (PCFC), and then in 1993 to the new Higher Education Funding Council (HEFC), which also covered the old universities. Thus there is a symmetry in that there is both a further education funding council (FEFC) and a higher one. The FE funding council largely covers the FE and sixth form colleges with a residual amount of FE in the HE institutions, while the HE funding council caters for the universities and colleges of higher education with a small amount of HE in the FE colleges.

The 1992 Further and Higher Act gave birth to the separate further education funding councils for both England and Wales. (The Scottish FHE Act created the Funding Council for Scotland.) The English Council was preceded by an FEFC Unit, which completed some of the initial work of setting up the new sector. The FEFC formally took over responsibility for funding of the 465 English further education, tertiary and sixth form colleges on 1 April 1993. It is based in Coventry, and there are also nine regional offices where most of the Council's 100 inspectors are based.

The Further Education Funding Council was established on 17 July 1992. It has a membership of 15, including the Secretary of State's representative. The Chief Executive was formerly Chief Executive of the Polytechnics and Colleges Funding Council. The Secretary of State for Education placed on the Council certain statutory duties:

i) under Section 2 of FHE Act 1992 to secure the provision of sufficient facilities for full-time education suitable to the requirements of 16–18 year olds (taking into account education for that age group provided by LEA maintained schools, grant-maintained schools, non-maintained schools and CTCs); and

ii) under Section 3 to secure the provision of adequate facilities for part-time education suitable to the requirements of persons over compulsory school age, and full-time education suitable to the requirements of those aged 19 and over, where such education falls within the scope of Schedule 2 to the Act.

In fulfilling its duties under sections 2 and 3 of the Act, the council will have to strike a balance between securing maximum access to the widest possible range of opportunities in FE and avoiding a disproportionate charge on public funds. The duty on the council to avoid provision which was too expensive was not intended to rule out education that is by necessity more expensive (such as that for students with special educational needs); rather its purpose was to exclude expenditure which was out of proportion to the need being met.

The English Funding Council may give financial support to the governing body of any institution within the further education sector (or the higher education sector) in respect of:

- the provision of facilities for further education and higher education; or

- the provision of facilities, and the carrying on of any activities, which the governing body of the institution consider necessary or desirable to be provided or carried on for the purpose of or in connection with the provision of facilities for further education and higher education.

Excluded from this support are local education authorities, the governing body of a grant-maintained school or a person maintaining or carrying on a city technology or city college for the technology of the arts. Allocations may include funding for:

- institutions and bodies outside the further education sector which have made successful applications under Section 6(5) of the Act, i.e. they are sponsored by FE colleges;

- courses of further education provided by institutions in the higher education sector;

- courses of higher education within the new further education sector, although such funding should normally be limited to those courses which are not the responsibility of the Higher Education Funding Council for England.

The guidance to the Funding Council from the Secretary of State for Education in July 1992 made clear that the key aims of the funding should be:

- to secure greater efficiency as student numbers increase. While public funding will remain the main source of income for expansion, the council should encourage institutions to take advantage of opportunities for funding from private sources. The Government, for its part, will not reduce public support in the light of institutions' success in attracting other funding;

- to provide a direct incentive to colleges to expand participation by relating an element of colleges' funding to actual student enrolments: the Government, for its part, has undertaken that the total resources available to the council, and hence to colleges, will be determined in part by the actual numbers of students recruited in the year in question;

- to encourage the development of flexible and part-time modes of delivery, including distance learning;

- to maintain and enhance quality by relating funding to the council's assessment of quality;

- to maintain the diversity of missions which currently exist among institutions which will enter the new sector;

- to secure stability of funding for institutions as they enter the new sector. Allocations should take account of academic and financial viability – in particular they should not lead to year-on-year changes in income greater than institutions can be required to accommodate.

The financial support can take the form of grants, loans or other payments and may be given on such terms and conditions as the council sees fit. However, as loans will require the consent of the Secretary of State, in practice this power is likely to be used only very rarely. The council was asked to advise the Secretary of State of which new institutions might be incorporated into the new sector. The council is required to make an annual appraisal of the financial position and requirements of the institutions which it funds, which will inform the Government's consideration of public expenditure.

The Treasury announced planned expenditure for the new sector for the first three years as £2,549 million, £2,734 million and £2,943 million in 1993–94, 1994–95 and 1995–96 respectively. That increase in funding will allow for a projected 25 per cent increase in student numbers between 1992–93 and 1995–96. The figures were based on surveys of what the 116 local authorities spent on further education in the preceding year, 1992–93, and the trend over the three year period 1990–93 to iron out any fluctuations in the last year. This was because a number of local authorities cut college budgets in the last year of financial delegation prior to incorporation.

In announcing the figures for England, the Secretary of State for Education said that the Government's aim was to provide many more people with urgently needed technical skills. 'This will be a large step towards achievement of our national education and training targets and should lift us towards the top of the international league table in staying-on rates for 16 to 19 year olds with the next three years.' In qualification terms, this means that 80 per cent of students will leave education with NVQ Level II (GCSE grades A to G in four subjects) and 50 per cent will reach Level III (A levels or equivalent vocational qualifications).

Further education is competing with higher education for a share of national funds. The higher education sector has the advantage that the Government has made a commitment to increase student numbers by 300,000 by the end of the decade and has maintained an open-ended policy of paying fees for all students recruited into the HE sector. Nevertheless, the Government has throttled back on the rise in higher education since the new sector had increased its student numbers in excess of the targets outlined in the Government's 1991 White Paper **Higher education: a new framework** (DES *et al.* 1991b). The projected three year increase in students is 13 per cent, which assumes that the proportion of young people entering higher education will remain at the 1992 level.

The money from the funding council goes to colleges incorporated as further education corporations (FECs). The colleges, as corporate bodies established under sections 15 and 16 of the FHE Act, have been approved by the Secretary of State for the purpose of establishing and conducting an educational institution. The principal powers of the further education corporations are (a) to provide further and higher education, and (b) to supply goods or services in connection with their provision of education. The Act states that:

goods are supplied in connection with the provision of education by a further education corporation if they result from (a) their provision of education or anything done by them under this Act for the purpose of or in connection with their provision of education, (b) the use of their facilities or the expertise of persons employed by them in the fields in which they are so employed, or (c) ideas of a person employed by them, or one of their students, arising out of their provision of education.

In addition:

A further education corporation may (a) acquire and dispose of land and other property, (b) enter into contracts, including in particular (i) contracts for the employment of teachers and other staff for the purposes of or in connection with carrying on any activities undertaken in the exercise of their principal powers, and (ii) contracts with respect to the carrying on by the corporation of such activities, (c) borrow such sums as the corporation think fit for the purposes of carrying on any activities they have power to carry on or meeting any liability transferred to them under sections 23 to 27 of this Act and, in connection with such borrowing, may grant any mortgage, charge or other security in respect of any land or other property of the corporation, (d) invest any sums not immediately required for the purposes of carrying on any activities they have power to carry on, (e) accept gifts of money, land or other property and apply it, or hold and administer it on trust for any of those purposes, and (f) do anything incidental to the conduct on an educational institution providing further or higher education, including founding scholarships or exhibitions, making grants and giving prizes.

Auditing

While a funding council could provide the majority of the income of a college, the college itself has various other sources. For example, a largish English FE college might derive its funding as outlined below. Since funding now comes through a Government department (the Department for Education covers England and Wales), there is a statutory duty to examine and report to Parliament on the accounts of the department as well as attached public funding bodies such as the FEFC. The statutory duty is carried out by the Comptroller and Auditor General assisted by the National Audit Office. There is also a statutory right of access to the books of colleges in the further education sector.

Audits by the Comptroller and Auditor General are wider than basic financial ones as they include a 'regulatory' element which requires him to certify whether any terms and conditions attached to public funds have been complied with and whether monies have been used only for the purposes intended by Parliament. Additionally, there is a further statutory duty to investigate economy, efficiency and effectiveness through value for money studies. The National Audit Office does not conduct a regular audit of colleges. It will determine its own programme in the light of assessment of audit risk across the whole of the public sector. Where it decides to carry out an audit examination in the FE sector, it is likely to conduct its fieldwork in a sample of colleges.

The chief executives of the funding councils are the councils' accounting officers who are accountable to Parliament for:

- ensuring that public funds are safeguarded;
- securing value for money from public funds; and
- monitoring colleges' compliance with any terms and conditions attached to their funding.

To fulfil these responsibilities, whilst avoiding an excessive audit burden on colleges, the accounting officer relies to a large extent on the audit work

---

carried out by the college's external auditors. Colleges incorporated under the FHE Act had to select and appoint internal and external auditors. Prior to April 1993 internal audits were performed by local education authority staff. External audits were carried out by the local authority's external auditors. Since then the colleges have had to make their own arrangements for internal and external auditing.

Sources on income for colleges of further education

Recurrent grant from FEFC:
- the main allocation and all other recurrent grant from the council allocated in the financial year;
- other grants for recurrent funding as notified by the council.

Release of capital grants.

Education contracts:
- from the local education authority (to include all non-Schedule 2 and Links income);
- from the TEC (to include work-related further education income, youth training income, training for work (formerly ET) income, and any other including training credits);
- from the English Higher Education Funding Council for HE courses run at the college and from HE institutions where courses have been franchised;
- from other authorities such as the health authorities and the Home Office (Prison Education).

Tuition fees and charges:
- income from all tuition fees and income from partial cost recovery and full-cost recovery short and special courses, including registration fees.

Grant income:
- income from the European Social Fund and other funds such as Erasmus, Euroform, Petra;
- other funds including Section 11 (Commonwealth immigrants), TVEI, and Section 210 (travellers).

Research grants and contracts:
- all income in respect of research carried out by the college for which expenditure has been incurred.

Other income generating activities:
- income not covered under other headings in respect of services

rendered to outside bodies such as payment for consultancy.

Residences and catering operations:

– income from student residences and college catering operations.

Other income:

– investment income;

– examination fees;

– other income.

Profits from subsidiary companies:

– amounts paid to the institution by deed of covenant out of the net profits of any subsidiary company.

(Derived from FEFC **Circular 92/16**, FEFC 1992e)

Funding pre-1993

As I stated earlier, up to 1993 most of the money devoted to the operation of a college came from its local education authority, which used a mixture of income from government grant and local taxation to fund it. Up to and including the 1980s local taxes were levied in the form of rates which were assessed on the use of land and buildings. From 1989 in Scotland, and 1990 in England and Wales, local taxes were based on a community charge (more commonly referred to as the poll tax), replaced in 1993 by the new council tax. During the 1980s the percentage of local expenditure covered by government fell from 60 per cent of council spending to 46 per cent.

The proportion of the block grant that is actually spent on the different kinds of local services, including education, is a political decision for elected local councillors. For example, in the past, the education authority might have wanted to spend more on the education of pre-school children rather than post-school students and could have re-allocated finance destined for colleges to nurseries. The removal of further education from this process should result in a more uniform national level of FE spending than the wide diversity that was provided by different local councils.

During the 1980s successive governments had grown impatient with having to work second hand through LEAs and sought an increasing say in where money was spent in education. A system was designed for the former Department of Education and Science to provide specific grants, called Education Support Grants (ESGs), on top of the block Revenue Support Grant to ensure that some funds were devoted to particular government priorities.

Local authorities vary greatly in what they currently spend on each school pupil or used to spend on a further education student; there was no mandatory minimum level. The accountancy body for the public sector, the Chartered Institute of Public Finance and Accountancy (CIPFA), publishes annual league tables of local authority spending levels which are used for purposes of comparison.

Before the new régime of national funding councils providing for incorporated colleges took effect in 1993, FE colleges (but not sixth form colleges or colleges in Inner London) had had three years experience of delegated budgets. The 1988 Education Reform Act had introduced the new measures to rationalise financial procedures for the delegated funding of further education colleges. The changes showed a recognition of the increasing complexity of course provision and funding arrangements as well as the Government's wish to give colleges more autonomy from their local authorities.

Under the previous ERA arrangements, there was a duty placed on every local education authority in England and Wales to prepare a scheme of financial delegation which the Secretary of State had to approve. The scheme had to outline the principles and procedures which the authority was going to use to plan the education provision to be made in the further education colleges which it maintained or substantially assisted. The local authority then had to specify the method of determining the annual budget for each college and provide for the delegation by the authority of the management of the budget to the governing body of the college.

The schemes of delegation, which lasted from 1990 to 1993, were a useful rehearsal for full independence. Each scheme had to:

- give colleges as much freedom as possible to manage their affairs and allocate their resources as they thought best within the strategic framework set by the LEA;
- promote responsiveness by colleges to the changing needs of students, employers and the local community;
- promote good management and the effective and efficient use of resources in colleges;
- provide for college budgets to be based on an objective and equitable allocation of available resources;
- be as simple and clear as possible (in particular, the formula for calculating budgets) so that college governors, staff and students, and the community in general, could understand how it operated;
- give colleges appropriate incentives to earn additional income by providing courses and other services and facilities for the local community, including in particular the business community.

The 1988 Act did not specify how each local authority should have determined what proportion of the total funds available for the education service in its area should be allocated for the use of its further education colleges. The DES guidance only noted that different authorities would use different methods, partly depending on the structure of their further and higher education service. The Act did, however, specify that the authority should make clear the share that each college within the LEA should have of the further and higher education budget. The budget was decided by the application of a formula, which took into account student numbers, laid down by the scheme for the allocation between colleges. The procedure was known as formula funding.

The main duties of the governing body under local financial management were:

- to manage the budget allocated to them effectively and efficiently;
- to fulfil any statutory duties;
- to avoid incurring a deficit;
- to comply with the relevant financial regulations and standing orders of the authority;
- to maintain college premises.

Funding post-April 1993

Following incorporation, both the FEFC and the FEFCW instituted a temporary 16-month funding régime based upon the historical levels of funding provided through the LEA funding formulae. This provided time for a thorough examination of possible funding methods. A working group was established by the FEFC which published a consultation document **Funding learning** (FEFC 1993a). This spelled out six possible options for funding colleges. The document pointed to two possible ways of measuring the student activity to be funded – by continuing with student enrolments as the measure, or by moving to a system which funds each of the three basic elements of learning programmes, entry, programme attendance and exit. It also identified the basic elements of a funding system as the units of activity to which funding is attached; the mechanisms to establishing the amount of activity to be funded; the mechanism for determining the rates at which various types of activity are funded; and the mechanisms to maintain some year-on-year stability in the system.

The options posed by the FEFC included funding based on enrolments, whether established by rates of growth or by bidding systems, but distinguishing between core and marginal funding; and on separate funding for each of the basic learning elements; while one of the options was for a voucher system. After consultation, the FEFC decided to implement the option which funds each of the three programme elements – entry, attendance on programme and achievement (FEFC **Circular 93/14**, FEFC 1993b). The allocation system is based on colleges' proposals for a volume of provision, measured in standard units of provision, funded at a rate set by the council annually (**Circular 93/16**, FEFC 1993c). A Tariff Committee proposes the weightings of these standard units, by subject area and qualification aim (**Circular 93/32**, FEFC 1993d).

Year-on-year stability is achieved by adopting a core and margin system. The core funding is a percentage of each college's previous year's allocation, linked to a fixed amount of core activity. Colleges are then invited to bid for additional marginal funding, from a fund and using criteria established by the council.

The new system means that colleges are responsible for deciding which programmes to offer, but the councils decide the volume that they will fund, the rate at which those programmes will be funded, and any priorities which will attract differential funding. The councils enter into annual agreements with their colleges, in which minimum volumes of provision are specified in return for the funding provided.

FEFC has also established a formula-based approach to the allocation of capital funds to colleges. As with recurrent funds, the initial allocation system is a temporary one, with colleges invited to comment on ways in which the longer term capital funds might be allocated. In particular they are asked to comment on whether the formula should include a bidding element in future. The capital funds cover three elements: a) capital equipment to be applied to the purchase and installation of equipment for teaching and learning, for student and staff support services, or administration of the college; b) minor building works, including urgent health and safety works as identified in the Hunter and Partner's survey; c) major projects, defined as any capital project costing more than £1m including VAT but excluding fees, furntiure and equipment. In Scotland work is in hand to develop a funding methodology which is related to the level of student activity and takes account of the modular nature of the Scottish FE curriculum. For 1993/94 colleges were funded on an historic basis.

The FEFCW published a consultation paper entitled **Funding further education in Wales** (FEFCW 1993c). The paper, produced by a working group of college principals and Funding Council officers, identified three stages in the education process which were regarded as particularly significant in the development of appropriate funding mechanisms. The recruitment, learning and attainment stages form a three-part framework which, the paper suggested, offers the greatest potential for the future funding of further education. At each stage, primary factors could be used to calculate the core allocation of funding and associated growth, with secondary factors being taken into account to recognise additional costs.

At stage 1, the primary factor used could be student enrolments; one or more secondary factors could enable the Funding Council to recognise the recruitment of particular categories of student, or to encourage participation in particular types of programme. Proposals for funding stage 2 aim to take account of the increasing modularisation of the curriculum and more flexible methods of delivery: standard learning hours and weighted student learning units derived from them would provide the primary basis of funding. Emphasis on outcomes at stage 3 may be based on standardised attainments. Within the framework, the Funding Council is anxious to ensure that institutions are supported in rendering accessible their provision to students with learning difficulties and/or disabilities.

The FEFCW's capital funding grant has been distributed over the financial year 1993/94. Major capital project support has included only those projects for which commitment was inherited from pre-1993 agreements between the Welsh Office and the LEAs. Following consultation with the sector, the Funding Council has established procedures for the submission and evaluation of new major projects to be funded from March 1994 onwards.

Allocations for minor works in 1993/94 have been made partly on a formula basis and partly on the basis of a building condition survey of the sector. Consultation on the longer term strategy will include the suggestion that a procedure be established for minor capital projects costing less than £1 million.

Allocations for capital equipment were calculated in 1993/94 using a temporary formula. Additional support was being made available to enable students with learning difficulties and/or disabilities to access further education programmes. From 1994–5 the annual capital allocation is in three categories, for equipment, major projects over £1 million, and minor works, with a particular initial emphasis on health and safety issues.

Monitoring

Government funding to local education authorities for further education colleges in their area was based on the Further Education Statistical Record (FESR). The FESR comprised an annual survey of college enrolments using individualised student records at the beginning of November, which the local authorities returned to the government by the following January. The FESR snapshot was extended to a full academic year from 1984 by the introduction of an Annual Monitoring Survey (AMS) return of aggregate numbers which all colleges complete at the end of the year.

The Annual Monitoring Survey is designed to provide information for various groups and bodies which are concerned with the provision of further and higher education. The data are used in the calculation of the degree of spending outlined in public expenditure surveys. The Annual Monitoring Survey is also used to derive student:staff ratios (SSRs) as well as cost weightings in the measurement of staff deployment and student contact hours. The same indicative numbers of full-time equivalent staff and students, together with the ratios covering average class size, average lecturer hours and average student hours, are used by both the college and the Department for Education in preparing student:staff ratios.

College management information systems

This information has increasingly been recorded on computer packages which form part of college management information systems (CMIS). The Government used education support grants to encourage local authorities and colleges to computerise their further education information systems at the end of the 1980s and pump-priming funding was made available. In Scotland a CMIS project is being funded by the SOED to equip all colleges with a compatible system to meet the needs of incorporation. In England the FEFC proposes to assist colleges in developing their management information strategies and systems, through a central register of information systems, together with support through seminars and user groups (FEFC **Circular 94/05**, FEFC 1994).

Chapter 12
The governance of FE

Background

There is a division of responsibility between the partners involved in further education (which was partly described in Chapter 10):

- the national Further Education Funding Council and its regional committees act as agents on behalf of the Government to finance the further education corporations;
- the governing body of the FE corporation has an overview of the general direction of the college, within its legal powers to provide further and higher education, and supply goods and services in connection with their provision of education;
- the principal or chief executive officer has responsibility for the internal organisation of the college and its day-to-day management and discipline;
- the academic board has an involvement with the planning, co-ordination, development and oversight of the academic work of the college;
- a students' union or other body representing students must be established under arrangements made by the governing body to conduct and manage its own affairs and funds in accordance with a constitution approved by the governors.

The governing body plays a crucial role in the overall management and direction of a college of further education or sixth form college. The strengthening of the powers of the governing body has been a major factor in the process (which started in the mid-1980s) of getting colleges to plan as independent bodies. Now that colleges have become autonomous corporations, the board of governors now resembles the board of directors of a company rather than the large consultative forum of the past dominated by local councillors.

In England and Wales the legal basis and guidance for governing bodies stemmed from the 1968 Education (No. 2) Act and DES **Circular 7/70** (DES 1970). This legislation and guidance stood for two decades before being overtaken first by the governance of colleges provisions of the 1988 Education Reform Act and then the regulations relating to the new FE corporations set out in the 1992 Further and Higher Education Act (FHE). In Scotland, the college councils were also reformed: first by similar powers as those under ERA by Part II of the Self-Governing Schools etc. (Scotland)

Act of 1989 (known, in Scotland, as 'The Et Cetera Act'); then by the 1992 Further and Higher Education (Scotland) Act.

The new governing bodies of FE corporations

Each college must have both an instrument of government, which provides for the constitution of the governing body of the institution, and articles of government, in accordance with which the institution is to be conducted. The articles also set out the relative responsibilities of the principal/director, the governing body and the academic board. In Scotland and Northern Ireland there was no requirement to have a college academic board, so not all colleges introduced them – some relying instead on academic councils.

The 1992 Acts for England/Wales and Scotland altered the definition of the composition, role and powers of governors from the 1988 legislation. With the establishment of further education corporations, new instruments and articles of government were necessary when the 'shadow' corporations were established on 30 September 1992. These were laid out in the Education (government of further education corporations) (former further education colleges) regulations (Statutory Instrument 1963).

The corporations were required to have not more than 20 members and not less than 10, except by permission of the Secretary of State. In the handover from the old style governing body to the new corporation, all members transferred over except for any governor nominated or appointed by a local education authority, who was an elected member of a local authority or who was employed by a local authority other than a teacher (including a head teacher or principal) or who was a member of a fire brigade. These regulations were to remove the direct influence of local education nominees who had dominated most governing bodies prior to 1990. Their maximum membership was restricted first to one-fifth of the total under ERA and then removed altogether by the FHE Act. It was then left up to the new corporation to decide if it wanted to co-opt up to two local authority nominees onto the board.

The membership of the corporation must be based on the categories laid down in the Statutory Instrument (SI 1963), which gives quite a lot of scope. The groupings are as follows:

(a) not more than 13 members who are, or have been, engaged or employed in business, industry or any profession or in any other field of employment relevant to the activities of the institution (to be known as 'independent members');

(b) one member nominated by the training and enterprise council for the area in which the institution is situated;

(c) not more that five members (to be known as co-opted members) co-opted by the members of the corporation who are not co-opted members, of which not more than two may be employed by a local authority, other than as teachers (including head teachers or principals) or as members of a fire brigade maintained under the First Services Act 1947 or be elected members of a local authority;

(d) not more than two members who are members of the staff of the institution elected and nominated by the staff of the institution (to be known as the 'staff members');

(e) not more than one member who is a student at the institution elected and nominated by the students at the institution (to be known as the 'student member');

(f) not more than two members nominated by a body or bodies within the local community nominated by the other members of the corporation;

(g) the principal of the institution unless he chooses not to be a member.

The clear intention was that the members under (a) and (b), to be known as the 'business members', would dominate the corporation. The corporation had to ensure that at least half of all the members were business members. A governing body can vary from a minimum of 10 members based only on the business members and/or the principal to the maximum 20 members with representation from each of the seven categories.

A transition period was fixed from 30 September 1992 to 1 April 1994 for the new corporation to achieve its desired size and composition. The corporations were asked at their first meeting to decide on size and composition, which could be different from the membership carrying over from the previous governing body. During the transition period, any vacancies could be filled or left vacant depending upon the relationship of the initial composition of the corporation to the determined size. If at the first meeting of the corporation after 1 April 1994 the membership did not conform in number and composition to the number and composition determined at its inception, then the regulations require that:

(1) the independent members shall decide at that meeting on which independent members are to be removed from office so that the number of independent members does so conform; and

(2) the members of the corporation excluding the independent members shall decide at that meeting on which members, other than independent members, are to be removed from office so the number and composition of such members does so conform.

Sixth form colleges

In contrast to the FE colleges, the sixth form colleges which entered the FE sector had a different composition. Prior to incorporation, the governing bodies of sixth form colleges included elected parent and teacher representatives, the head (if he or she chose), LEA representatives, and either a number of co-optees or (for controlled colleges) one co-optee and a number of foundation governors. Governors had to make sure that the local business community was adequately represented on governing bodies, whether by co-option or otherwise. After the reforms, instruments of government no longer provided for an LEA representative, although, as with FE colleges, governing bodies could make two additional co-options if they wished. The relationship with the local business community was reinforced by a representative of the local TEC.

For the voluntary aided sixth form colleges, the governing bodies had members from among the same groups, but composition was not otherwise standardised. There previously had to be at least one LEA representative, and foundation governors had to have an overall majority of two or three, depending on the size of the school. The Government preserved the foundation's majority position. By removing LEA appointees and allowing for a TEC representative, the size of the governing body remained the same, or was reduced, so foundation governors retained or increased their majority. The Government intention was that voluntary aided and voluntary controlled sixth form colleges continued to make their particular contribution to the education of pupils over the age of 16.

The regulations for sixth form colleges are listed below.

(1) The corporation shall consist of not less than 12 and not more than 20 members appointed in accordance with the following provisions of this Instrument and shall include the person who is for the time being the principal of the institution, unless he chooses not to be a member.

(2) Of the appointed members:

(a) up to 12 (referred to in this Instrument as the independent members) shall be persons appearing to the appointing authority to be, or to have been, engaged or employed in business, industry or any profession or in any other field of employment relevant to the activities of the institution;

(b) not less than three and not more than five, or in the case of a former voluntary controlled school, not less than three and not more than 10 (referred to in this Instrument as the initial nominee members) shall be persons nominated in accordance with this Instrument otherwise than by other members of the corporation; and

(c) up to three, of which up to two may be employees or elected representatives of a local authority (referred to in this Instrument as the co-opted members) shall be persons nominated in accordance with this Instrument by the members of the corporation who are either independent members or initial nominee members and the principal of the institution (if he is a member).

The initial nominee members of a corporation shall consist of:

- up to two parents of students at the institution;
- up to two staff nominees;
- one student nominee;
- up to five foundation nominees (in the case of former voluntary controlled schools only); and
- one TEC nominee.

Up to incorporation, the sixth form colleges had concentrated mainly on academic courses with little provision of vocational education. With the transfer to the new sector, sixth form colleges were asked to review their range of activities and increase their offering of vocational education. They are also able to provide education for adults. If there is a major change in emphasis, then the Secretary of State can make adjustments to increase the representation from employment interest governors.

Impact of the new governing bodies

At the time of writing, it is too early to know how the new governing bodies will settle down. A governing body of 10 to 15 members may become the norm. Small governing bodies can act in a more executive way. A Staff College research study (Graystone *et al.* forthcoming), yet to be published, revealed that there was some scepticism among existing governors about the ability of the governing body to be quorate if senior industrialists are away on business; the need to cope with the heavy demands of the meetings of the governing body, sub-committees and working parties might take a toll. Initial indications are that many colleges have not put staff and student governors on the new governing bodies, arguing that to have staff as directors of a company is incompatible with decisions on sensitive personnel matters and that student governors are too young and inexperienced to make any significant impact.

It is ironic that in the former polytechnics, now universities, which broke away from local government in 1989, a quarter had more than 25 members and six out of 10 had 20 or more.

Duties and responsibilities of the new governing bodies

The role of the governing body of the FE corporation in the period after 1993 is laid out in its articles of government.

The corporation shall be responsible (a) for the determination of the educational character and mission of the institution and for oversight of its activities; (b) for the effective and efficient use of resources, the solvency of the institution and the corporation and for safeguarding their assets; (c) for approving annual estimates of income and expenditure; (d) for the appointment, grading, suspension, dismissal and determination of the pay and conditions of service of the holders of senior posts; and (e) for setting a framework for the pay and conditions of service of all other staff.

Prior to the 1992 FHE Act, a major responsibility of the governing body was staffing. Governing bodies were empowered to: decide staffing requirements; select senior staff for appointment; dismiss staff; determine the duties to be performed by members of staff; judge the hours of work of part-time staff; determine the grading of full- and part-time posts; exercise any discretion over the remuneration of staff; and handle employee grievance and discipline matters. From 1993, the governors are responsible for appointing those people designated as senior staff, which could be either just the principal/chief executive or could include the principalship and the next tier of management. However, principals, in their new roles as chief executives, oversee all other appointments and gradings.

Governors have a legal liability for their acts. Normally if a member of a governing body acts in a bone fide way and is intra vires (i.e. within the permitted powers of the corporation) then there should be no fear of personal liability. But there is still potential for a breach of the law which is by no means simple as it has not been codified by statute and depends on interpretation by courts establishing case law. Schemes have been set up for members of governing bodies to benefit from professional indemnity and other insurance policies. The four main areas of potential liability identified by solicitors Wedlake Saint were outlined as follows.

- where governors actively participate in an act which is beyond the powers of the corporation – members are under a duty to see that the corporation's powers are properly used;

- governors must act honestly and exercise that degree of care and skill that may reasonably be expected of them having regard to their knowledge and experience – if wrongful acts are committed wilfully, maliciously or recklessly, members will be liable;

- in relation to criminal liability, certain statutes provide that where a corporation has committed an offence its officers shall, in certain circumstances, be deemed guilty of that offence;

- where any corporation disobeys a judgement or order of the Court which requires it to abstain from doing something or, being required to do an act within a specific time, refuses or neglects to do it within that time, its property (and the property of its officers and members) is liable to sequestration.

Size and composition of governing bodies: 1988–92

There is little research on the work of FE college governing bodies. At the beginning of the 1990s, studies were done by HMI as part of the review of the ERA and by The Staff College (Graystone 1991). The HMI report, **The impact of the ERA on further education** (HMI 1991d) noted that ERA had resulted in a significant change in the composition of governing bodies, and in most cases a reduction in their size. Governing bodies had reduced to between 18 and 23 members, and were up to 30 per cent smaller than previously. All the bodies had at least half their membership drawn from outside education and the local authority, with the majority representing employers. The employers represented a range of local industry and commerce and there was often a trades unionist nominated by the local trades council. In all but two colleges of those inspected, one or two co-opted members represented the non-vocational work of the college such as adult and continuing education.

In 1990 (the first year of the delegated powers) local authority representatives accounted for only 20 per cent of the membership of governing bodies having previously formed over a third. The remaining 30 per cent of the governing body was filled with representatives of college staff, of students, of headteachers and higher education representatives and, in several instances, a broad constituency had also been achieved by including a parent, a representative of the ethnic minority communities or a member of an agency providing for students with special educational needs. Between 10 and 25 per cent of governors were women. In most cases, at least one member of the governing body was also a member of the board of the local TEC.

In research conducted by John Graystone of The Staff College as part of governor development (Graystone 1991), he found that of 190 colleges surveyed after ERA, the average size of the governing body was between 18 and 19 with the largest having 23 members and the smallest 10. A typical governing body of 19 or 20 might contain nine employment interest governors, one co-optee, four LEA nominees, two staff, one student, one educational institution, possibly one community organisation and the principal. The Staff College survey discovered that most governors were male (82 per cent); white (98 per cent); and able-bodied (99 per cent). Only eight per cent of governing bodies were chaired by women, 49 per cent were chaired by local authority nominated governors and 47 per cent by employment interest governors. Almost two-thirds of female chairs of governors were LEA-nominated governors, who largely disappeared as a category of membership after 1993.

Her Majesty's Inspectorate (HMI 1991d) found that the governing bodies that their inspectors saw had created sub-committees to consider particular areas of their work. Every governing body had a finance and general purposes sub-committee and in nearly all colleges this had been complemented by up to three other sub-committees dealing with personnel, resources, student affairs, strategic planning or curriculum issues. Some governors also sat on specialist advisory committees. The chair of the governing body at that time was most likely to be an elected member of the LEA.

In terms of the effectiveness of governing bodies, HMI found that in the colleges inspected, most principals and LEA officers said that the meetings of the new governing bodies had been purposeful and well managed. Governors had shown commitment and enthusiasm in fulfilling their remit. The working relationship between the principal and the chair of the governing body had been particularly important in enabling the governing body to fulfil its remit. It was established that governing bodies had demonstrated some independence from both the LEA and the college senior management. Governors generally were making decisions and not merely confirming those proposed by college staff.

Governor training

With the increasing responsibility of governors, governor training has become an important feature. The HMI review (HMI 1991d) found that in most cases training had been provided in two ways. First through briefing papers for governors meetings, and training materials produced by the Department for Education or the local education authority. Second, training sessions were provided for governors at which issues relevant to the work of the college and LEA were covered. These were sometimes complemented by a tour of the college and its resources and meetings with college staff and students.

Up to 1993, most LEAs and colleges jointly provided training, while from 1993 onwards colleges have been responsible. Principals have been keen to ensure that governors gain an appropriate understanding of the issues specifically relating to their college. HMI reported that training had been seen as having mixed effectiveness. Some governors had shown little enthusiasm for training. Some industrial representatives in particular had claimed that they could not spare the time. It was thought that training sessions closely related to the work of the college were received more enthusiastically by governors than those which tackled wider educational issues.

The Association for Colleges

Governing bodies in the further education sector have had their own professional body for many years through the Association of Colleges for Further and Higher Education (ACFHE). Its remit covered the whole of the United Kingdom and it was largely a lobbying and updating organisation. The tertiary colleges had a separate arrangement via the Tertiary Colleges Association (TCA). In 1992, ACFHE and TCA came together with the principals' associations for the FE and tertiary sectors to establish the Association for Colleges (AfC). The Association is governed by a council and a board of three governors and three principals.

The Association has its head office in London, a regional structure in England, and national branches in Wales, Scotland and Northern Ireland. It supports and promotes the interests of colleges nationally and internationally. Its aims are to:

- identify with, and campaign for, the interests of the colleges, recognising that unity and concerted action is the best way of affirming the sector's diversity;
- represent those interests to government and Parliament, and to national and international organisations in education, industry and commerce, presenting a focal point and a strong voice for the sector;
- promote the colleges' activities and achievements to the public in the press and broadcasting media, creating a positive image for member institutions and the FE sector generally;
- assist the development of programmes which are relevant to the needs of the post-16 population and support measures to assure the quality of that provision;
- conduct and support research into the organisation and delivery of courses in colleges, using the outcomes to disseminate best practice and to influence policy-makers in their decisions;
- link the colleges in a national network of information, support and strategic development, and in branches representing Wales, Scotland, Northern Ireland and the regions of England;
- offer the colleges technical, legal and commercial advice and services, in all areas save that of employment conditions;
- establish working relationships with sector bodies in schools and higher education in order to promote coherence throughout the service.

Chapter 13
The management of FE

The day-to-day running of a college is delegated by the governing body or college council to the principal or director. The responsibilities of the principal are laid out in the 1992 Regulations for the government of further education corporations (SI 1963). They state that, subject to the responsibilities of the corporation:

> The principal shall be the chief executive of the institution, and shall be responsible (a) for making proposals to the corporation about the educational character and mission of the institution, and for implementing the decisions of the corporation; (b) for the organisation, direction and management of the institution and leadership of the staff; (c) for the appointment, assignment, grading, appraisal, suspension, dismissal, and determination, within the framework set by the corporation, of the pay and conditions of service, of staff other than the holders of senior posts; (d) for the determination, after consultation with the academic board, of the institution's academic activities, and for the determination of its other activities; (e) for preparing annual estimates of income and expenditure, for consideration and approval by the corporation, and for the management of budget and resources, within the estimates approved by the corporation; and (f) for the maintenance of student discipline and, within the rules and procedures provided for within these articles, for the suspension or expulsion of students on disciplinary grounds and for implementing decisions to expel students for academic reasons.

Staff roles

In small colleges, the principal may be the sole senior manager operating with heads of department or he/she could have a vice-principal (depute principal in Scotland). A medium-sized college will have one or two vice- or assistant principals, who usually split functional management responsibilities with the principal. It is common for one person to be responsible for resource allocation while the other looks after curriculum matters. In larger colleges there may be a team of senior staff, often called the principalship or directorate. One of the team will usually be the official deputy to the principal/director, although there is an increasing tendency to farm out these duties. Each college works out its own arrangements and there is no standard national pattern.

Mergers

One management problem that has to be addressed in the 1990s is that of college size. Some college principals fear that their institutions will be unable to survive in the more competitive atmosphere under the new funding régime. A survey in 1992 revealed that one in 10 colleges was engaged in talks on merger proposals or collaborative arrangements, which could include sharing the burden of administration, marketing and advertising. On the run up to incorporation in 1992/3, the FEFC warned colleges that they would have enough to do to get themselves ready for independence without being distracted by merger talks. Some colleges, such as those that are specialised and largely monotechnic, feel that they do not have the width to move resources around if the market that they are in is affected by adverse outside circumstances.

From 1993 colleges faced many new challenges; **Figure 10** shows the contrast, as described by the KPMG group.

Figure 10: Contrast in colleges pre- and post-incorporation

Pre-incorporation	Post-incorporation
Administrative culture	Managerial culture
Hierarchical or complex matrix structures	Management by performance
Centralised finance from LEA	Decentralised financial systems
Limited flexibility	Flexibility with autonomy
Traditional contractual terms	Wide range of contractual terms
Funding largely guaranteed	Funding based largely on outcomes

Colleges in the 1990s have to react to new markets, changed funding arrangements and anticipated rising demand but will also have to overcome professional conservatism among some college staff, a skills gap in certain parts of the college and a redistribution and better use of resources. In order to develop a dynamic overall strategy, colleges have been asked to prepare a mission statement and strategic and business plans.

Strategic and business planning

The Staff College/Longman's **Guide to college management** (Turner 1991) defines strategic management in the following way:

It is a concern about surviving and thriving which is based on a clear understanding of where you are, informed by a vision of where you want to be, a clear focus of the business you are in, and which operates throughout with a meticulously sensitive relationship to its various environments. Its purpose is to get a near enough fit between the expectations of the stakeholders and both the planned and the achieved service of the college.

The principal has to lead the senior management and staff in a continuous process of review and development. Factors that should be monitored include:

- student enrolment by mode of attendance, sex, age, curriculum and/ or discipline area, geographical distribution, etc. over several years;
- the product or service provided via the range of courses over several years;
- educational outcomes in terms of completion rates, pass rates, progression into higher education, employment, destination of students, future performance in careers;
- staff information, e.g. numbers, ratio of full- to part-time staff, proportion of different categories of staff, (e.g. teachers, managers, technicians, administrators), skill mix, overtime, sickness leave, etc.;
- efficiency data such as staff:student ratios, average class sizes, lecture contact ratio, unit costs;
- financial information such as expenditure analysis over some years, sources of income, end of year balances;
- analysis of physical plant and buildings such as equipment levels and condition, buildings conditions;
- other assessments such as those from FEFC, HMI, validating and examining bodies, local employers' opinions;
- information on the organisational culture;
- internal morale via good feedback systems and careful observation.

Strategic plans are usually expressed as rather general, long-term objectives. The process of defining medium-term targets is often known as business planning. The three distinguishing characteristics of business plans are that: they describe specific, quantifiable targets achievable in one or, at most, two years; they specify which part of the organisation is responsible for achieving the targets; realistic estimates of the resources necessary to achieve the targets, and the financial or other benefits accruing from them, are spelt out in the form of a budget.

Academic board

For England and Wales the Secretary of State stated in DES **Circular 9/88** (DES 1988c) on local management that it was appropriate for all colleges to have a forum for discussing issues relating to the academic life of the college. This forum is normally the academic board, which is chaired by the principal. While academic standards and organisation of the college are the ultimate responsibility of the governors and the principal, the academic board is responsible for advising the principal on the standards, planning, co-ordination, development and oversight of academic work, including arrangements for the admission, assessment and examination of students.

College structures

In the past, most colleges of further education were organised into departments for the delivery of courses. A survey at the beginning of the 1990s by The Staff College (Graystone 1991) showed that this applied to over 70 per cent of further education colleges in the UK. A typical organisational framework for a further education college might be based on departments covering engineering, management and business studies, science and mathematics and general education. It could have further departments such as catering, construction, motor vehicle, community care or adult and community studies. The head of department is a line manager responsible for the delivery of a group of courses. A medium-sized department would have two or more senior lecturers responsible for sections of the department. At course level within a department there will most likely be a course tutor, who will lead the course team and be responsible to the head of department for the quality of the course.

Up until the beginning of the 1990s there was a growing trend for small and medium-sized colleges to abolish departments and set up alternative systems of middle management. In tertiary colleges some form of matrix system was popular, with only just over 40 per cent of this kind of college retaining a departmental structure. A typical matrix structure operates on the basis of groups of courses being run by section leaders who are responsible to assistant principals with functional responsibilities across the college. The term 'matrix' is used because of the separation of academic leadership and resource control, both of which came under the head of department in traditional structures. In larger colleges it is common to have faculties or schools under which departments, sections or programme areas are grouped. There is no nationally recommended pattern and most structures tend to be modified over several years as demands and pressures alter.

Increasingly, colleges have come to recognise that organisational structures should be based on the tasks facing the college. Turner (1991) lists a range of decisions that the college will need to take:

- specification of work to be undertaken;
- supervision of that work;
- differentiation of operations and work groups into separate manageable sub-groups – manageable in that they are within the span of control of specified managers; and
- integration and co-ordination of decision-making and work operations with and between those sub-groups.

The payment of principals, vice-principals, assistant principals and heads of department has been based on salary scales related to a range of unit totals, which themselves are based on calculations of student hours with various weightings. Following ERA, the management side of the National Joint Council for Further Education proposed the abolition of the unit total method of salary estimation. The employers wanted instead to recognise the change over to forward funding in line with forecast or target student numbers, rather than basing salaries on a calculation of the previous year's student volume. They have secured the abolition of the current salary grades falling below the level of principal and above the senior lecturer grade, and their replacement by a spinal column of salary points from which the principal or governing body would be able to determine four-point salary scales in the light of local circumstances. The new 35-point scale is called the 'management spine'.

Cross-college posts

In all colleges there will be a number of people with cross-college responsibilities. The non-academic employees, such as clerical, administrative, technician and catering staff, will come under a person with the title of chief administrative officer, college secretary or registrar. There is usually a staff development officer who is charged with arranging in-house and external staff training, although increasingly this post will come under the general human resource development. Under health and safety legislation, the college should have a safety officer who advises the principal on the safe operation of buildings, teaching and working accommodation and dealing with hazardous substances and situations. The increasing complexity of colleges has generated all kinds of other posts which are based on the equivalent of functional middle managers: a management information systems co-ordinator will generate computerised information and provide statistics; a marketing officer will be responsible for improving the responsiveness of the college to new needs and demands; a student liaison officer will advise on relations with the student body; an enrolment officer will ensure a systematic approach to recruitment. There is a growing trend to have enhanced customer care facilities so there may be a student services unit dealing with applications, guidance, careers and counselling.

The transfer of colleges from the LEAs has meant that a number of functions that were previously undertaken by the LEA are now performed by the college or its agents. This applies to financial management, personnel management, premises management, payroll systems, internal and external auditing, legal advice, banking, insurance and taxation.

It is not the remit of this book to deal in detail with the management of further education. There are much better texts such as the **Guide to college management** (Turner 1991), which I would recommend to readers.

Chapter 14
The teaching of FE

The different routes into FE teaching

College lecturers generally have backgrounds which differ from those of school teachers; they also work in different ways. These differences are often difficult for newcomers to comprehend, who have little knowledge of how colleges function. Since most staff in further education colleges teach vocational subjects, it is common for new lecturers to have had an average of 10 years in industry or commerce in a vocational field relevant to the one in which they are going to teach. Thus the majority do not enter further education until they are in their late 20s or 30s. This is obviously in sharp contrast to the bulk of school teachers who go straight into teaching after either a degree course and one year of teacher training (the Postgraduate Certificate of Education) or a four year teacher training degree (the Bachelor of Education).

The method of entry to further education teaching is also different from schools. Most FE lecturers are likely to have started teaching on a part-time basis while they were still employed by a local company. They then have the option of either applying for a full-time post when one comes up in their subject area or, alternatively, resigning from their job and taking a one year course at an FE teacher training centre. There are four such centres in England: located in London, Wolverhampton, Bolton and Huddersfield. My own background is typical of FE teachers. After five years' employment in the gas industry, I taught for two years on a part-time basis and did a one year pre-service course at Huddersfield before getting a full-time lecturing post.

Not all staff, of course, follow the above route. Some lecturers, who teach general education subjects similar to those offered in schools, might have transferred from a school or even gone straight into a post after training to teach in schools, although this is unusual. Where there has been a reorganisation of post-16 education in a local authority to form a tertiary college, some of the staff in that tertiary college will be former sixth form teachers from schools or a sixth form college. Some lecturers who teach higher level work similar to that in a college of higher education or a university may have been recruited because of their academic qualifications at Masters Degree or Doctorate level, rather than their industrial experience. An increasing number of people who work in various kinds of training agencies are now trying to find employment in further education owing to the better pay and conditions available in colleges.

Conditions of service

The way working arrangements are laid down in further education shows its difference from both schools and universities. These conditions are contained in the so-called Silver Book, which was up for renegotiation from 1993. A lecturer's working week is not measured in days but in hours and sessions. All lecturers are required to attend for 30 hours per week, or 10 sessions. There is a general limit of two evening sessions for mainstream college staff, but some adult education organisers may work more evenings. A lecturer could thus have a timetable which entails working from 09.00 to 21.00 on Monday and Tuesday of each week and having a day off in lieu.

A session should not normally exceed three hours but could go up to four. An evening session is normally for a maximum of three hours. Where regular evening or weekend work is required, a separate local arrangement is made about time off in lieu or extra payments. The normal maximum for a member of staff is 21 hours in any week. This could be 'averaged' over a term so that in some weeks the lecturer does more than 21 hours, but with a lighter load at another time.

The lecturer is assumed to do marking, preparation and a range of other duties in the nine hours left within the 30 hours; most lecturers do many more hours than this. Although the normal academic year extends from the beginning of September until the beginning of July, many staff work on an extended year basis outside of this period – although they are still limited to 36 teaching weeks. Lecturers are required to be involved in two weeks of administration, usually at the beginning and end of the academic year.

There are restrictions on both the maximum period of teaching and the minimum time off for holidays in the conditions of service agreement. There is no obligation to teach for longer than 14 consecutive weeks without a two-week holiday break. Classes usually close at Christmas and Easter for at least seven consecutive days. There is an entitlement to not fewer than six weeks' continuous holiday between the beginning of June and the end of September. These and similar regulations can lead to highly complex discussions between managers and lecturers in putting together an annual programme.

The arrangements for the work load of lecturers show the flexible nature of further education. The annual pay discussions over the last few years have involved the management side trying to loosen up some of the limitations on flexibility which the lecturers' side sees as essential to prevent exploitation. The difficulty is that the range of teaching in FE colleges varies from school-type courses, through full-time vocational courses, part-time and evening courses, short training packages, block release sessions and training on company premises, to higher education work comparable with universities and colleges of higher education. No standard pattern covers everyone. It is likely, however, that there will be pressure from governing bodies to negotiate local deals on working arrangements which could be coupled with incentive schemes. The Government has expressed its wish to move to performance-related pay in the 1990s.

Part-time staff

Further flexibility is given to FE by the widespread use of part-time lecturing staff. At one time about 20 per cent of the total hours in a college would be taught by a large number of part-time teachers who were on contracts allowing for only one week's notice. This percentage varied from almost nil in some highly technical areas where it was difficult to get part-time staff during the day, to nearly 100 per cent in adult education which could be run by full-time and part-time heads of centre and staffed almost entirely by part-time teachers.

The ratio of part-time teaching compared to full-time has been on the increase. As colleges moved to financial independence there has been a growing tendency to use more part-time staff or to use temporary staff on full-time renewable contracts. Temporary contracts are particularly common where people teach on programmes which only have short-term funding or are pilot projects.

The make-up of the teaching staff

Until recently it was difficult to give an accurate figure for staffing in the FE sector since published government statistics lumped lecturers in the FE colleges together with those in polytechnics and colleges of higher education. Although the two sectors were separated in 1989, the 1993 edition of **Education statistics for the United Kingdom** still did not disaggregate the sectors

In 1990–1 (from the data in the 1993 edition) the combined FHE workforce was 88,000 in the United Kingdom, of whom 58,000 were men (62 per cent). Of these lecturers 48 per cent were graduates, 60 per cent of whom were teacher trained. This compares with university lecturers (99 per cent graduates) and the school teachers where 38 per cent of primary school teachers and 67 per cent of secondary teachers were graduates.

The age profile of the lecturers showed that, on average, the workforce is getting older. Only three per cent of the lecturers were under 30 years of age, with 43 per cent in their 40s and 30 per cent over 50. Since then, due to the extensive use of enhanced early retirement schemes in 1992/3 prior to incorporation, there has been an increase in staff turnover and more recruitment of younger lecturers.

The gender balance of the lecturing force has only changed by 11 percentage points in the past two decades. In 1970/71, when there were only 69,000 staff, men represented 81 per cent of the lecturing staff. In the 1990s the proportion of men had dropped to 70 per cent, with a consequent 30 per cent of women. Percentages of women in senior managerial posts are even lower than the 30 per cent of lecturers.

There are no reliable statistics published on the ethnic balance of the lecturing force although the DFE now collects the information. Generally speaking, however, with the exception of some inner city colleges in the major cities, staff from ethnic minority backgrounds are not significantly represented in the full-time teaching force in FE colleges.

Pay structures and teaching standards

The structure of college staffing in England is the same as that in Wales and Northern Ireland, but differs in Scotland. In England there are only two current grades of teaching staff: the lecturer and the senior lecturer. In 1986/87 the main lecturer grade accounted for three-quarters of the estimated 53,000 lecturing staff. There were nearly 12,000 senior lecturers (22 per cent) and over 1,000 on the former principal lecturer grade (two per cent). The employers' side in the national salary discussions negotiated the replacement of the principal lecturer grade by a small range of points on a management salary spine at the beginning of the 1990s; this had already happened in Scotland. Lecturers are expected to teach up to an average of 21 hours for 36 weeks, but senior lecturers with significant management responsibilities could be limited to 18 hours (or 15 hours if protected under previous arrangements).

The HM Senior Chief Inspector of Schools report **Education in England 1990–91** (HMI 1992) gives some general views about the success of further education teaching. In looking at post-16 education, the inspectors observed that FE enrolments had increased by 3.6 per cent compared with the previous year. Over 4,200 lessons had been inspected and 90 per cent of classroom practice was satisfactory or better. Standards of work on all courses were good or at least satisfactory, and reflected the requirements of the various national examining and validating bodies. In a range of vocational areas, the standards of practical work were often high and students responded well to the demand of extended assignments and project work. In contrast, much written work was less satisfactory. The introduction of NVQs has led to an improvement in standards in office studies and in craft work in construction and improved student motivation in hairdressing.

There was no clear correlation between poor practice and poor resources; some good classroom practice took place despite poor resources and reflected the efforts of individual teachers. An increasing number of colleges had identified performance indicators, usually covering enrolments, wastage rates, examination results, employment destinations and student:staff ratios. More colleges were developing their own quality assurance systems in order that the quality and standards of learning could be fully monitored. Some of these systems were proving effective without incurring high cost or complex administration.

From 1965 to 1987 the payment systems for college teaching staff in England and Wales were governed by statutory machinery under the 1965 **Remuneration of Teachers Act**. The Committee that governed advanced and non-advanced further education was known as the Burnham Further Education Committee. Following industrial action by lecturers in 1987/88, changes were made in the bargaining structure covering lecturers' pay and conditions of service. A National Joint Council for Lecturers in Further Education in England and Wales, which operated on a voluntary collective bargaining basis, was brought in to replace the old statutory machinery, but it lasted only until 1993, when colleges replaced local authorities as the employers.

The colleges set up a Colleges' Employers' Forum (CEF) in 1992 to conduct collective bargaining at national level on their behalf. The CEF took over from the Local Government Management Board after the 1992 pay round in education. In Scotland, a decision was made in 1992 to set up a new employers' association, the Scottish College Councils' Forum (SCCF), with a structure akin to that of the CEF. The CEF is a voluntary body relying on subscriptions from colleges. At its inception, the CEF hired the Polytechnics and Colleges' Employers' Forum to conduct its negotiations. The Association for Principals of Sixth Form Colleges (APVIC) selected the Local Government Management Board to bargain on behalf of sixth form colleges at national level.

Salaries for further education staff in Northern Ireland are negotiated at the Northern Ireland Further Education Negotiating Committee. Although there are some small differences, the scales are the almost the same as in England and Wales.

Trades unions

The main trade union and professional association for staff in colleges of further education is the National Association of Teachers in Further and Higher Education (NATFHE). NATFHE now calls itself the University and College Lecturers' Union. The union covers England, Wales and Northern Ireland, but not Scotland. The vast majority of full-time and many part-time academic staff are members. NATFHE is affiliated to the Trades Union Congress, as are most British trade unions. NATFHE acts both as a trade union in the conventional sense and as a professional association. The trade union function is represented mainly in the negotiation of pay and conditions through the National Joint Council. The union has at least one branch based on each college, which negotiates with college management. NATFHE's decision-making structures are based on regional groups, feeding into a National Executive Committee.

NATFHE, the university and college lecturers' union, fought a test case in the High Court to support the fact that lecturers were protected by a European directive in transferring to further education corporations. The lecturers kept their pay, conditions and collective agreements in the transfer.

NATFHE plays a major role in further education policy making through its representatives on most of the major examining and validating bodies, the Further Education Unit, The Staff College, the National Institute of Adult Continuing Education and so on. The Association frequently issues policy statements on major issues and its subject sections organise conferences and courses and publish journals and newsletters. NATFHE also recruits in higher education, penal education departments, adult education institutes, continuing education and in training organisations. It has joint agreements with the Agricultural Colleges' Association, the teachers of home economics, the main Scottish lecturers' union and the National Union of Teachers.

Other associations recognised in England and Wales for pay bargaining are the Association of Agricultural Educational Staffs and the National Society for Art and Design Education. Many college managers are also members of the Association of College Management, which recruits at head of department level and above. The Association of Principals of Colleges was formerly a trade union recognised for pay bargaining and part of the national machinery but it chose to deregister and act as a professional association. Principals and senior staff will have their salary package governed by the remuneration committee of the college's governing body.

In Scotland, the major union in further education is the Further Education Lecturers National Section, a self-governing association within the Educational Institute of Scotland, the main Scottish school teachers' union. There is a smaller association called the Scottish Further and Higher Education Association.

Responsibility for staffing matters within colleges

Under the ERA legislation college governing bodies (or, in Scotland, college councils) took on a number of powers in relation to staffing that were formerly the prerogative of the local education authority. Under the FHE Act, many of these became the responsibility of the principal as chief executive. For example, under an Order issued by the DES in 1989 to modify the employment arrangements, the governing body must: not discriminate unlawfully with regard to race or sex; recognise at least all the trades unions recognised by the LEA; not dismiss staff unfairly; handle trade disputes arising from governing body decisions; disclose information to trades unions; consult unions before any redundancy of staff employed in the college; not pressure staff on union membership matters; re-employ women after maternity leave; allow secret union ballots on college premises.

After incorporation the main powers in relation to staffing passed to the principal/chief executive. He/she became responsible in 1993 for the appointment, assignment, grading, appraisal, suspension, dismissal, and determination, within the framework set by the corporation, of the pay and conditions of service, of staff other than the holders of senior posts.

Staff appraisal

The work of college lecturers has not been formally appraised until recently. There were suggestions, as long ago as 1973, for the introduction of an annual interview for all staff, with job specification as the focus, as a means of identifying staff development. The Government introduced the idea of appraisal of teachers and lecturers in the 1986 Education Act, when it laid down enabling clauses for the introduction of appraisal to secure the performance of teachers in discharging their duties and in engaging in other activities connected with the establishments at which they are employed. The definition of teachers included those employed at any further education establishment maintained at that time by a local education authority.

The 1988 pay settlement in the further education sector contained a plan for the introduction of appraisal schemes for lecturing staff. While a few kinds of appraisal arrangements operate in some colleges, there is no official national scheme. Pilot schemes operated in six local education authorities under the direction of a working party of the National Joint Council (FE). The National Foundation for Educational Research was appointed to evaluate the schemes on behalf of the Department of Education and Science. An interim report was published in October 1989 (Bridgwood 1989). The outcome of the pilots was fed into the national negotiations from 1990 onwards.

The major issues coming from the pilot schemes included formalisation of the tasks of individual lecturers within their job descriptions, the training of appraisers, self-appraisal, the appraisal interview, classroom observation, an agreed statement of outcomes and an appeals procedures. Local authorities were asked to agree local schemes by the summer of 1992 which allowed for all lecturing staff to be included in the process by 31 August 1994 at the latest.

The productivity of teaching staff in the colleges as a whole has been measured by the student:staff ratio (SSR). The ratio is constructed from figures for average class size, average lecturer hours and average student hours. While these figures are artificial constructs they are used as a guide and colleges were asked to achieve SSRs of at least 12:1 by the early 1990s.

Section Four
Where are the boundaries of FE?

Chapter 15   *Locating the boundaries*

Chapter 16   *FE and the labour market*

Chapter 17   *FE and training structures*

Chapter 18   *FE and skills training*

Chapter 19   *FE and youth training*

Chapter 20   *FE and adult training*

Chapter 21   *FE and higher education*

Chapter 22   *FE and schools*

Chapter 15
Locating the boundaries

Background

I suggested in earlier chapters that it is difficult to define a college of further education since, although there are legal interpretations about what courses might be funded, it is not a precisely delineated institution. Instead, one can paint a picture of the surroundings of a college and try to explain what might fall within the college boundary and what would probably be outside. Much of this boundary definition is helped by an explanation (often historical) of how the boundary has been managed. It is true to say that further education has no natural boundaries because it has no range of courses for which it is the sole provider, although it is the major provider for full-time vocational courses such as BTEC/SCOTVEC.

The history of further education is rather like that of a country in the middle of a land mass, which is not bounded by a coastline, a mountain range or a major river. In 1985, when I gave a lecture about the changing nature of vocational qualifications, I used the analogy of the evolution of further education as being similar to the historical problems of Poland. At the time I had been reading James A Michener's epic novel of the development of Poland and had in my mind the image of this country in the 18th century, sandwiched between its giant neighbours: Russia to the east, Germany to the west, Austria and the Ottoman Empire to the south. At times, like the end of the 18th century (and again later, during the Second World War), Poland has been partitioned by its large neighbours but has bounced back with a spirit of independence and a will to survive. That survival and expansion has been by clever alliances and good boundary management with its large neighbours.

The major difficulty for a small country sandwiched between large empires is that those neighbours can use their strength to push back the frontiers at any time, unless they are prevented by hostile public opinion.

In the case of further education, one could imagine that higher education is the Russian Bear to the east and the school system is the German Eagle to the west. To the south are the various types of training organisations that have come and gone in the post-war period. All of them compete to some extent with further education and there are overlaps of student and trainee populations. In the post-war period, further education has succeeded in pushing back the boundaries as it has expanded. The chapters in this section examine the nature of the boundaries and the role of FE.

Other training providers

The first boundary to be examined will be the one to the south. In the 10 years from 1945 the technical colleges, as FE institutions were then called, were in competition with Government training centres. These centres were gradually wound down, allowing FE to push outwards. From the mid-1960s onwards colleges prospered in partnership with the industrial training boards. In the 1980s government attempts to set up an alternative network of publicly-subsidised training agencies to service youth and adult training schemes met with only partial success in the competition for customers with the colleges. That boundary was stretched but remained intact. In the 1990s the cuts in Youth Training have weakened the private training organisations. Further education has maintained its frontier, although some colleges have pulled away from a reliance on youth training as the arrangements for resourcing it have changed. Even though FE colleges have gained more favoured status during the 1990s, many colleges as incorporated institutions would not see the provision of youth and adult training as economic if full-time lecturing staff are involved in the training.

Higher education

The second boundary is with the higher education sector. This boundary was affected in April 1989 when the English polytechnics and colleges left the local government world for independence within a newly expanded higher education service. Five years later, in 1993, a new unified sector was created by putting together the old universities and the new universities (i.e. the former polytechnics) under the umbrella of the Higher Education Funding Council. At the same time, FE and sixth form colleges achieved their own independence within the Further Education Funding Council sector in England, Wales and Scotland.

It was thought at first that after 1989 the polytechnics would want to jettison their residual FE, in line with other previous examples of upwards academic drift. Nevertheless, there was no great throwing out of FE ballast and the change did not greatly benefit FE colleges as the receivers of discarded FE provision. Neither did the FE colleges have to surrender their HE courses. In contrast, the rush of polytechnics/new universities to expand, and the adoption by many of them of a community role to replace the former LEA influence, meant a franchising downwards of higher education to the FE colleges.

The situation was different in Scotland because the central colleges had not been attached to the education authorities but came under the national Education Department. Northern Ireland's only polytechnic, Ulster Polytechnic, had merged with a university in the mid-1980s to form the second university in the province, so was not involved in the changes.

It is worthwhile dwelling for a moment on the countervailing trend mentioned above – the growth of HE with FE. The higher education boundary has started to be affected by new pressures such as the growth of non-traditional access courses pushing some HE-type work back into the colleges. In 1992 there were over 1000 such examples recorded. It remains to be seen whether the FE colleges will develop like the two-year community colleges in the USA, where the first part of a degree can be done in the local institution. In addition, the amount of franchising of higher education work from HE to FE institutions is increasing significantly, as HE institutions try to cope with the Government's growth targets for the 1990s. The management of boundary problems has now fallen to the FE and HE funding councils to oversee from 1993. The three year growth targets of 25 per cent for FE and 13 per cent for HE may reverse the trends as colleges struggle to find more room for FE growth.

Schools

The third boundary, to the west, is with the school system. Further education has gradually pushed that frontier outwards into post-16 school territory in a number of localities. The debates in the late 1970s and early '80s about the merits of tertiary colleges recognised, not only a wider set of opportunities in a college environment for young people in the 16–18 age group, but also the emigration of part of the former natural population from schools to FE. In some local authorities this process was legitimised by putting in a new tertiary boundary at 16 and annexing post-16 work to the FE sector. Conservative governments did not wholeheartedly support this clarification nationally and continued instead to protect their favoured outposts – the school sixth forms of 'proven worth'.

Summary

These three boundaries are not static and are constantly changing. The 1992 Further and Higher Education Acts did go further than ever in defining the 'natural boundaries' of the further education sector and even increased its size by bringing in the sixth form colleges. The sense of 'nationhood' for FE in the three mainland UK areas has increased by the removal of the funding role from the local city states and provinces to national bodies having an overview of the system.

Up to the 1990s the national tendency to ignore further education as a mainstream part of UK education had meant that the boundary changes had been evolutionary. It says something of the self-confidence of further education that it had managed to grow at the expense of the former great empires without much official encouragement. The question for the 1990s is whether the nationalisation of FE under the funding councils will cause it to grow into a major respected part of education in the United Kingdom which could be seen as the pinnacle of its development.

Chapter 16
FE and the labour market

The role of further education has always been intrinsically linked to developments in the labour market. The heart of an FE college is in its vocational work. This is what distinguishes it from a sixth form college or an adult education institute. An FE college's vocational profile is shaped by the nature of the local and sub-regional labour markets. Colleges have changed since the 1960s and '70s when large engineering and construction departments totally dominated the institution; the relative decline of these sections of industry has been mirrored by the loss of staff in these areas through retraining or retirement. Many senior staff in the management of the former technical colleges came from this kind of background. They have been replaced in many instances by staff from general education, business and management or service trades environments.

Going further back in time, the evolutionary paths of education and the labour market over the last century have been closely inter-linked. The demand for literate and numerate workers during the last century can be compared with the development of compulsory education and the rise of vocational education. The process of excluding children and young people from employment often coincided with a requirement for their compulsory attendance at school.

Additionally, employers and Government have been aware that the level of training that can be given to a school leaver is built upon the foundations laid by the school in literacy, numeracy and scientific understanding. The recent pattern of a decline in many industries in the demand for craft-level and unskilled workers, but with an increased need for technological specialists, has exerted pressure on both the school system and the training networks for higher quality vocational education and training, which in turn is reliant on a better base of general and technical education within schools. The Government has responded to these pressures with programmes such as the Technical and Vocational Educational Initiative (TVEI).

The shape of vocational work in colleges in the first part of the 1990s is very much moulded by the local labour market. The work-related further education exercise that colleges have had to carry out for the TECs and the Employment Department has been based on local labour market information. Prior to 1993, local education authorities and their colleges had up to a quarter of the monies from central government held back unless they satisfied the Employment Department's Training Agency (now TEED) that the courses being mounted catered for changing employment needs in their area and that courses needed by local employers were not being cut.

This line-up of the colleges allied to the national Education Departments and the Training Agency (in Great Britain), which came under the Employment Department, illustrates my point about empires and alliances. The situation is similar in Northern Ireland, where colleges are associated with the education and library boards and employment and training come under the scope of the Department of Economic Development. Given the relationship of further education colleges to the labour market, an examination of some of the trends in the labour market will throw some light on the trends in further education.

The workforce

At the beginning of the 1990s the Labour Force Survey (ILO definitions) showed that the size of the workforce of the United Kingdom was 28.7 million people. This was from a population aged 16 and over of 45 million. Of this group of people, 58 per cent were in employment, including 7.6 per cent self-employed. Another 5.3 per cent of this total were unemployed at the time of the 1991 survey and further 36.5 per cent economically inactive. The percentages did not differ massively between the different parts of the United Kingdom. The occupational groupings are shown in **Figure 11**.

The civilian labour force in 1991 was made up of 24.25 million people in England, 1.34 million in Wales, 2.49 million in Scotland and 0.69 million in Northern Ireland. Of those actually in employment, there were 16.30 million men and 12.47 million women. The growth in the workforce over the previous two decades was largely accounted for by the increase of females from the 1971 figures of 9.53 million – an increase of nearly three million or almost 31 per cent. This should be contrasted to a growth of only two per cent in the male part of the labour force.

The workforce is becoming increasingly concentrated in the 25 to 54 year old age range. Two-thirds of the labour force are now in this age group. A major change in the structure of the labour market is the decline in the 16 to 19 population which fell by over one million between 1983 and 1993, resulting in the number of young workers under the age of 25 falling by 1.2 million between 1987 and 1995. This obviously affects FE recruitment in the traditional apprenticeship age range. Employers will not be able to recruit as many young people, especially well qualified young people, as they have in the recent past. They will have to rely on the retraining of older employers and the recruitment of more adults. Women will play a greater role by filling new jobs. It is also expected that more people from the ethnic minorities will be in employment. Colleges can obviously play a leading role in all these processes.

Figure 11: Population aged 16 and over: by occupational grouping (percentages)

Occupational grouping	England %	Wales %	Scotland %	N Ireland %	UK %
Managerial and administrators	6.6	4.5	4.4	3.7	6.2
Associate professional and technical	4.7	4.0	4.3	4.4	4.6
Clerical and secretarial	4.4	3.4	4.5	3.3	4.3
Craft	9.0	7.6	7.8	8.0	8.8
Personal and protective services	6.3	6.4	7.3	6.5	6.4
Sales	4.8	5.3	5.8	4.0	4.9
Plant and machine operatives	4.2	3.9	3.9	3.5	4.2
Other	5.3	5.7	5.5	4.4	5.3
Self-employed	7.8	7.1	5.6	7.5	7.6
All in employment	58.8	53.2	56.4	52.9	58.2
Unemployed	5.2	5.5	5.7	7.2	5.3
Economically inactive	36.0	41.3	37.9	39.9	36.5

Source: Labour Force Survey, Employment Department in **Regional trends 27** (Central Statistical Office 1992)

The job market

The general increase of jobs in the period of economic growth of the 1980s was particularly favourable to service industries and to the south of England. Studies of regional employment changes show that Yorkshire and Humberside, Wales and Scotland lost jobs twice as quickly as the English south in the 1979–83 recession. In the recession which developed from 1989, the south of England suffered much more. The vast majority of the net jobs growth in Britain since 1983 has been in southern England. Over two million employees were lost from the workforce between 1979 and 1983, while 750,000 were gained in the following four years.

Service sector employment has grown most significantly in four main areas – banking, finance and insurance; public administration; education;

and wholesale distribution and repairs. Manufacturing employment is still on a downward trend, although not as steep as in previous years. In 1987, when the economy was expanding prior to the recession at the end of the 1980s, employment had fallen most in metal goods, engineering and vehicles while there had been some growth in non-metallic mineral products; office machinery, data processing equipment; timber and wooden furniture; and other manufacturing which includes jewellery and sports equipment. Self-employment increased in the 1980s by about 100,000 people every year. Even though the United Kingdom was in recession in the early 1990s, skill shortages have been in evidence with particular difficulties experienced in recruiting professional engineers, machinists, managers, computer and management service staff, welders and mechanics. The construction industry has persistent problems in finding bricklayers and carpenters/joiners although this has been less obvious in the building industry recession in the early 1990s.

Over the last 25 years, the number of trainees and apprentices in manufacturing has declined far faster than the rate at which jobs have been lost in the sector. Only 90,000 employees in manufacturing were being given formal training at the beginning of the '90s, a fifth of the peak reached in 1968. Between 1979 and 1990, jobs in manufacturing fell from 7.1 to 5.1 million, while numbers in training dropped from 266,300 to 89,300 – a fall of 67 per cent.

An OECD report on the employment outlook at the beginning of the 1990s stated that the 1980s were characterised by an increase in the number of part-time and temporary workers, and the growth of jobs in the service sector. In the 1990s, the report thought that there could be big changes in labour supply signalled by the slowing tendency of women to join the labour force and the decline in numbers reaching working age. There would be decreased labour mobility, a rise in the proportion of the long-term unemployed and further increases in temporary and part-time working and self-employment. **Figure 12** shows employees in employment in Great Britain, analysed according to the Standard Industrial Classification as at the end of 1988, prior to the latest recession.

Figure 12: Employment in the UK (1988)

Employment sector	Numbers (thousands)
Agriculture, forestry and fishing	296
Coal, oil and natural gas extraction	168
Electricity, gas, other energy and water	288
Manufacturing industries	5,177
Construction	1,020
Wholesale distribution and repairs	1,292
Retail distribution	2,230
Hotels and catering	1,149
Transport	942
Postal services and telecommunications	476
Banking, finance and insurance	2,601
Public administration	2,018
Education	1,714
Medical and other health services	1,306
Other services	1,662

Source: Department of Employment.

The effects on colleges

All these changes have been reflected in colleges. The major influence is the move away from a heavy concentration on manufacturing and into service trades. One obvious example of this is the change in the gender balance of the workforce and thus of the student population. Departments in colleges have been wound down and often amalgamated and staff have diversified into new fields. In engineering, for example, the decline of foundry and pattern making has been matched by the growth of electronic engineering. A major influence has been the expansion of business and finance courses, but within this there has been a decline in full-time secretarial courses. These factors can be followed through in most parts of the local FE college and, indeed, are part and parcel of the adjustments reflected in the annual work-related further education plans.

The balance of further education provision is obviously tied in to the current educational qualifications of the local workforce and the future needs. **Figure 13** shows the breakdown of qualifications at the beginning of the 1990s.

Figure 13: Educational qualifications of the workforce (1991). Percentages

Educational qualification	England %	Wales %	Scotland %	N Ireland %	UK %
Degree or equivalent	10.0	7.5	7.5	8.6	9.7
Higher education below degree	6.3	6.4	8.3	6.1	6.5
GCE A level or equivalent	20.0	18.1	25.5	16.0	20.3
Apprenticeship	6.7	8.1	11.1	12.3	7.3
GCE O level or equivalent	19.3	20.5	14.3	16.6	18.8
CSE below grade 1	4.5	4.5	N/A	2.8	4.1
Other qualifications	6.5	4.9	3.8	4.9	6.2
No qualifications	25.9	29.1	28.5	32.2	26.4

Source: Labour Force Survey, Employment Department in **Regional trends 27** (Central Statistical Office 1992)

The careers service

Further education colleges work closely with the careers services. The careers service is controlled by the LEA and acts as a funnel for young people wanting to enter employment. Its main focus used to be on school and college links with companies. The careers service has statutory backing arising from the Employment and Training Act (1973), which placed an obligation on all local education authorities to introduce a careers service from April 1974 in England and Wales, and from May 1975 in Scotland. The same Act of Parliament extended the work of the careers service to cover young people aged 18 and over who were still in full-time further and higher education. The service is funded via the Employment Department. Central government discharges its responsibility for providing careers information through the Careers and Occupational Information Centre.

The Centre is part of the Employment Department and issues a wide range of careers publications and guides.

The main task of the careers service is to help those in full-time education to reach informed decisions on a choice of career, to help them find suitable employment or training and to monitor their progress during the early years of their transition from full-time education to employment. Each college will have at least one careers adviser attached to it. The service plays an important part in placing young people on Youth Training and in the advice relating to Training Credits. The careers service normally comes under the control of a principal careers officer and is operated by a network of careers staff.

In a government review of the careers service in 1991, the Secretary of State for Employment said that he was not convinced the organisational arrangements were still appropriate. He wanted a greater role for employers, through training and enterprise councils, in managing the service and the introduction of market disciplines to sharpen managerial practice. He put forward three options for the future:

– placing the careers service under TECs;
– placing it under partnership between LEAs and TECs; or
– contracting the service out to the private sector.

Chapter 17
FE and training structures

Responsibility for training

Training is primarily a responsibility of employers. This is sometimes forgotten in the discussions about government interventions in the vocational education and training processes. Employers who want to produce quality products or provide good service must make available the necessary training of their company workforce. It has been one of the failings of industry and commerce in the United Kingdom over the last century that sizeable proportions of the nation's employers have not delivered that training and the national government has not intervened sufficiently strongly to ensure that enough inducements are offered or penalties threatened to overcome this reluctance to train.

Local government played its part up to the 1990s in that it made available further education and training for local employers via FE colleges. The role of the technical colleges in the post-war period (described in Chapter 1) has been a major influence in the training process. However, the placement of the training functions of colleges under the remit of the national departments of education has separated the colleges from the national government-led training structures which come under employment ministries. In one sense there is no need for colleges to be involved in training. Employers could provide the vast majority of their own training if they were large enough to support a training school, or they could band together to fund common facilities under their control, as happens, for example, in Germany where the Chambers of Commerce run vocational training institutions for local groups of employers.

In addition to company training, if the market was sufficiently large and profitable enough for training employed workers, the private sector could move in to provide a service. That they have not done so in large numbers, except in certain specialised fields or where they have been subsidised by government grants, could be indicative of either the general malaise, underfunding, or alternatively, the respect that employers have for their local college.

Too many United Kingdom governments have adopted a *laissez faire* attitude towards the provision of training, relying on market pressures and competition to force companies to train their workers. Colleges have often relieved employers of the need to have their own training sections. Government reports have periodically voiced concern about the failure of British industry and commerce to train enough skilled employees to allow the country to compete internationally. These reports have ranged from the

Samuelson reports of the 1880s through to the National Economic Development Office/Manpower Services Commission/Department of Employment reports of the 1980s.

Investigations into training in the past have usually concentrated on the development of the craft apprenticeship or higher technical/professional training and have involved debate about the number of years that had to be served, the quality of training provided and the future numbers needed to supply the demand for a well trained workforce. Concentration on the skilled worker has meant that training for women in the non-manual areas, and for operatives, has taken second place. It was only with the introduction of mass programmes such as the Youth Training Scheme that this began to be rectified.

The start of training in the United Kingdom can be traced back to the Middle Ages. The Guilds promoted apprenticeships as far back as the 12th century. In 1563 the Statute of Artificers marked the beginning of statutory apprenticeships which flourished until 1814 when voluntary systems were introduced after pressure from manufacturers. The major growth in vocational education stemmed from industrialisation in the late 18th century.

In the 20th century, mass unemployment between the two World Wars made government and companies reluctant to train enough skilled staff for anything other than immediate needs. It was only with the advent of the Second World War that government intervened to provide trained workers for the armaments industries. In a crash programme the number of Government Training Centres (currently called Skillcentres) was increased from 16 to 38, with the result that they had trained 500,000 people by 1945. In this same period, the technical colleges also grew rapidly to try to answer the need for training.

Legislation

The attitude of post-war governments and of employers' organisations towards training was very patchy, with some of the major companies providing excellent training but others doing little or nothing. The government, under growing criticism about the problems of maintaining an adequate supply of well trained, skilled labour, passed the **Industrial Training Act** in 1964. This Act was a landmark in that it gave legal backing to new industrial training boards (ITBs). Representation on the boards was made up of equal number of employers and trades union representatives with a smaller group representing the education service, often drawn from the senior staff of colleges. The system of balancing both sides of industry (the social partners) with a third group of educationalists was known as the tripartite system. (ITBs are described in more detail later in this chapter.)

The Manpower Services Commission and its successors

The 1964 Act also created a Central Training Council, representative of employers and workers, to advise Ministers of Employment (as the office was then known) on training trends. The lack of impact of this body in the 1960s led to the belief that it was too weak to be effective. In 1974 a more powerful and far-reaching national training authority, the Manpower Services Commission (MSC), was created to supervise employment as well as training. As the MSC was responsible to the employment departments and not the DES, it ensured a structural divide between colleges and training organisations.

The Manpower Services Commission was the first manpower body with real power to plan national training. It was a non-departmental government body which technically performed its functions on behalf of the Crown. The Commission was responsible to Parliament via the Secretary of State for Employment who required the Commission to ensure that its activities were in line with his proposals and that its financial affairs were conducted in accordance with his memorandum of financial arrangements. The MSC did not cover Northern Ireland.

The work of the Commission grew very quickly because of the rapid rise in unemployment after 1974. While the debates on training in the 1950s and '60s had been about labour shortages and the best methods for training the employed, discussion in the 1970s and '80s centred on job creation and training for the increasing numbers of unemployed. The MSC devised a series of programmes for adults, such as the Community Programme, which were based on job creation. It also launched a comprehensive range of opportunities for the young unemployed from 1977, which culminated in the Youth Training Scheme in 1983.

The Manpower Services Commission was also responsible for revitalising the employment service. A new management framework was established so that the service became a self-managing unit with work on behalf of the employed being separated from that for the unemployed. Employment offices were brightened up and made 'self-service' for vacancies based around local labour market areas. Part of the responsibility for guidance was passed over to the local authority careers service. The new local offices began to collect local labour market intelligence, which was used in planning training programmes.

At the beginning of the 1980s the government published its **New training initiative** (MSC 1984). It set an agenda for the 1980s, supported by the MSC, which covered major vocational education and training objectives for skill training, foundation education and training for young people and the training of adults. These three categories form the basis of the next three chapters. The Government expressed the three 'objectives' (as they came to be known) as follows:

1. We must develop skill training, including apprenticeship, in such a way as to enable young people entering at different ages and with different educational attainments to acquire agreed standards of skill appropriate to the jobs available and to provide them with a basis for progression through further learning.

2. We must move towards a position where all young people under the age of 18 have the opportunity either of continuing in full-time education or of entering training or a period of planned work experience combining work-related training and education.

3. We must open up widespread opportunities for adults, whether employed, unemployed or returning to work, to acquire, increase or update their skills and knowledge during the course of their working lives.

The Commission was a major innovative body in designing new schemes of both training and education, often in the teeth of enormous opposition from the sections of local government and the education service. In some ways it was used by Conservative government ministers as a means of bypassing (as they saw it) unresponsive education departments. In fact it was not only Conservative political pressure: in the second half of the 1970s, the then Labour prime minister had launched a 'Great Debate' on education, during which he attacked so-called progressive teaching measures and education's failure to meet the needs of industry.

The 1980s thus saw government backing for a whole range of MSC programmes linking education and industry, before the Commission ran out of steam in the late 1980s and was dismantled. It set up schemes to improve vocational education in schools (the Technical and Vocational Education Initiative), in further education colleges (work-related further education) and in higher education (the Enterprise Initiative). In conjunction with the National Council for Vocational Qualifications, the MSC set up a five-level system of National Vocational Qualifications. These are all described elsewhere in this book.

There were a number of criticisms of the Commission based on its alleged concentration on quantity rather than quality, its emphasis on getting people signed off the unemployment registers rather than enhancing skill training, and concern about its position as a massive semi-independent bureaucracy. The Government decided to answer part of this criticism by splitting the training and employment functions of the MSC, with the training going into a new Commission and the employment service, including the JobCentres, being transferred to the Department of Employment.

A new body, the Training Commission, was established in June 1988 as a result of the 1988 Employment Act. The most obvious public effect of the Act was to change the name of the old Manpower Services Commission to the Training Commission. Less publicly, it increased the membership of the governing body of the Training Commission to include more employers' representatives. This upset the carefully planned balance between employers, trades unionists and local government and education commissioners, achieved under the tripartite arrangements for the MSC and common in mainland Europe, and signalled the start of a period of employment interest domination of sections of education and training. Tripartite arrangements had existed in Britain and Western European countries in the post-war period and marked the right of employees and their trades unions to act as equal social partners with employers.

The Training Commission had a very short existence. The Secretary of State for Employment wound up the Training Commission in September 1988 after a decision of the Trades Union Congress to withdraw support for the Employment Training programme. The Government claimed that the membership on the Commission of three trades union leaders who were opposed to its main adult training programme would make the Training Commission unworkable. The Commission's staff were transferred to the Department of Employment and the body was renamed the Employment Department Training Agency. It is currently known as the Training, Enterprise and Employment Directorate of the Employment Department (TEED). TEED is the fourth structure of its kind in a decade. Hardly a recipe for stable policies and in sharp contrast to the well established systems of most of the UK's partners in Europe. At the time of writing, TEED was responsible, usually in partnership with the TECs, for Youth Training, Training For Work (TFW), the industry lead bodies, the Technical and Vocational Educational Initiative, the development of work-related further education, the compacts, and Higher Education Enterprise. TEED has a brief to work in conjunction with the TECs/LECs, with employers, the education service, voluntary organisations, training providers and individual trade unions to improve the training system and help make the education system more relevant to the world of work.

Further reorganisations

Along with the disbanding of the Training Commission, a number of other tripartite bodies were abolished which supervised Training Commission programmes: the Youth Training Board, the TVEI Steering Group and the Non-Advanced Further Education Steering Group. The NAFE Steering Group particularly affected further education since it had an overview of (what was then called) the work-related non-advanced further education programme. The 58 area manpower boards were also abandoned. In their place the Government moved over to a system of local employer committees, in England called training and enterprise councils

(TECs), to take over the planning and oversight of vocational education and training. The councils were based on the American model of private industry councils, which are responsible for delivering government-sponsored training programmes. One hundred new bodies took over the work of the area manpower boards in Great Britain, thus passing more control to the local level and giving a better base for building local partnerships. It also marked a significant change in the philosophy from the large national schemes of training, which previously were totally centrally determined. (TECs and LECs are described in more detail further on in this chapter.) The Department of Employment under various ministers has thus had a reputation during the 1980s and early '90s of being seen to make things happen by reorganising its bureaucracies and launching new schemes and initiatives.

Training policy in Wales

The Secretary of State for Employment has the lead responsibility in Wales for training policy generally and for the national framework within which that policy will be pursued. The Secretary of State for Wales contributes to the formulation of national policy and will ensure that it remains fully relevant to distinctive circumstances and requirements in the Principality. The Welsh Secretary also approves the annual training programme and budget for Wales and is involved in liaison with the TECs. There is close liaison with the Welsh Office and Welsh local education authorities for their education and enterprise programmes.

Training policy in Scotland

In Scotland, the Secretary of State for Scotland takes responsibility for the training and approves its annual plan. The Scottish Development Agency (SDA), which was established in 1975 for the purpose of stimulating the economy and improving the environment, works in parallel. The Government brought training, enterprise and environmental activities formerly administered by the Training Agency and the Scottish Development Agency into a new agency, Scottish Enterprise. The combined organisation operates the network of 22 area-based local enterprise councils (LECs) which plan local and sub-regional training and industrial needs.

Training policy in Northern Ireland

In Northern Ireland, the Department of Economic Development (part of the Northern Ireland Office) is responsible for training, since TEED operates only on the mainland. The Department of Economic Development

(DED) provides virtually all of the money spent on government-organised training. The Department is responsible for training centres, the Management Training Unit, a system of training grants, various schemes for the training and employment of the unemployed and the administration of the Youth Training Programme (jointly with the Department of Education).

The Northern Ireland Training Authority (NITA) provides administrative services to eight industrial training boards, reviews the training needs of industry and encourages cross-sectoral training and training in sectors where there is no ITB. The Department of Economic Development has called the current system fragmented and proposed a new single training organisation which would embrace the training functions and responsibilities of the Department, the Northern Ireland Training Authority and the industrial training boards – with provision for a strong industrial input.

Monitoring quality

The quality of training in Great Britain is monitored by the Training Standards Advisory Service (TSAS). The service is totally separate from the various education-based inspectorates, which have a quality monitoring function for public sector institutions. The Advisory Service was established in 1986 as part of the Government's proposals to extend Youth Training from a one year to a two year scheme and establish it as a permanent route for transition from school to work. The main role of the Training Standards Advisory Service was initially to assess the overall effectiveness of YT by carrying out surveys of individual schemes and to use its findings to influence central development policy, particularly in relation to programme quality. The remit of TSAS has been extended to cover quality assurance on Employment Training.

TSAS is separate from the TEED structures and independent of its field staff. TSAS has divisions in Scotland and Wales. It consists of a small head office team together with divisional managers and Training Standards Inspectors for YT and for adult training. Though operating as a generalist, each TSI has expertise in at least one industrial or commercial field or specialist area of education and training; collectively they provide a spread of expertise across most training disciplines. The role of the Training Standards Advisory Service is advisory only. It does not have an executive function in relation to approved training organisations or YT. In Scotland the majority of reports were produced as a result of joint visits by TSAS and HM Inspectors.

The Government's White Paper **Employment for the 1990s** (DE 1988a) set out the view that a system of employer-led organisations should identify and establish standards and secure recognition of them, sector by sector, or occupational group by occupational group. Its objective was to see established throughout industry and commerce standard setting bodies created by employers themselves, to which they could subscribe and which would secure their continuing voluntary support. This approach was in contrast to that of the ITBs, which were viewed by government as being too much involved in regulation and compulsion. It has been pointed out by critics of Government policy that in some ways, since the Government has failed to either cajole or persuade the bulk of British employers to provide training at European levels, it is now handing over control of training to employer-dominated boards at local and industry level.

Industry lead bodies

Each of these new employer-led organisations, usually called industry lead bodies (ILBs), or lead industry bodies (LIBs), must secure and retain the demonstrated commitment of senior management within its sector; it has to act as the means by which key skill requirements and training needs can be defined, monitored and periodically reviewed; it must provide the lead in establishing standards for key occupations and arrangements for assessing and accrediting learning achievements; and it must have the ability to influence a significant part of the sector and be seen as the body which can deal with government on training and vocational education matters. The Government publishes updated guidelines by which each sector training organisation may judge its progress and from which it can identify the objectives it should be trying to achieve. The employment departments are responsible for reviewing progress, sector by sector.

In the 1990s, there has been adverse comment about the large number of lead bodies. In particular, the loose nature of many of them, their overlapping remits, the fragmentation of many initiatives and the inability of the Employment Department to keep giving pump-priming funding to them all for such work as standards setting, has forced a rethink about the numbers. The Department of Employment floated the idea of a scheme for some 15 or so Occupational Standards Councils in 1992. These would eventually incorporate the 160 lead bodies.

Non-statutory training organisations

While a lot of work has been done in the early 1990s , there is still a long way to go for many of the sector training organisations, which are not part of the ITB system. These bodies are usually called non-statutory training organisations (NSTOs). A study of these bodies was completed by the Institute of Manpower Studies for the former Training Commission and its findings were reported in 1987 (IMS 1987). The study concluded that many NSTOs were too small to take on board the range of tasks expected of them as LIBs. They did not match up to tasks such as the gathering of information about their sector, setting occupational standards or liaising with other sectors and national bodies.

The Institute of Manpower Studies recommended that a central support unit should be created as a focus for the NSTO system. The National Council of Industrial Training Organisations (NCITO) helped industry-level training organisations improve their standards. The National Council carries out research and development, the implementation of new methods of training and the marketing of training and materials. It is controlled by the training organisations themselves but funded by government.

Industrial training boards

The creation of the industry lead body represented another step away from the traditional organisation of the last two decades, the industrial training board. The boards were set up as a result of the 1964 **Industrial Training Act** on the basis that they would levy moneys from employers in their sector to spread the cost of training across the industry and give grants to encourage employers to train. Where employers did not carry out proper training, the levy would be a tax from which they would not directly benefit. This system was streamlined with experience into one where employers carrying out satisfactory training were exempted from the levy/ grant system. The creation of ITBs reached its peak at the end of the 1960s when 27 boards covered 15 million employees.

The industrial training boards had very broad ranging powers which are worth recalling. They were responsible for the following:

- establishing policy for training in industry, including such questions as admissions to training (apprenticeship or otherwise), length of training, registration of trainees and appropriate attendance at colleges of further education;
- establishing standards of training and syllabuses for different occupations in the industry, taking into account the associated technical education required;
- providing advice and assistance on training to firms in the industry;
- devising tests to be taken by apprentices and other trainees on completion of training and, if necessary, at intermediate stages;
- establishing qualifications and tests for instructors;
- establishing and running training courses in its own centres;
- paying grants to firms to reimburse all or part of the costs incurred in the provision of improved training;

- paying allowances to trainees not taken on by firms while being trained in public, or the board's own, centres;
- collecting money from firms in the industry by means of a levy.

In the early 1970s criticism of the work of the ITBs led first to restrictions on their powers and later to abolition of 16 boards in 1982, leaving only seven in operation. The restrictions amounted to modifying the boards' original mandatory duties to the level of enabling powers, excluding small firms from the levy, limiting the levy to one per cent of payroll and introducing exemption schemes. Most of the seven remaining boards exempted most companies from their levy payments. They reduced their dependence on levy income by recovering growing proportions of their costs by charging for their services. The Government then consulted with each of the statutory industrial training boards and organisations representing employers in their sectors and drew up a programme and timetable so that they became independent, non-statutory bodies.

Even before the Government placed restrictions on them, the ITBs had started to make changes for themselves. For example, the Engineering Industry Training Board (EITB) which started life in July 1964, was reconstituted in July 1988 at the start of a new three year cycle. The Board's composition changed as a result of the Government's desire to move from the former tripartite arrangements to a system where employer representatives are in the majority. The original composition of nine employers, nine trades unionists and five educationalists was replaced by a new board of six trades unionists, six employers directly representing companies, three employers representing specialist interests and four educationalists. Under previous arrangements, only two per cent of companies within the scope of the Engineering Industry Training Board paid the full levy. The levy only applies to firms in the industry which have over 40 employees (this equates to approximately 30 per cent of firms). When the EITB was reconstituted it agreed to reduce levy income and replace it with money raised by selling training services and packages to individual companies. The Board concentrated on reaching franchise agreements with 'out-of-scope' companies – firms employing engineering workers who do not have to pay the levy because they are not regarded as part of the engineering industry. The new bid for extending its commercial activities includes providing an EITB standards-based training system and materials for craft apprentices.

The Engineering Industry Training Board was replaced by a new industry level training organisation – EnTra. EITB believed that the interests of industry would be best served by a single successor body. EnTra is a company limited by guarantee with charitable status and which took on the assets of the EITB. The new organisation does not depend on the levy for funding, thus reducing its activities to the core elements of standard setting, research and analysis of manpower needs, and promotion of training. EnTra staff take on more of a consultancy role to replace their previous inspection function. Companies are advised about the best ways to identify training needs and what help the association can give them. New voluntary codes of practice to ensure standards have replaced the assessments carried out as part of the system of exempting companies from the returnable part of the levy. In future, companies will have to give details of their training policy which EnTra will monitor.

Northern Ireland has eight ITBs financed by levies raised from industry, by sales of services, by grants from the Department of Economic Development and the European Social Fund. A proportion of levy income must be passed back to the industry, either in remission for approved training or in the form of training grants. The boards cover construction, road transport, engineering, catering, food and drink, textiles, clothing and the distributive sectors.

The Government, while recognising the quality of training provided in the traditional craft sectors and within the areas under particular boards, has produced similar criticisms of ITBs in the Province as it has on the mainland. Difficulties cited in the 1988 Department of Economic Development consultative document (DED 1988) are as follows:

- as boards naturally tend to provide services primarily for levy payers, they do not always provide cover for all their sectors;
- the income of some boards severely limits their ability to respond to training needs. A high proportion of some board's income is spent on administrative costs, including the costs of remitting levy;
- the financial strength of boards and thus their ability to offer training does not necessarily relate to the economic importance of the sectors with which they are concerned;
- the effectiveness of the levy system and levy remission in securing training where it is most required is uncertain.

The Government has reduced the role of the boards in Northern Ireland. They are subordinate to a new single training organisation and have the job of ensuring that the needs of the respective sectors of industry are properly identified and adequately reflected in the new organisation's plans. The boards are serviced by specialist officers who link with corresponding personnel in industrial development agencies and with training providers. The Department of Economic Development is looking at the training levy in terms of its effectiveness in securing, promoting and providing training, the financial implications of raising or not raising levies, the possible coverage and level of any levy system and alternative means of securing an appropriate industrial contribution to training costs.

The Skills Training Agency

Another arm of training policy operated through the Skills Training Agency (STA). STA operated 60 Skillcentres throughout Great Britain. STA was an operational arm of the former Training Agency. The main function of the Skillcentres was to train unemployed adults in craft skills, particularly in engineering and construction, but they also trained employed people through contracts with employers. The Skillcentres competed with colleges.

Skillcentres originated in the retraining of ex-servicemen disabled in the First World War. As unemployment grew in the 1920s, the emphasis changed to training unemployed adults. In the Second World War the Government Training Centres (as they were then called) expanded rapidly to cater for the munitions industry. In the 1950s the centres were run down and catered mainly for the disabled.

In the 1970s and early '80s, Skillcentres were used to train the increasing numbers of adult unemployed on government schemes. But the Government did not like the idea of one wing of the then Manpower Services Commission providing work for another, and having to 'buy' training courses from the Skillcentres. The Skills Training Agency was forced to prepare a commercial training plan with the aim of breaking even by the end of the 1980s. When this proved unsuccessful without large amounts of work from the MSC, the Government started to investigate moving the STA into the private sector. Since the agency was losing £20 million on a turnover of £55 million in 1988/89, and a third of its centres had excess capacity, major cutbacks were made. Finally the centres were offered to a group of managers in a management buy-out helped by an £11 million government subsidy. A new body, Astra Training Services, took over most of the privatised network and has since gone into receivership due to the effects of recession on training demand.

Local planning and supervision

Mechanisms for the planning of local training have taken various forms in the United Kingdom. There is no equivalent of the German Chambers which have a statutory local role in the regulation and provision of training. Nor has local government ever been entrusted with the co-ordination of training. Instead, the usual British ad hoc systems have come and gone over the post-war period.

When the Manpower Services Commission was split in 1988, and a new Training Commission created, the Government reviewed the role of local advisory bodies since they would have to concentrate on vocational education and training. It was suggested that since the work of the area manpower boards had largely consisted of approving projects and programmes from sponsors and managing agents, new local advisory bodies should be charged with planning the Commission's local efforts in the context of actual and potential needs of the local community, assisting the delivery of that plan and overseeing quality.

The process of consultation about new local advisory bodies was overtaken by the Government's decision to scrap the Training Commission before it could get into its stride. The function of supervising the local bodies was given over to an employer-dominated National Training Task Force (NTTF). This move was reflected at local level where the Government invited local groups in England and Wales, led by employers, to submit proposals for the establishment of training and enterprise councils (TECs) to contract with the Government to plan and deliver training and to promote and support the development of small businesses and self-employment.

Training and enterprise councils

The White Paper, **Employment for the 1990s** (DE 1988a), listed the key functions which the training and enterprise councils had to fulfil. They have to examine the local labour market to assess key skill needs, prospects for expanded job growth and the adequacy of existing training opportunities. They must draw up a plan containing measurable objectives for securing quality training and enterprise development that meets both government guarantees and community needs, tailoring national programmes to suit area needs and to achieve agreed performance outcomes. They manage training programmes for young people, for unemployed people, and for adults requiring new knowledge and technical retraining. They are responsible for the development and provision of training and other support for small businesses relevant to local needs. This activity includes the planning and administration of the Enterprise Allowance Scheme, and the counselling currently provided in England through the Small Firms Service. This service continued to be provided in Wales by the Welsh Development Agency.

The prospectus for the TECs required that each had to develop a rolling three year business plan that defined its vision and role within its particular community; set strategic objectives; described the economic and social characteristics of the area in the context of national and international skill trends; identified priorities for training and enterprise in terms of sector, level and location of service; set objectives for promoting equal opportunities and the health and safety of trainees; laid out an agenda of new activities which the TEC will undertake; and described the organisation needed to carry out its objectives.

Training and enterprise councils were established over a three year period from 1989. The councils can have a membership of nine to 15 members, two-thirds of whom must be drawn from private sector employers. Other council members are drawn from local education, training and economic development activities and from voluntary bodies and trades unions which support the aims of the council (this last phase giving a possible vetting mechanism). A survey of TEC directors published in the January 1992 issue of **Employment Gazette** (1992a) showed a breakdown as follows. There were 1,014 men compared to 122 women, with 40 people from ethnic minority backgrounds with 805 representing the private sector compared to 331 non-private sector. Of these, 99 were from local authorities, 48 from LEAs, 27 from other education, 58 from trade unions and 42 from the voluntary sector.

There are 82 TECs in England and Wales and 22 local enterprise councils (LECs) in Scotland. The resources available to each TEC range from £15 million to £50 million tied into a contract with the TEED. TECs do not run programmes themselves but subcontract training and enterprise activities to local providers. TECs are responsible for Youth Training, Training For Work (TFW), TVEI and work-related FE in their local patch.

In relation to work-related further education, the TECs initially contracted with the local education authorities, who had to generate operational and strategic plans on behalf of, but in conjunction with, the colleges. The exercise had been designed to increase the responsiveness of public sector further education provision to the needs of employers, and to improving efficiency and cost effectiveness. Since the withdrawal of LEAs from control of colleges, the TECs have to liaise directly with colleges. For the TECs and the Employment Department, the FE sector is important as a contributor to meeting the Government's target of 'a world class work force' as it is estimated to deliver half of formal off-the-job training.

Local enterprise companies

In Scotland, local enterprise companies (LECs) were created to work in conjunction with Scottish Enterprise. The LECs have more powers in the economic and environmental spheres than the TECs, but still function within the UK framework. The LEC local offices can assist in development of rural areas. However, the majority of LECs' expenditure will still be taken up with YT, TFW and similar programmes. The underlying idea of the LECs is that they will hasten the reinvigoration of local economies.

TECs and National Providers Unit

The Government's TECs and National Providers Unit (TNPU) liaises between the 82 training and enterprise councils and 22 local enterprise companies. However, unlike with the previous central manpower agencies, the unit did not initially conduct national negotiations with the very large national training bodies, such as the Construction Industry Training Board, which has something like 10,000 trainees under its wing. Instead, these industry-wide organisations have had to hold discussions with up to 104 different local bodies.

In 1992 the Government decided that the TNPU would become a managing agent which would negotiate with national bodies on behalf of the TECs/LECs. In order that it can conduct these national negotiations, the unit has been privatised so that it can charge fees for its services.

Many of the private sector members of TECs and LECs come from local chambers of commerce, the Confederation of British Industry (CBI) or the local employer networks (LENs). The LENs were established in 1987 by the CBI and the Association of British Chambers of Commerce, with the aid of Government subsidy. Their main aim was to bring together employers to identify training needs in local authority areas and to provide a means of dialogue about this with the education service, including the FE colleges. It was hoped that the LENs would provide a local focus which could give some coherence to the various publicly funded initiatives which often had widely different aims, objectives and funding mechanisms. The original aim was for the networks to be self-financing within two years but this was not achieved. Funding was conditional upon an equal amount being found by the networks themselves, and the presentation of a three year business plan demonstrating how they will move to self-sufficiency. The most successful networks were based on chambers of commerce in the major cities but their work has been largely superseded by the TECs.

Chambers of commerce

The local chambers of commerce are Britain's oldest employers' organisations. The Association of British Chambers of Commerce has a network of 96 local chambers in Britain and Northern Ireland. Unlike the German Chambers of Commerce, membership is voluntary. Sixty of the Chambers of Commerce are YT managing agents, 15 are running compacts between education authorities and local business, and half the local employer networks were based on them.

Chapter 18
FE and skills training

Data collection

It is perhaps significant that it is only in the last decade that there has been any attempt systematically to quantify the level of total training in the United Kingdom. It is not that training was not measured in the recent past, but it was done to meet particular needs such as those of industrial training organisations. Although the Department of Employment has issued various series of statistics, especially where training involved public money, it is significant that the annual government publication, **Training statistics** (DE), only started to be produced in 1990. It was possibly a suitable date for a new HMSO publication in that, although that year was in the recession at the beginning of the 1990s, it marked a growing concern about the quality of education and training for all, as well the understandable apprehension to make sure that large Government schemes for the unemployed were delivering to the large numbers who were eligible.

The author of the introduction to the 1992 edition of **Training statistics** highlighted the fact that there was still no standard definition of training. Virtually every source drawn upon used its own definition and many definitions lack clarity. The author noted that a great deal of effort was being taken by a number of organisations, both within the UK and on an international basis, to improve the situation. In an attempt to establish a definition which was precise, could be applied consistently, and would be easily understood, training was viewed as, 'intentional intervention to help the individual (or the organisation) to become competent, or more competent, at work'. Nonetheless, it is recognised that there are a number of indistinct boundaries within the training market: for example, between training and education; between training and work experience; and between initial and continuing training.

This chapter relates to skill training. It is recognised that skills can be learned in a variety of settings and are not limited to a particular training programme. **Training statistics** remarks that both education and training intend, among other things, to help the individual to acquire skills of wide applicability, such as learning how to learn, learning how to apply what has been learned in one context to another one and acquiring communication skills of all types. It notes that even the most academic subjects can have varying degrees of applicability for work.

The most wide-ranging study of vocational education and training in Great Britain in recent years was **Training in Britain** (TA 1989), a study of funding, activities and attitudes. It is now a little dated because its main reference year was 1986/87, but it attempted to give an in-depth view of where 'UK plc' was in the training league tables. In that year it was estimated that 350 million days of training were undertaken. The working definition of training used was, 'the process of acquiring the range of knowledge and skills that are related to current or future work requirements by formal or structured or guided means'. About a third of these days (115 million) took place on employers' premises. Of the remaining two-thirds, 145 million days were sponsored by employers. The vast majority of the off-the-job training took place in colleges.

The further and higher education system provided 220 million days of education and training in 1986/87. About one-third of all 16–18 year olds were in full-time education. Not all the students were young people on pre-employment courses, although the under 25s accounted for more than half of all students. The over 25s were most commonly found in part-time and further education. The higher education sector awards over 300,000 qualifications each year.

Job training in the private sector

The private sector's share of off-the-job training, which covers some 4,500 private training organisations, was estimated to deliver only 15 million days annually in 1986/87 (TA 1989), with management subjects forming one of the largest categories. A further survey of these private providers estimated their total income at £1.2 billion per year for providing training to 2.4 million people, both in the workplace and outside. Of the training provided, nearly three-quarters involved off-the-job release, two-thirds made use of on-the-job training and 40 per cent used both modes.

One-third of employees in private sector manufacturing received training, roughly half in private sector services and half in the public sector. In 1987 about two-thirds of economically active adults aged 19–59 claimed not to have received any job-related training or education in the previous three years, although about half admitted to some learning experiences related to work. Employers reported giving training in the survey year to 48 per cent of their employees, each one getting an average of 14.5 days. In terms of the total accounting costs of training, including the implicit cost to trainees of earnings foregone while in training, Britain spent some £33 billion in 1986/87. As a national investment, it was equivalent to eight per cent of Gross Domestic Product, compared with 17 per cent devoted to investment in physical capital.

There is a growing trend for the starting point for training activity to be the individual assessment of training needs and the appropriate means of meeting them. Such assessments are becoming an integral part of the initial entry of individuals on to government funded training programmes. Each individual will have a training plan arising from discussion of the needs analysis. Many initiatives such as Investors in People and National Training Awards are designed to encourage increased employer commitment to this process.

The cost of training

Direct spending by trainees on their own training is relatively low. They can incur substantial costs with respect to earnings foregone while in training, but most of these costs were accounted for by students in full-time education. Employers' net costs were in the order of £18 billion, with labour costs accounting for 85 per cent of this total. Most of the training costs were met from business revenues. While these figures seem large, they do not match those of many of our international competitors and have not done so for many years.

The Government has in recent years been trying to move more of the cost of training on to the individual who benefits while providing tax incentives for those incurring such costs. In 1988, the Government, in co-operation with a consortium of three national banks, launched the first of its subsidised loan schemes for education and training. The Career Development Loans applied to vocational courses lasting between one week and a year. Successful applicants could borrow between £300 and £5,000 (increased to £8,000 from April 1994). The loans covered 80 per cent of course fees, the cost of books and equipment, and living expenses for full-time students. Traditional higher education courses, which attract mandatory awards, were excluded. Courses qualifying for the loan are those which would be eligible for local authority grants. The range of courses could include full-time and part-time attendance at a college, or distance learning, and may cover some postgraduate degrees.

The participating banks vet applications, using normal commercial criteria and grant the loans. Initially, the interest due on the loan during the period of the course and for three months afterwards was met by the Department for Education with the borrower paying back the loan on the fourth month after completion of the course at a fixed interest rate. However, this 'interest free holdiay' was cut to four weeks from 1 April 1994 and career development loans can no longer be considered a 'soft' loan.

Skills shortages

Initiatives such as training loans have only really addressed the question of who pays, not the size of the total national training budget. Numerous reports over the last 100 years have pointed out the inability of the British to keep up with their major industrial competitors in securing a well trained workforce. The United Kingdom has suffered skill shortages every time its economy has expanded in this century. Employers shed skilled workers during the inter-war slump and during the recessions of the 1970s, '80s and early '90s, and did not make up for it by recruitment in the following years. This reflects the short-term thinking of many companies which do not view training in the same light as other long-term investments.

For example, in the five years following the upturn in the United Kingdom economy in 1983, numerous skill shortages were reported. The recessions in the UK economy over the last two decades led to reductions in skill training by employers who were anxious to cut costs. This is illustrated by the fact that the number of apprenticeships was cut by half, a far bigger proportional decline than the fall in employment in the industrial sectors where apprenticeships were to be found. Similarly, the number of adults receiving formal training fell from seven per cent in 1974 to four per cent in 1984. A skills survey by the CBI and the MSC of manufacturing industry when the economy was expanding in 1987 (CBI 1989) found that 37 per cent of companies were suffering from skill shortages which constrained output – an increase of 18 per cent on the previous year.

The Employment Department produces quarterly reports on the labour market and skills shortages from regular statistical surveys and a variety of ad hoc sources. Their July 1988 report, **Training for employment** (DE 1988b), pointed out that shortages of skilled labour and recruitment difficulties appeared to have increased significantly during 1987, in line with the exceptional 4.8 per cent growth in output during that year. Although causing concern, the reported difficulties remained well below those recorded in the 1960s and '70s. The problems were worst in the south of England where economic expansion had been fastest.

Comparative figures for particular industries demonstrate equally bleak figures. A 1988 study of vocational training at craft level for electrical and mechanical engineering showed that only 30,000 people qualified in 1987, a drop of 6,000 over the previous year. France trained three times as many people and West Germany four times the number. While 38,000 youngsters started engineering training under the one year Youth Training programme in 1985/86, only 8,800 of them passed the City and Guilds Part 1 Examination, as compared with 13,600 in 1982 – the year before Youth Training started. In vehicle manufacture, the numbers achieving the three year craft certificate fell from 2,500 in 1984 to 700 in 1987.

Figures 14–17 (based on the Labour Force Survey of 1991) show information about employees receiving job-related training during the last four weeks. The figures indicate that off-the-job training is running at nearly twice the level of that in the workplace. Professional groups get the most training and the lowest skilled also get the lowest training. Further education also provides the largest slice of training.

Figure 14: Employees of working age receiving job-related training in the last four weeks (by standard occupational group). Great Britain – thousands and percentages

Occupational group	Total number of employees	% receiving on-the-job training only	% receiving off-the-job training only	% receiving both on and off training	% receiving any training
All employees	21,264	4.3	8.2	2.3	14.8
Managers and admin	2,709	4.4	9.7	2.3	16.4
Professional	2,002	8.2	17.8	5.1	31.1
Associate professional and technical	1,875	7.6	13.5	5.2	26.3
Clerical and secretarial	3,769	4.4	8.0	1.6	14.0
Craft and related	2,758	2.7	5.8	2.7	11.2
Personal and protective service	2,096	4.7	7.9	2.0	14.6
Sales	1,785	3.8	7.2	1.2	12.2
Plant and machine operatives	2,299	2.5	2.4	0.8	5.7
Other occupations	1,926	1.6	3.0	0.4	5.0
No answer	45	*	*	*	*

Source: Labour Force Survey, Spring 1991

Footnotes: 1. Employees are those in employments, excluding the self-employed and people on Government schemes
2. Training includes both on-the-job and off-the-job training
3. * less than 10,000 in cell: estimate not shown

Figure 15: Employees of working age receiving job-related training during the last four weeks (by industry and type of training). Great Britain – thousands and percentages

Occupational group	Total number of employees	% receiving on-the-job training only	% receiving off-the-job training only	% receiving both on and off training	% receiving any training
All employees	21,264	4.3	8.2	2.3	14.8
Agriculture, forestry and fishing	246	*	4.1	*	6.1
Energy and water supply industries	545	4.7	10.3	3.0	18.1
Extraction of minerals and ores other than fuels; maufacture of metal goods, mineral products and chemicals	763	4.1	7.3	1.5	12.9
Metal goods, engineering and vehicle ind.	2,319	4.1	7.5	2.3	13.9
Other manufacturing industries	1,952	2.7	3.7	1.0	7.4
Construction	1,099	2.5	6.1	2.7	11.3
Distribution, hotels and catering; repairs	4,205	3.0	6.3	1.3	10.6
Transport and communication	1,397	3.9	6.0	1.6	11.5
Banking, finance, insurance, business services and leasing	2,406	5.5	10.5	3.2	19.2
Other services	6,244	6.0	11.2	3.2	20.4

Source: Labour Force Survey, Spring 1991

Footnotes: 1. Employees are those in employments, excluding the self-employed and people on Government schemes
2. Training includes both on-the-job and off-the-job training
3. * less than 10,000 in cell: estimate not shown

Figure 16: Employees of working age receiving off-the-job training during the last four weeks (by location of training). Great Britain – thousands and percentages

Main place of training	Number receiving off-the-job training	Percentage
Total	1,745	100
Own employer's premises	485	27.8
Other employers premises	63	3.6
Private training centre	137	7.9
Skillcentre	*	*
Employment rehabilitation centre	*	*
Community project	*	*
Government/local authority training workshop	20	1.1
Information technology centre	*	*
Open University	18	1.0
Other correspondence course	104	6.0
College of further education	569	32.6
Other educational centre	138	7.9
None of these	195	11.2
No answer	*	*

Source: Labour Force Survey, Spring 1991

Footnotes: 1. Employees are those in employment, excluding the self-employed and people on Government schemes

2. Training includes both on-the-job and off-the-job training

3. * less than 10,000 in cell: estimate not shown

Figure 17: Proportion of employees of working age receiving job-related training in the last four week: by social class

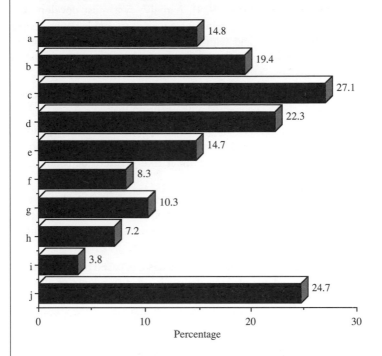

Percentage

Total number of employees (000s) = 21.264

Social class

a All persons (21,264)

b Non-manual (12.242)

c I Professional etc. (1,241)

d II Intermediate (5,595)

e III Skilled non-manual (5,405)

f Manual (8,880)

g III Skilled manual (4,511)

h IV Partly skilled (3.200)

i V Unskilled (1,170)

j Armed forces, inadequately described/no rely (142)

Source: Labour Force Survey, Spring 1991

Footnotes: 1 Employees are those in employment, excluding the self-employed and people on Government schemes

2 Training includes both on-the-job and off-the-job

Meeting the MSC's new training initiative objectives

The pattern of skill training in the 1980s fell within Objective 1 of the **New training initiative** (MSC 1984), namely: 'we must develop skill training, including apprenticeship, in such a way as to enable young people entering at different ages and with different educational attainments to acquire agreed standards of skill appropriate to the jobs available and to provide them with a basis for progression through further learning'.

The Manpower Services Commission prepared an **Agenda for action** (MSC 1981b) which was concerned with ensuring that:

- young people receive adequate and proper initial occupational training, particularly in occupations requiring more extended periods of education and training, to meet likely future demands from industry;

- initial occupational training is appropriately comprehensive in coverage and systematic in application and gives a sound basis – skills, knowledge, understanding and experience – on which future learning can be built;

- occupational training, initial or otherwise, is based on achievement of agreed standards of competence; is open to people of all ages; results in general recognition by industry and commerce of competence achieved; and helps individuals to progress to jobs or to further training and education.

These three strands link with the second and third objectives. Young people learn the occupational skills needed for many jobs as part of their two year Youth Training or through other foundation training or education. Youth Training and other vocational education initiatives thus help to meet the skill supply aspects of Objective 1. Youth Training also provides a platform for further occupational or job specific training necessary to complete apprenticeships or traineeships.

Objective 3 is concerned with adults who have been in the labour market for some years but may not have had the access to vocational education and training previously open only to young people entering employment. Adults need the opportunity to adapt their existing skills and to learn new ones to meet employment demands. Training arrangements under Objective 3 need to be developed in such a way as to encourage employers and individuals to make the necessary investment – both in time and resources.

In 1981 the Manpower Services Commission laid down a target, to be achieved by 1985, that training should be to standards without regard to age and that this should be accepted and implemented in both national agreements and local practice. Substantial progress was made but resistance was met both from employers and trades unions in some sectors. This modernising of initial occupational training arrangements was helped by the collapse of apprenticeships in manufacturing industry in the 1980s. The development of YTS meant that a flexible two year traineeship was introduced into many sectors of industry and commerce, even though it was age restricted.

The Standards Programme

The Manpower Services Commission looked at further problems in implementing Objective 1 in its position statement (MSC 1984). There was a feeling that it was necessary to eliminate unnecessary entry restrictions to training – such as age or irrelevant educational qualifications. Further action was needed to persuade employers to base recruitment and selection on recognised and tested competence rather than on criteria which are honoured by tradition but may have less occupational relevance than agreed training standards. The Standards Programme was set up to try to implement the MSC's 1981 target, but updating it to take account of work on competency. The aim of the Standards Programme is principally to encourage and support the development of standards of competence by lead industry bodies. The Training, Enterprise and Education Directorate of the Employment Department (TEED) gives help, guidance and technical advice and shares the cost of new development projects. The timescale was linked to the target set by NCVQ to have the bulk (80 per cent) of the reformed system of qualifications in place in England and Wales by the end of 1992.

At the beginning of the 1990s, the Secretary of State for Employment issued strategic guidance to the new TECs under the title of **1990s: the skills decade** (DE 1990). In amplifying this, he suggested that there were five identifiable areas where TECs could be active:

- motivating people to undertake training;
- providing effective information and guidance;
- making training and development opportunities readily accessible;
- measuring and recording the skills of individuals, that is, assessment and accreditation;
- providing, in appropriate cases, help via career development loans for those people who do not have all the resources to hand to pay for training and who are not receiving support from their employers or elsewhere.

The NVQ system was used in July 1991 as the basis for constructing targets for education and training for the 1990s. The National Training Task Force (NTTF) and the CBI launched a series of 'national education and training targets'. They were drawn up with the agreement of over 100 organisations, which committed themselves to bringing about what was called a 'skills revolution'. The targets were recognised as being ambitious but there was a strong determination to concentrate resources at national and local level to achieve them. The targets actually put the United Kingdom at the front of developed nations in establishing goals for the whole range of education and training, from initial training right through working careers (CBI 1991).

The national targets for 'foundation learning' are:

1. by 1997, 80 per cent of young people to reach NVQ II (or equivalent);
2. training and education to NVQ III (or equivalent) available to all young people who can benefit;
3. by the year 2000, 50 per cent of young people to reach NVQ III (or equivalent);
4. education and training provision to develop self-reliance, flexibility and breadth.

For 'lifelong learning', the targets are:

1. by 1996, all employees should take part in training or development activities;
2. by 1996, 50 per cent of the workforce aiming for NVQs or units towards them;
3. by 2000, 50 per cent of the workforce qualified to at least NVQ III (or equivalent);
4. by 1996, 50 per cent of medium to larger organisations to be Investors in People.

The lead bodies, in conjunction with examining and validating bodies, have been establishing the standards and putting in place a series of competency-based NVQs up to Level V approved by NCVQ. In Scotland, SCOTVEC has modularised its National Certificate to give ease of access and a basis for credit accumulation. SVQs are available in large numbers.

Although the Standards Programme is principally about standard setting, it also assists the development and accreditation processes. Standards need a properly structured assessment system to gain credibility, and accreditation is a vital part of the wider objective of establishing a comprehensive coverage of vocational qualifications. TEED monitors the sectoral organisations concerned with training, which cover three-quarters of the employed population. Cross-sectoral standards work has been developed through the lead bodies covering management and supervision; administrative, business and clerical occupations; and information technology.

The Training and Development Lead Body set new standards and qualifications for training and development with a code of good practice.

The standards can be used by training professionals to:

- establish basic requirement specifications that can be used in the purchase of training services;
- indicate the kinds of criteria that should be used to evaluate the progress and outcomes of training programmes;
- act as an operational guide to the design, development and delivery of training programmes;
- underpin the introduction and use of innovative non-traditional training methods, systems and materials;
- incorporate best practice in human resource development planning and strategy design approaches;
- provide a basis for workplace assessment to nationally recognised standards by qualified assessors and verifiers.

The range of Employment Department activities concerned with improving British vocational education and training includes:

- the improvement and dissemination of labour market information, (mentioned in Chapter 16);
- stimulating the responsiveness of the education and training system to employers' needs;
- helping to improve employer and training networks and the organisational infrastructure generally;
- using major programmes to develop a wider training competence and interest on the part of employers;
- promotional work to get the vocational education and training message to employers and to assist employers to help themselves.

Other initiatives

Various initiatives have been used to fund new employer training, one of which is the Business Improvement Initiative. The initiative replaced overlapping grant programmes which had grown in a piecemeal way. Under the Business Improvement Initiative, the Employment Department will help to develop business training to meet the needs of owner/managers of very small firms for business start-ups. For firms with up to 500 employees which are working to produce a plan for managing business change, including the preparation of a systematic forward plan for developing its people, the TEED will offer half the cost up to a contribution of £15,000. Innovation projects help support and encourage companies to embark on major innovative training and development and to disseminate the results widely. TEED will support selected employers by meeting up to half the total costs, up to £100,000 a year. Skill projects encourage employers and their representative organisations to tackle skill supply problems by selectively funding short-term pump priming to reinforce employers' ability to deal with the problem in the longer-term.

The Group Training Association (GTA) plays a major role in the co-operative efforts of employers in an industry to pool some of their training resources. The term covers a wide variety of organisations, set up by employers, who have joined together to promote the training of their employees. They range from associations with their own training centres and training staff, to those with only one specialist peripatetic training officer. Of 260 GTAs involved in TEED programmes at the end of the 1980s, 190 were YT approved training organisations, 21 were working in other YT activities and 72 were participating in Employment Training.

GTAs differ in their origins, funding, constitution and control. Links between GTAs and their industry training organisations also vary. Some were very much creatures of their industry training organisation, as in construction where in all but a few cases the group training officers were training board employees. Others, for example in the chemical and furniture and timber sectors, have no formal links with the industry training organisation in their sector. There are indications that GTAs are beginning to establish themselves as separate and identifiable pressure groups; for example, in road transport and engineering, independent groups have been set up in the last decade to put pressure on the industrial training organisations.

GTAs include bodies receiving TEED operating cost support, others who have received support in the past but no longer do so, and yet others who have never received it. The picture relating to funded GTAs is generally of a phased withdrawal from the need for funding, which is given on the basis of activities carried out rather than general institutional support.

In order to increase the availability of information about skills training, TEED funds the Training Access Point (TAP), a computer terminal providing information on education and training. By the end of the 1980s a network of TAPs had been built up in England, Wales and Northern Ireland, which could provide details of over 60,000 nationally available and 3,000 locally available courses. Early experience showed that men have been the main users but a campaign has been launched to try to find ways of encouraging more women to use TAP. The service is managed locally by agents who are responsible for building comprehensive databases on locally available learning opportunities, looking after the terminals, and arranging advice and support on training and education for individuals and companies.

Chapter 19
FE and youth training

Young people at the age of 16 in the United Kingdom have several routes open to them. The first one is to stay in full-time education and this has already been discussed in Section 2. The second path is to try to find a job, an option which has been become more difficult in the late 1980s and early 1990s. The third option is to enter a government training scheme for young people. The young person can enter a college on any of these routes, either on a full-time course, or on release from work (or after work in the evening), or as part of the training programme of the scheme. These alternatives noticeably impact on each other. For example, the introduction of a training allowance with YTS in 1983, reduced the proportion of young people entering full-time education. The figures did not return to their pre-1983 level until the end of the decade.

In the 1990s, there has been an attempt to be forward-looking in education and training of young people by the introduction of 'foundation learning targets' as part of the national education and training targets. The Government aims are that:

1. by 1997, 80 per cent of young people should reach NVQ II (or equivalent);

2. training and education to NVQ III (or equivalent) should be available to all young people who can benefit;

3. by the year 2000, 50 per cent of young people should reach NVQ III (or equivalent);

4. education and training provision should develop self-reliance, flexibility and breadth.

These targets have taken over to a large extent from the Government aims for young people in the 1980s, which were outlined in the second 'objective' of the White Paper, **A new training initiative** (DE 1981). It stated that, 'all young people under 18 should have the opportunity either to continue in full-time education or of entering a period of work experience combined with work-related training and education'. While the Government made little public comment during the 1980s about which of the two routes it preferred – full-time education or training – its policy was to fund training through the Department of Employment, rather than to fund colleges and post-16 school providers through the national education departments and the local education authorities.

Training credits

In order to encourage young people to take up further education and training, the Government brought in the idea of training credits at the beginning of the 1990s. This move followed pressure from the Confederation of British Industry, which advocated the introduction of credits for young people in its influential document **Towards a skills revolution** (CBI 1989). Similar support was given by the Trades Union Congress.

The credits build upon the foundation of YTS. Training is to approved standards and skill levels, through recognised qualifications generally at National Vocational Qualification Level II, III and IV. Young people without jobs continue to be guaranteed an offer of a training place and the appropriate minimum training allowance. Credits differ from YT in some important ways. Public funding is routed through the young person rather than a training provider. Each credit scheme includes enhanced careers education and guidance so that young people can make the best choices about use of their credits. The emphasis of the whole scheme is on flexibility and TECs have considerable freedom to develop their own ideas.

Ten TECs and one LEC began development work in 1991. A further nine TECs and LECs joined the second round in 1992. They cover approximately 10 per cent of the 16 and 17 year olds leaving full-time education. In the second round, the scheme in Calderdale and Kirklees offered both education and training credits. By April 1994, training credits are expected to cover 30 per cent of all 16 and 17 year olds.

Public funding for the pilots comes from a variery of sources: existing resources for YT; extra money for additional careers advice and guidance (to allow for more and higher levels of training to be delivered); and money that previously went to pay for part-time provision in colleges for 16 and 17 year olds. In 1991/92, the allocation for Great Britain was £109 million.

A training credit is an individual entitlement to train to approved standards for 16 and 17 year olds who have left full-time education to join the labour market. Each credit displays a monetary value and can be used by a young person to obtain training with an employer or training provider. The aims of training credits are:

- to expand and improve training by motivating more young people to train and to train to higher standards;
- to increase the quantity and quality of training provided for young people by employers; and
- to establish an efficient market in training.

The evaluation report on the first year of pilot schemes in 1992 (Employment Department 1992) found widespread support for training credits among employers, trainers, educational establishments and, most significantly, young people. Awareness of training credits was high. However, the report suggested that more could be done to improve understanding through more effective and continuing local marketing. Training credits had not influenced the priority of young people leaving school which was to get a job, with training only a secondary option. Nearly 60 per cent of eligible 16 to 17 years olds had begun to use their credit, close to the original projection of around 65 per cent take up in the first year.

The Government's aim, spelled out in the 1991 White Paper **Education and training for the 21st century** (DES *et al.* 1991a), is that the offer of a credit will be extended to all 16 and 17 year olds by 1996 with the phasing out of YT.

Figure 18: Training credits (issues and starts), December 1991

TEC/LEC	Issued	Starts
Birmingham	3,387	2,565
Bradford	3,159	2,105
Devon and Cornwall	7,193	4,579
Grampian	5,168	941
Hertfordshire	3,086	672
Kent	541	172
NE Wales	463	226
Northumberland	1,189	1,292
S&E Cheshire	4,134	981
SOLOTEC	795	650
Suffolk	2,391	1,489
TOTAL	31,506	15,672

Source: **Employment Gazette** February 1992 (1992b)

Youth Training (YT) and the Youth Training Scheme (YTS)

The vehicle for work experience and training for 16 and 17 years olds in Britain has been Youth Training (YT) or the Youth Training Scheme (YTS) as it was known in the 1980s. The first details of YTS were announced in 1982 in the wake of the White Paper, **A new training initiative** (DE

1981). YT started as a one year scheme in April 1983. It replaced a varied series of initiatives which were designed primarily to counter the 25 per cent unemployment for 16 and 17 year olds at the beginning of the 1980s. At that time the main scheme was the Youth Opportunities Programme. YOP was based on Work Experience on Employers' Premises, a scheme which gave trainees an allowance from the Manpower Services Commission for up to six months, with no cost to employers. YOP had a bad reputation because employers were not obliged to offer any form of structured training to the young people taking part. Alongside YOP was the much smaller Unified Vocational Preparation (UVP) programme in which employed young people in clerical and semi-skilled manual jobs could have some off-the-job training and further education funded by government grants. At its peak, YOP attracted some 240,000 entrants in 1981/82, while UVP catered for only 15,000.

During the first three years of its operation, YTS offered one year of basic vocational training to all unemployed 16 and 17 year olds. It involved planned work experience, off-the-job training and further education. The organising body, the Government's Manpower Services Commission, hoped that employed young people would be brought into the scheme as well, but the proportion was never significant. The scheme was extended to two years' duration from April 1986, by which time some 26 per cent of all 16 year olds were in YT – just under half of those not in full-time education.

By the end of the decade YTS offered a guarantee of a two year place for all 16 year old school-leavers, based on a training programme of at least 20 weeks' off-the-job training and 17 year olds were eligible for a one-year programme with at least seven weeks' off-the-job training. All trainees were given a training agreement which detailed what was involved in the training programme, including the rights, responsibilities and protection of the young person. Greater emphasis was placed on the achievement of recognised vocational qualifications based on competence and success within the outcomes of the programme. The addition of a second year meant that numbers were over 40 per cent higher than for the one-year scheme, although the cyclical nature of recruitment makes comparison difficult.

A survey of two year YTS, completed in March 1988 after its second year of operation, gave a snapshot of the scheme. On the mainland of Great Britain, there were 538,800 contracted places with an average of 376,000 young people in training. The figures represented a national place occupancy rate of just under 70 per cent. The lowest occupancy rate in England was in the London area (62.8 per cent), while the highest was in Yorkshire and Humberside (76.9 per cent). The rates for Wales and Scotland were 78.9 per cent and 75.5 per cent respectively. The scheme does not operate in Northern Ireland. By 1992, the number in training had fallen to just over 250,000.

The largest number of places were in the administration/clerical area (70,000), followed by construction (58,000). Entrants still tended to follow the traditional male/female occupations, although there were some signs that this was beginning to change. The figures for recruitment to YT in the period April–June 1988 showed that, on standard schemes, 70 per cent of all starters were in the private sector, 24 per cent in the public sector, five per cent with voluntary organisations and one per cent in specialised Information Technology Centres (ITECs). For the training programmes which attracted extra funding because of difficulties with the client group or the expensive nature of the training (known as premium schemes), only 14 per cent were in the private sector, 38 per cent in the public sector, 39 per cent in voluntary organisations and nine per cent in ITECs.

ITECs provide young people with training and work experience in new technology. More than 170 centres offered training in electronics, computing and modern office skills. The young people recruited have a wide range of abilities. ITECs have a high occupancy level, long work-placement periods and good records of placing trainees in jobs, but are expensive to operate. Their prime target group is young people in inner city areas. In some 90 per cent of ITECs, all trainees study for a recognised vocational qualification and for this reason they exercise greater selection among trainee applicants than do other schemes. In the 1990s, more of the ITECs have been attached to colleges and have either been slimmed down or become more integrated into the information technology provision of the college.

Perceptions of YT

In terms of outputs from YT, in England in 1990–91 when surveyed three/sixth months after leaving, 57.5 per cent had full-time or part-time work; another 9.6 per cent entered a different YT scheme. 5.9 per cent moved into further education. Finally, 19.8 per cent became unemployed on leaving YT and 7.4 did not answer. The rates fluctuate depending on the general state of the labour market.

Trainees interviewed about their attitudes to various aspects of YT thought that the scheme as a whole was useful (74.4 per cent), with more finding on-the-job training useful (78.45 per cent) than that off-the-job (61.0 per cent). The lower figure for off-the-job training epitomises the continuing problem of persuading young British people of the value of further study once they have left school. This seems to be part of a cultural barrier which is less prevalent in other industrialised countries. After leaving YT, only 58.4 per cent of the trainees questioned thought the scheme had helped them with their current job.

YT and employed trainee status

The way that YT has operated has failed to increase significantly the number of trainees given employed status. This lack of success, especially when linked with the collapse of apprenticeships, has given support to critics who say it is primarily a scheme to get young people off the unemployment register rather than to provide genuine training. The Government answer to this criticism has been to introduce the targets for training to various NVQ levels.

Despite strong efforts since the introduction of two year YT to persuade companies to employ their trainees from the start, the share of employed status places only increased from nine per cent in 1986 to 16 per cent in 1988. Surveys by the Department of Employment have found that many placement providers were reluctant to employ another member of staff. Companies were concerned about the time and cost of administration in issuing contracts of employment and dealing with tax and national insurance; nor did they like having to release employed trainees for college training. Employed status has only thrived where there were previous apprenticeship agreements or, more recently, where companies can only attract young people by offering them some job security.

Companies questioned about the advantages of employed status trainees referred to the stopping of the rotation of placements, which gives non-employed trainees more varied experience. Without placement rotation companies had two full years to train a young person systematically to their own company standards – rather than to more general YT standards. It also gives companies a longer period in which to observe and assess an employed trainee's ability and potential, and therefore longer to develop and mould their skills, knowledge and personality to suit company requirements. Other advantages are that the company would have a more motivated and enthusiastic trainee as a result of the security and extra financial reward of employed status. Companies offering employed trainee status continue to receive the weekly subsidy from the approved training organisation.

Who operates YT schemes?

The direct operation of Youth Training is in the hands of over 3,000 approved training organisations (ATOs) to whom trainees are attached. ATOs must have:

- the ability to arrange a two year training programme;
- a previous record in training;
- adequate resources;

- competent staff;
- the right premises and equipment;
- appropriate trainee assessment schemes;
- an effective programme review system;
- financial viability;
- a positive commitment to equal opportunities; and
- a positive commitment to health and safety.

ATOs recruit trainees with the help of the careers service. The ATO decides who is recruited to a particular scheme, subject only to adherence to recruitment policies laid down in their contract. ATOs have a responsibility to provide training to each entrant sufficient to meet the trainee's full entitlement.

Outcomes of YT

The original one year YT did not concern itself greatly with the achievement of vocational qualifications by trainees, but concentrated instead on individual training programmes. It was not until 1986, with the establishment of the NCVQ that an effort was made to make suitable qualifications available to all trainees. This change of philosophy was brought about by pressure from employers who were used to judging the quality of potential employees by the certificates they brought along, rather than by examining detailed records of achievement and profiles. This change of emphasis tied in with the development of the national standards programme.

YT is firmly based on the idea of occupational competence delivered through four training outcomes. The four outcomes are: competence in a range of occupational skills; competence in a range of transferable core skills; ability to transfer skills and knowledge in new situations; and personal effectiveness. TEED defines the main YT outcome of occupational competence as the ability to perform the activities within an occupational area to the levels of performance expected in employment. The other three outcomes are partly a recognition that employers want adaptable, versatile and enterprising recruits, and partly an attempt to minimise the risk that the definition of occupational competence will be viewed narrowly at a task or job skill level rather than at the broader level of employment competences. Competency has the added dimension of giving an understanding of how and why things are done – rather than just what is done.

The process of defining competence starts with the identification of the lead industry body (see Chapter 17). First the lead body produces industry-defined standards for the occupational areas to be covered, usually in the form of competence statements. Then it can produce a preferred training pattern, which sets out the ways that a trainee who is entering the industry can achieve the stipulated competences. Performance criteria are added to each competence statement, so that an assessor can determine whether a person can perform a particular defined task. Finally, the lead body works in partnership with the examining and validating bodies, which arrange for the certification of the competences. Competence statements will usually be grouped to make assessment modules – blocks of skill which those in the industry can easily recognise.

YT and special needs

Youth Training has had to cater for young people with special training needs. During 1987/88, 8,600 young people with disabilities joined YTS as first-time entrants. From February 1988 a code of practice has been available for YT special training needs to emphasise the importance of flexibility in the design and delivery of training programmes for these young people. They include those with physical disabilities, learning difficulties, behavioural and emotional problems, or who need help with literacy or numeracy, or for whom English is a second language.

YT and initial training

From September 1988 the new concept of initial training was introduced into YTS. It allowed eligible young people to be recruited into specially tailored programmes designed to achieve a number of specified objectives chosen to fit individual cases. Initial training has been used where: trainees seriously lack motivation or vocational commitment; trainees are disabled or have learning difficulties which require careful assessment; trainees face severe initial language difficulties or literacy/numeracy problems; trainees wish to explore non-stereotypical vocational options before deciding on a conventional YT scheme; it is apparent that trainees need help and detailed assessment. Entry is via endorsement by the careers service or any other person designated by the TEED. Time spent on initial training by YT trainees is in addition to their normal YT entitlement. The first initial training programmes were for up to three months' duration and exceptionally up to four months. The programmes should, where possible, contain an element of work experience which allows the trainee to experience a range of training occupational categories and environments.

YT and state benefits

In 1988 the Government removed the right of young people to opt out of education or training after leaving school and claim income support (the former supplementary benefit) if they could not find a job. In effect it said that, since it was guaranteeing places on YT for all who needed them, there was no need for any 16 or 17 year old to be unemployed. The 1988 **Social Security Act** removed income support for young people under the age of 18, except in certain limited circumstances such as for those judged to be severely mentally or physically disabled. The Regulations allow those assessed as not yet ready for YT to claim income support for a period of 12 months, which can mean college attendance as they are deemed incapable of work. There is also provision for a bridging allowance to cover short periods between one YT place and another or between a job and a YT place. Parents can receive extended payments of child benefit for specified periods until the young person has found a suitable job or a YT place. In certain circumstances a new bridging allowance will be available to young people themselves.

The demographic downturn in the 1990s, the increase in staying on rates in full-time education and the consolidation of initiatives for the adult unemployed into TFW has put pressure on the size and emphasis of the YT programme. In the 1980s the central thrust of YT was to get a strongly directed national programme in order to maintain minimum standards. In the 1990s various agencies have been competing for a reduced supply of young people. It is the view of the Employment Department that unless YT is seen to be flexible and coherent, it will not be a preferred alternative. The Government asked TEED to allow shorter schemes with less than 20 weeks' training, provided they are operated by training organisations with a good track record and the trainees leave with an approved vocational qualification.

YT in the 1990s

For many youngsters in the more affluent parts of the UK, the end of the 1980s initially offered the opportunity of a job coupled with education and training on a scale not seen in the period 1974–87. However, the continued recession at the beginning of the 1990s reversed this trend and young people moved in increasing numbers into full-time study. The National Economic Development Office warned employers not to drop training in order to find more money to pay attractive rates for initial recruits. It suggested in that schools should be warned of the danger of a return to the 1960s when many school leavers went into jobs which involved low levels of skills and little associated training. The shortage of young people is not reflected on a national basis, however. Between 1989 and 1991, the number of 16 year olds going on to either YT or jobs fell every year, except in Scotland where there was a slight increase. In contrast to the rise of the proportion of 16 year olds staying on in education from 48 per cent to 61 per cent, the percentage involved in YT fell from 22 to 15 per cent while the proportion employed fell from 18 per cent to 10 per cent.

At the beginning of 1990 the scheme became officially known as Youth Training (YT). To meet the demand for raising the general level of qualifications and the need to secure more high level craft and technician training, new qualification targets are being set. These are monitored by the local TECs (or LECS in Scotland) rather than a national governmental agency as in the 1980s. YT must now provide all young people with the opportunity to achieve qualifications which are at least at or equivalent to NVQ Level II. There will also be local targets for higher level skill training at NVQ Level III or its equivalent and above.

To meet the requirements of a more buoyant labour market, trainees who are not employed or who do not have a firm job offer by the start of their final six months in training are offered extra help to gain employment. This is done without damaging the chance to obtain a vocational qualification. Young people with learning difficulties have been categorised as trainees with special training needs, in parallel with the definition of special educational needs that operates in colleges and schools. They receive special training plans or else fit within the initial training design framework.

The Government's guarantee of a training place for young people continues under the YT programme. Under the guarantee all young persons under 18 years of age not in full-time education or employment must receive an offer and, if necessary, a re-offer of a suitable YT place. The guarantee under YT is extended to include an offer of a suitable place to older persons whose availability for YT has been delayed by disability, ill health, pregnancy, language problems, custodial sentence or care order. There has been considerable political argument in the early 1990s over the alleged failure of the Government to fulfil the guarantee for significant numbers of youngsters.

Provision in Northern Ireland

Youth Training does not operate in Northern Ireland because the Department of Employment's Training, Enterprise and Education Directorate operates only in mainland Britain. Instead the Northern Ireland Department of Economic Development, in co-operation with the Department of Education (Northern Ireland), devised a similar scheme under the title of the Youth Training Programme (YTP) which started in 1982, a year before the mainland YT. High levels of unemployment in Northern Ireland make it difficult to find employer-based training places. For example, even before YTP started, the Youth Opportunities Programme in the Province had only 12 per cent of its places composed of work experience on employers' premises, compared to 60 per cent in mainland Britain.

The first year of YTP offers a mix of broad-based training, an introduction to skills and the opportunity to develop interests and to test aptitudes. It is based on a combination of work preparation and work experience, provided by partnerships of government training centres, FE colleges, community workshops and employers. The second year involves more specialised training, offering the trainee the opportunity to acquire a recognised vocational qualification in a specific occupational area. The YTP has become increasingly like YT in recent years.

Community Industry

Many disadvantaged young people who have not participated in YT can take advantage of a scheme run by a group called Community Industry. Community Industry is a national YT managing agent and operates under the same terms as all other managing agents, but it is also responsible for operating an alternative scheme for those with special needs. Up to 7,000 16–19 year olds are referred to the 55 Community Industry units in England, Wales and Scotland by the careers service. The younger ones must have failed to benefit from YT. Projects should have some kind of community benefit and young people generally remain on the scheme for up to 12 months; 16 and 17 year olds receive wages in parity with YT, and 18 and 19 years olds receive a larger amount. Community Industry has been funded by a grant from the Department of Employment since 1971 and is aided by local authorities. It also raises funds from industry, commerce, charitable trusts and other sources. Community Industry operates as a group of companies limited by guarantee and which are separately registered as charities. The training covers a wide range of skills and work experience is provided. Attempts are being made to target the scheme more directly at the needs of the labour market.

The youth service

The youth service forms part of the education system and is concerned with promoting the personal development and social education of young people through a wide and diverse range of leisure activities. It comprises a partnership between statutory authorities and voluntary agencies which reaches some six million young people, the voluntary sector contributing 90 per cent of provision. The piecemeal historical development of the youth service means that a large number of distinctive organisations contribute. The range of provision includes clubs of various kinds, adventure pursuits and other tests of enterprise, help for unemployed young people, counselling, community service and international contacts. Young people take part on a voluntary basis. The service is staffed by a small number of professional officers supported by part-time paid and unpaid workers.

A 1982 review of the youth service stressed the importance of extending the range of experiences open to young people and of giving them opportunities to participate in decision-making in their organisations. The review discussed the need for the development of political awareness with which young people can influence the society in which they live and have a say in how it runs. Although most young people face the problems of growing up without undue difficulty, and have wider horizons and greater opportunities than ever before, for a significant and growing minority the process is far from easy. The personal development of many young people is blighted by unemployment, urban deprivation, rural isolation, racial discrimination and homelessness. The need was recognised for girls to be given greater encouragement to play a full part and for efforts to be made to counter those attitudes in society which prevent them from achieving their full potential.

The Government accepted a number of the review's findings and itself stressed the need for better planning, co-ordination and management in order to get the best return from existing resources. It established the National Advisory Council for the Youth Service in England and Wales to advise Ministers and others on the scale and direction of youth service activity. It has also taken new initiatives concerned with staff training and is giving financial support for experiments in management innovation. It agrees that the involvement of young people in decision-making should be encouraged.

Many of the issues raised by the review of the youth service in England are particularly pertinent to Northern Ireland where the youth service is seen as having a very important role in contributing to greater understanding between the two traditions which divide the community.

Chapter 20
FE and adult training

The training of adults has been a central part of the work of further education right back to its origins in the mechanics institutes. Although the training of adults is intrinsically a part of the overall training provision of colleges, I have separated this chapter out in order to highlight the range of Government-funded schemes. The structure of these schemes impacts on the way colleges relate to adult training since the colleges themselves do not usually manage the schemes but merely act as subcontractors to other bodies. In the 1980s, colleges suffered from the Government's hostility to the public sector in general, and in particular the reluctance to let colleges be managing agents for the Government-funded training schemes.

The Government has funded many private providers to manage Government training schemes on the assumption that the private sector is cheaper and more flexible than colleges. It has been a sign of the strength of colleges that they have come through this and now contract with the TECs and LECs and subcontract with various kinds of managing bodies and small training companies. The private trainer has not challenged FE to a great extent except in what might be called 'niche' markets – hairdressing, retailing etc. – at the cheaper end of the market. (A cynic might say that adult training does not generate sufficient profit to tempt the private sector into the training market.) The other small training companies and training consultants are at the top of the market in high cost management training where profit margins are larger.

In contrast to the Department of Employment, the Department for Education established schemes like REPLAN and PICKUP which have supported the work of colleges in further and higher education by helping with development money for colleges to try new things. These schemes do not have the massive bureaucracies associated with large programmes for the unemployed.

Like YT, the heyday of the adult training schemes came in the late 1970s and 1980s as the MSC reacted to large scale unemployment. The framework was laid down at the beginning of the 1980s with the three main objectives, contained within the White Paper, **A new training initiative** (DE 1981) which were discussed in the previous two chapters. Objective 3 aimed to, 'open up widespread opportunities for adults – whether employed, unemployed or returning to work – to acquire, increase or update their skills and knowledge during the course of their working lives'.

In its 1983 discussion paper, **Towards an adult training strategy** (MSC 1983), the MSC stressed that many adults had not benefited from a sound initial training and needed assistance to improve their employability and/or make the most of their talents. The MSC saw an urgent need to increase awareness of the necessity for learning to be a continuing process for people of all ages, not a once-and-for-all matter concerned only with training new entrants to the labour market. It wanted to encourage thinking about the development of individuals who can cope with and benefit from education and training throughout working life.

The Commission looked at the background factors involved in training people to do their jobs during the 1980s. It pointed out that the number of unskilled and semi-skilled operatives had fallen by a million over the previous 10 years, and predicted a further fall of another million by 1990. Non-manual workers had come to outnumber manual workers. The traditional apprenticeship system was in decline. There was a growing demand for people with technical and professional skills and a shift of jobs from the manufacturing industries to service and commercial work.

Initiatives during the 1980s

A whole series of initiatives came and went in attempts to make some progress on an adult training strategy. Local collaborative projects, the National Priority Skills Scheme, local consultancy and training grants, Training for Enterprise, the Job Training Scheme and Access to Information Technology were all tried in the 1980s. The proliferation of schemes coming under the umbrella of 'Objective 3'(DE 1981) up to 1988 caused concern about their ad hoc nature. There was widespread worry about the inadequacy of British adult training provision: in particular, the large number of programmes available, the absence of coherence between these programmes and the lack of freedom for individuals to choose their own training. Most of the programmes had evolved by accident rather than from policy decisions and this confirmed the need for a new approach.

Employment Training (ET)

The Employment Training (ET) programme was proposed by the MSC as a single coherent scheme which would overcome the fragmentation of the wide variety of schemes existing at the time. ET, as it has come to be known, was claimed by the Government to be the largest adult retraining programme in the world. It was projected to have an annual budget of £1.5 billion to pay for training for up to 600,000 unemployed adults at all levels of skills. The scheme was devised by an MSC Task Group of Commission members in the early part of 1988. They proposed five principles as the foundation of ET: participation should be voluntary; high quality training should be provided; schemes should be individually tailored to meet client needs; there should be an incentive to take part; programmes should be locally planned and delivered.

It was originally envisaged that the development of ET would be overseen by an adult training board, similar to the one existing at the time for Youth Training, which consisted of employers, trades unionists, managing agents, sponsors, local authorities, the education service and voluntary organisations. This was ruled out when the Government scrapped the Training Commission (the successor to the MSC) and all the tripartite bodies supervising its training programmes (see Chapter 17).

The Employment Training programme was cut back after only six months of operation. Only three-quarters of the 600,000 places on the scheme had been filled, despite sustained efforts to persuade the jobless to join it. The Training Agency offered to give employers and agencies in the scheme some of the money saved by the low take-up, to help them improve training. There was considerable criticism of ET from some trades unions, local authorities and training commentators. They said that to expect one-third more trainees to acquire skills for more or less the same money as was available for the old programmes suggested that quality may suffer. Additionally, if adults were to spend 60 per cent of their time working for an employer while on ET, they should be treated as temporary employees and paid the trade union rate for the job. In the past, when an employer had the chance to recruit people at the social security benefit rate with a small addition (the so-called 'benefit plus') as opposed to permanent employment, trainees were often used as substitutes for hiring properly trained and paid workers. The critics deny that subsidised travel, free meals and topping up of income support are adequate substitutes for reasonable pay. The Trades Union Congress called for a boycott and phased withdrawal from the scheme in September 1988. This resulted in their removal from any major influence in national training bodies and the end of the tripartite system.

Employment Training continued to decline. The handing over of training schemes to the TECs and LECs to control at local level at the beginning of 1990s did not halt the slide. In fact, the TECs have protested to Government Ministers about further cutbacks. The numbers in training in Great Britain fell from 174,800 in 1989 to 149,000 in 1992 – only a quarter of the original target figure (1989–1992 Employment Training Management Information telephone census). The effects of the recession in this period on the South of England are shown by the growth of those in training while the numbers have fallen everywhere else. The scheme had twice as many men as women participating, the majority have been unemployed for six to 12 months and the greatest concentration is in the 18 to 24 year olds males (25.9 per cent in a six year span) compared to 25 to 50 year olds (38.3 per cent for a 25 year age span).

ET did not have a great success rate when measured at the beginning of the 1990s. Only just over half completed the training – 65,700 from 130,500. Those who left the scheme between January and December 1992 fared little better. Only 35 per cent gained any sort of qualification and more than two-thirds were still unemployed three months after leaving the scheme (Employment Policy Institute 1994).

In terms of those attending further education colleges during their ET programmes, there were mixed reports. An HMI report in 1991, **Education responses to unemployed adults** (HMI 1991e), said that there was insufficient time and expertise on the courses available to provide initial assessment and guidance for those requiring help with basic skills. Only a few colleges had responded with specifically designed provision to meet the ET aim of providing learning programmes tailored to individual needs. Usually ET students joined mainstream courses at different times of the year. HMI also reported that 50 per cent never made it from referral from job centres and other agencies to the actual training agent. Much of the college provision lacked the flexibility to allow students to enter and exit at different times, and to receive accreditation.

However, on the positive side, many students expressed a high degree of satisfaction with the programme and are working hard. Relationships between staff and students were seen to be good almost everywhere and the staff working with unemployed adults were generally well-qualified, caring and committed. Even at the assessment stage, where there was a great pressure on time, students were invariably treated with courtesy, sensitivity and concern. The Inspectors noted 'where unemployed adults are enrolled in mainstream provision, a wide range of certification is available to them, and there are good examples of progression routes'. Some return-to-learn courses led into access courses and from there to higher education.

By March 1991 the Employment Department was considering ending the ET programme. Supplementary provision was announced that year (entitled Employment Action) which was intended to give the long-term unemployed periods of work experience. However, EA was short-lived and on 1 April 1993 it and ET were replaced by two new schemes – Jobplan Workshops and Training For Work. In its first year of operation, TFW was intended to provide 320,000 unemployed adults with an opportunity to undertake skills training or work of benefit to the local community.

Jobplan Workshops are based on the old Restart scheme. They require the long-term unemployed to attend a five day workshop to assess skills and form an action plan leading towards a job or further training.

Many colleges have not found ET or its successor, Training For Work, an easy scheme to provide for. The demands of roll-on/roll-off programmes and individual learning plans do not fit in with requirements to generate higher student:staff ratios and the income does not warrant individual care. In fact, many colleges have found it uneconomic to operate and have left it to a dwindling number of private and not-for-profit providers. HMI noted that many colleges found it necessary to subsidise their ET provision in order to respond adequately in terms of the guidance and course provision required.

The Industrial Language Training Scheme

Another part of the funded provision for adults from the Department of Employment is made through the Industrial Language Training Service (ILTS). As the name suggests, the original purpose of the scheme was to provide training in basic English for first generation immigrants in employment. In 1987 just over half of those trained by ILTS were employed by local authorities, with only 10 per cent coming from the private sector; the rest were employed in the National Health Service and the public or voluntary sector. The Employment Department suggested that a system should be established which encourages employers to identify and meet the training needs of employees in their organisation generally, and that this should include language and communications training, whenever necessary, in the interests of members of ethnic minorities.

PICKUP

The Professional, Industrial and Commercial Updating Programme (PICKUP) was launched in 1982 by the Department of Education and Science. The scheme was extended to Wales in 1984 and Scotland in 1986. It aims to increase substantially the amount of specifically designed training provided by colleges and universities for adult employees in business and industry. The PICKUP target was for a five-fold increase in college-provided adult training between 1984 and 1992. A national survey involving over 100 colleges and universities showed that about 750,000 people took part in PICKUP training in England in 1986/87. This marked an increase of nearly 40 per cent on the previous year. The Secretary of State for Education, while congratulating PICKUP on the increase, pointed out that the figures represented only one in 30 of the workforce. He set the new goal of one in 10 of the national workforce to receive PICKUP-type training each year by the early 1990s. He insisted that training for working adults was to become as much a part of the job of colleges as full-time education for school leavers or as research in universities.

The PICKUP programme focused on four key areas: better marketing and information; links with industry and business; developing more and better courses and training programmes and planning ahead; and staff development in colleges – training the trainers. PICKUP has a national database of course and training capability, operated by a team of 11 full-time regional agents in England and Wales, and an office in Scotland. The team of regional advisers was strengthened and a national network of regional technology centres has been introduced. However, by 1993 the government decided that PICKUP had fulfilled its purpose, and it was disbanded.

PICKUP (Scotland) was launched in 1986/87. Its aims were similar to the English scheme. College publicity advertised that innovative post-experience courses could be provided but conventional courses could also be adapted for new clients. Course were available across the range of professions, manufacturing and servicing industries, involving both the public and private sectors. Courses were available to meet the needs of operators, supervisors and technicians as well as administrative and management staff. A major expansion of the PICKUP programme in Scotland, announced at the end of 1988, meant a doubling of the funds from the Scottish Education Department for 'partnership projects'. Employers and other partners were expected to contribute further support in cash or kind, at a ratio of two to one to the £0.5 million put in by the Education Department, making at total of £1.5 million available. PICKUP was taken over by the FEFC in 1993.

REPLAN

REPLAN was another example of a central government programme funded by the Department of Education and the Welsh Office. It was established in 1984 and was intended to improve, increase and extend the educational opportunities available to unemployed adults. It tried to encourage and assist providers to review, adapt and change existing provision to meet changed community demand. The REPLAN programme was made up of five major components. The first was a team of eight regionally-based field officers who offered a consultancy service to local authorities, statutory and voluntary providers of education and a wide variety of other agencies and organisations concerned with unemployment, employment and training. This team sought to identify and promote good practice and to assist in development strategies for change. A second component was the appointment of development workers at local authority level whose role was to improve the co-ordination of existing provision and to encourage staff and curriculum development with a view to improving and extending provision. The third component was a national development programme aimed at staff from the wide range of agencies whose resources could be harnessed to meet the learning needs of unemployed adults. There was also a small programme of local development and curriculum development projects. The final component was the development of independent learning materials suitable for unemployed adults.

REPLAN workers acknowledged their inability to provide pathways to employment on a large scale for individuals, thus enabling them to focus on what they could realistically hope to provide. This was located within a five-point framework. Unemployed adults were assisted to develop knowledge, skills and attitudes which would: increase their chances of finding and keeping a job; help them cope with being unemployed; understand the extent to which responsibility for being unemployed rested with society rather than the individual; helped them make good use of their increased leisure time; and enabled them to create their own livelihood.

The programme was closed down after seven years in 1991. The Government said that the programme had largely fulfilled the purpose for which it was established. Instead, LEAs, TECs and colleges were encouraged to work together to improve the provision of adult literacy and numeracy skills.

Chapter 21
FE and higher education

Background

The dividing line between further and higher education is shaped by the highest school leaving qualification. It is an artificial concept but that is the nature of most boundaries. In the case of England, Wales and Northern Ireland, the boundary is marked by the GCE (General Certificate of Education) Advanced level. In Scotland, it is the Scottish Certificate of Education Higher Grade or Certificate of Sixth Year Study. In further education colleges, which of course also provide courses leading to the above qualifications, the equivalent vocational qualification is the National Certificate or Diploma of the Business and Technology Education Council or the Scottish Vocational Education Council.

In the 1980s those courses below the dividing line were known as non-advanced further education and those above were called advanced. These terms arose because the 1944 Education Act used the generic definition for further education which covered all courses in colleges outside the universities, so the former polytechnics largely did advanced further education courses while local colleges offered non-advanced further education. The 1988 Education Reform Act (ERA) simplified this divide when it redefined the former advanced courses as higher education. The courses which were previously defined as non-advanced have become known simply as further education. It is worth noting these definitions because old terms are sometimes still used interchangeably by different bodies.

Before the abolition of the categorisation of courses at the end of the 1980s, every course in an FE college was categorised for such purposes as the payment of part-time lecturers and the calculation of unit totals to determine college size. The categories ranged from I at the highest level to V at the lowest. Using these categories, the GCE Advanced level was graded as IV, while anything below was V. The first degree was set at Category II and the postgraduate qualification at I. Category III was anything falling below degree level and above GCE A level: this was mainly the Higher National qualifications of BTEC and SCOTVEC and lower professional examination courses. These Category III courses formed the biggest overlap between the colleges deemed to be in the higher education sector and those called colleges of further education.

BTEC courses

The Higher National courses sit astride the further/higher education divide. Full-time or sandwich courses fall under the heading of higher education and are funded by the Higher Education Funding Council. Part-time certificates, if offered in an FE college, count as local HE and are funded by the FEFC, despite the fact that the content is the same.

BTEC works closely with the various industrial and professional bodies concerned with qualifications at sub-degree level, which corresponds with Level IV NVQs. Among the range of courses at this level are people preparing for the examinations of professional bodies such as the Institute of Bankers, the Royal Society of Chemistry, accountancy bodies and so on. Some of this work does not meet the new definition of higher education but its location is often based on the historical fact of where the courses started and/or the range of institutions in the area.

Defining HE

At one time it was fashionable to talk of the 'seamless robe' of further and higher education in large local colleges which catered for everything from basic literacy to postgraduate professional qualifications. The removal of many colleges providing higher education from the control of local education authorities in 1989 sharpened the divide between further and higher education, but a number of colleges now under the auspices of the FE Funding Council still have a sizeable amount of higher education, for which they are funded by the Higher Education Funding Council (see below). Many more FE colleges have entered into franchising arrangements with an HE institution, whereby that institution's courses are taught at the FE college by FE staff. The HEFC directly funded over 70 FE colleges in 1993.

The Education Reform Act led to a Statutory Instrument which laid down the regulations for prescribed courses of higher education for England. These were:

1. all postgraduate courses;
2. all first degree courses;
3. all full-time and sandwich courses for the Diploma of Higher Education or the Higher National Diploma of the Business and Technology Education Council;
4. all full-time and sandwich courses of more than one year's duration providing education at a higher level which are not prescribed courses of higher education by virtue of 1 and 2 above;

5. all full-time courses of at least one year's duration and all sandwich courses and part-time courses (including block release and day release courses) of at least two years' duration, being courses providing education at a higher level (a) for the initial or further training of youth and community workers, or (b) for the further training of teachers.

In Scotland, the boundary line between further and higher education is at SCE Higher Grade or the SCOTVEC National Certificate.

Abolition of the 'binary line'

At the beginning of the 1990s, the United Kingdom higher education sector was the subject of a major reshaping. A radical White Paper **Higher education: a new framework** (DES *et al.* 1991b) was issued in May 1991 by the Department of Education and Science and the Welsh Office in conjunction with the Scottish and Northern Ireland Offices. The White Paper proposed the abolition of the dividing line between the older universities and the polytechnic and colleges sector – the so-called binary line. It also recognised the maturity of the institutions in the polytechnic sector in awarding their own degrees and abolished the Council for National Academic Awards (CNAA), which has been replaced by a single quality audit unit in which the institutions are major stakeholders. The White Paper was put into effect by two Further and Higher Acts for England/ Wales and Scotland in 1992.

Funding for all the institutions is on a national basis through the higher education funding councils. However, the councils are charged with keeping those universities, which were polytechnics prior to 1992, to their original mission of vocational higher education. Each funding council has its own quality assessment unit, operated in part by former government inspectors (HMI) and people from the wider academic world.

The rationale for these changes came from the Government's desire to make higher education available to one in three of the 18 to 19 age group by the end of the century. The White Paper had stated that the Government believed the real key to achieving cost effective expansion lay in greater competition for funds. The institutions are expected to cater for the increased demand from adults for part-time study.

Funding

The establishment of three national funding councils has involved more than the straightforward redistribution of existing institutions along national boundaries. In the case of the Higher Education Funding Council – England (HEFCE) it provided an opportunity to both expand the sector and consolidate collaborative arrangements between institutions. The process of merger and upgrading is expected to continue through the 1990s.

The composition of the HEFCE sector at its launch in 1993 consisted of 80 universities and 51 colleges:

- the 35 universities formerly coming under the Universities Funding Council (UFC);
- the 33 new universities created from the polytechnics and the larger higher education colleges formerly coming under the Polytechnic and Colleges Funding Council;
- the 49 higher education colleges also originally under PCFC;
- the Open University, the Royal College of Art and Cranfield Institute of Technology, originally funded by the Department for Education;
- the eight major institutions of the University of London, which will be treated as though they were independent institutions; and
- two colleges transferring from the further education sector – the Wimbledon School of Art and the Kent College for the Careers Service.

In Scotland, the universities are funded through the Higher Education Funding Council for Scotland. Its remit is to advise the Secretary of State for Scotland on university provision and on the implications of demand for Scottish higher education as it affects the balance between the university and college sectors. HEFC-S funds 13 institutions:

- eight old universities – Aberdeen, Dundee, Edinburgh, Glasgow, Heriot-Watt, St Andrews, Stirling, Strathclyde;
- four new universities – Glasgow Polytechnic, Napier, Paisley, Robert Gordon;
- Dundee Institute of Technology.

The Wales Higher Education sector was formed from:

- the University Colleges of Aberystwyth, Bangor, Cardiff, Lampeter, Swansea, Wales University College of Medicine;
- the University of Glamorgan.

In Northern Ireland, the Queen's University of Belfast and the University of Ulster remain unaffected.

At the end of 1992, the Chancellor of the Exchequer slowed down the previously accelerated expansion of the higher education sector in favour of putting more funds into further education. This was because the number of students on full-time and sandwich courses in higher education had expanded even faster than the rapid growth envisaged in the 1991 White Paper on which the Government's previous expenditure plans were based (DES *et al.* 1991b). The numbers of young people entering HE in 1992 were on target at 750,000 full-time equivalent students (FTEs). The Government envisaged a period of consolidation where the numbers entering the sector would remain broadly the same over the three year period 1993 to 1996 so that the targeted level of one in three participating would be achieved by the end of the decade. The revised expenditure plans provided for total FTE student numbers to rise by 13 per cent between 1992/93 and 1995/96.

The growth of HE

The story of higher education in the United Kingdom since the Second World War has been one of continuous expansion. Much of this expansion has been achieved by the hiving off of whole colleges or the splitting off of sections of colleges at the further education level. This exaggerated 'academic drift' has meant that the boundary between further and higher education has been as shifting as the seashore, but as the HE sea has advanced, the FE beach has reformed in front of it.

The tides of HE expansion were strong from the 1960s, but have been particularly high since the 1980s when the Government decided that it had to expand the higher sector in order to provide the stream of skilled people needed for the United Kingdom to compete internationally. During this period further education also changed quickly as described in the first part of this book and while the 1990s have seen a sharper divide between the further and higher education courses, it has also seen the rapid growth of HE provision being 'franchised' into further education colleges.

It is worth tracing the growth of the higher education sector, to enable the reader to understand the background to debates in the 1990s. In the early days of higher education, matters were relatively simple. For centuries the only accepted institutions of higher education were the ancient universities. In England, Oxford University was founded in the 12th century and Cambridge in the 13th. In Scotland, St Andrews, Glasgow and Aberdeen universities were established in the medieval period, followed by Edinburgh in the 16th century.

The widening of university education came very slowly. For example, in England the universities of Oxford and Cambridge were only modernised in the 19th century when the colleges were given new constitutions, the professorial system was reorganised, fellowships and scholarships were opened up, non-conformists were allowed to take degrees and women's colleges and halls were introduced. When the Charter for Durham University was issued in 1836, it followed the path of the ancient universities. The demand for a university which excluded religious teaching and provided scientific courses led to the formation of the University of London in 1836. London University was well known for its practice of granting external degrees to those who studied by correspondence courses, either privately or in all kinds of other institutions. This facility allowed the English provincial colleges to develop as awarding bodies prior to achieving university status.

Many attempts were made in the late 19th century to set up local universities in the large English cities. Manchester won the race in 1870 when Owens College became a member college of the new Victoria University. Liverpool and Leeds became constituent colleges of the federal university in the next decade. Birmingham, Manchester, Liverpool, Leeds, Sheffield and Bristol were allowed to found independent civic universities early in the present century. Other university colleges which had grown in association with the ancient universities became independent universities during the first half of this century. Charters were granted for Reading in 1926 and Nottingham in 1938. The remaining university colleges, at Southampton, Hull, Exeter and Leicester, achieved university status in the 1950s.

The national need for more graduates led to pressure for universities to extend their recruitment outside the usual catchment group of those from traditional middle class backgrounds. The reorganisation of schools brought about by the 1944 Education Act, which increased the number of qualified candidates, as well as the rise in the birthrate after the Second World War, led to greater numbers of eligible 18 year olds in the 1960s. By the beginning of the 1960s the number of full-time students had increased to over 100,000, as compared to just half that number at the end of the 1930s. The universities were finding it increasingly difficult to cope with demand, so the Government asked the universities funding body to recommend the formation of new institutions in other parts of England. This resulted in new universities at Brighton (University of Sussex), Colchester (University of Essex), Canterbury (University of Kent), Coventry (University of Warwick), Norwich (University of East Anglia), and Lancaster.

One unusual consequence of the 1960s wish to expand, was the creation of the Open University (OU), a non-residential institution which relied upon open learning techniques. The OU offers courses leading to degrees by a combination of television, radio, correspondence, tutorials, short residential periods and local audio-visual centres. The Open University has expanded to provide open access first degrees, post-experience and postgraduate courses. In 1988 the OU had more than 68,000 registered undergraduate students. It has always stood separate from the other universities and was grant-aided by the former Department of Education and Science until 1993, when its funding was transferred to the Higher Education Funding Countil. It has recently taken on a new role, picking up some responsibilities from the now-defunct CNAA (Council for National Academic Awards). The Open University Validating Service provides course validation for colleges which do not have the university status to accredit their own courses.

Unlike some other countries such as the United States, the United Kingdom did not encourage the growth of private higher education institutions as a way to cope with expansion. In fact England has only one independent university (at Buckingham) which provides a two year course based on eight terms of 10 weeks leading to a bachelor's degree. Its tuition fees are well above those in all other UK universities. It receives no financial support from government but its students are eligible for mandatory awards from local authorities.

The public funding of the higher education sector was obviously a key factor in growth. Originally, the universities established at the turn of the century struggled throughout their early years due to shortages of funds. Support from wealthy local business people, while sufficient to help their foundation as university colleges, did not cover running costs. From 1889 Parliament started to vote funds for distribution to the ancient universities and the university colleges. The award of grants was conditional upon each institution carrying out postgraduate research. The annual grant continued to rise until, in 1919, the University Grants Committee was established to make recommendations to the Government on its distribution, a task formerly carried out by the Board of Education. It carried out this role until the 1980s. The awarding of grants to the universities was based on development plans which were renewed every five years. The grants consisted of capital expenditure for new buildings and equipment, as well as funds to cover running costs. Within their five year plans the universities maintained their independence in respect of what was taught and examined.

Not all the growth in new universities after 1945 came from the traditional approach. In England the local authority institutions of higher education contributed to the process. The period of reconstruction after the Second World War, followed by sustained economic growth in the 1950s, led to concern about the low level of technological education. This resulted in the creation of an elite group of colleges to provide technological courses of university degree standard, with the courses being co-ordinated through regional advisory councils, under the umbrella of a National Advisory Council on Education for Industry and Commerce.

By the middle of the 1950s a clear stratification of colleges was becoming apparent. The colleges operating on a regional basis were offering full-time and sandwich courses on the same level as the universities at first degree and postgraduate levels. The area colleges offered a range of courses, including some advanced courses, mainly to part-time students. The local technical colleges offered largely non-advanced vocational courses, again mainly on a part-time basis. Finally, the adult education institutes offered mainly evening recreational courses, but with some vocational courses.

As a result of a White Paper in 1956, **Technical education** (Ministry of Education 1956), a number of regional colleges were designated as colleges of advanced technology specialising in advanced work under the control of an independent governing body. At the beginning of the 1960s the then Minister of Education took the colleges of advanced technology out of the local authority system under a régime of direct funding. By the end of that decade they had all become technological universities.

The removal of the colleges of advanced technology into the university sector left a gap in public sector provision. This was filled by the polytechnics, created by the 1966 White Paper, **A plan for polytechnics and other colleges** (DES 1966). The polytechnics were formed from the regional colleges which had not become colleges of advanced technology, often by amalgamating several colleges in a major town or city. The 29 polytechnics were expected to cater for the growing demand for higher education in vocational areas and they did this very successfully. Indeed, 25 of the 29 polytechnics passed the total of 5,000 students recommended by the **Robbins Report** (Ministry of Education 1963) as the minimum size for success for a university-type of HE institution. This was in contrast to the technological universities, only two of which had as many as 5,000 students. The polytechnics did not mimic the universities because successive governments wanted to protect their particular vocational emphasis.

From 1970, it was the polytechnics and other non-university HE colleges that accounted for the growth in student numbers. The reward for this 20 years later was that the polytechnics were awarded university status, so that at the end of the century most cities and major towns have two universities, when at the beginning they were struggling to found one.

Apart from the polytechnics, there were two other kinds of higher education institution that grew in the 1970s and 1980s. First, there were the big area colleges doing a significant proportion of higher education work. Second, there were the voluntary and other colleges funded by the DES which were already freestanding. These became part of the polytechnics and colleges sector from 1989 and were transferred to the HEFC in 1993.

From the middle of the 1970s, there was a debate about higher education in the public sector, that is, those colleges attached to local education authorities and not nationally funded like the universities. In the universities there was a clear remit to provide undergraduate and postgraduate courses, research and some continuing education in extramural departments. In the non-university sector, matters were more blurred. The problem of overlap with further education affected the polytechnics and colleges sector, since there was a strong tradition of colleges offering a wide range of courses across all levels of work. The arguments mainly centred around the issues of central government or local LEA control and funding. The planning for this new higher education sector, separated from the universities by what was called the binary line, began in earnest with the creation of a planning body, the National Advisory Body (NAB). The polytechnics and colleges sector of English higher education began life legally on 1 April 1989 under the umbrella of the Polytechnics and Colleges Funding Council. There were 350,000 students in the institutions, representing 279,000 full-time equivalents. General institutional funding was around £850 million.

The University Grants Committee was replaced by the new Universities Funding Council (UFC) as a result of the 1988 Education Reform Act. Like its predecessor, the University Funding Council was responsible to the Secretary of State for Education for allocating funding between universities, rather than the overall amount which was decided by Government. During the 1980s, the UGC had tightened the spending on universities by cuts in their income and academic staff. The Government insisted on looking at performance indicators such as student:staff ratios and a range of unit costs across the main categories of expenditure. Effectiveness was also measured by indicators such as income from research grants and contracts, the number of research and sponsored students, submission rates for research degrees and the first occupation of graduates. The block grant system was replaced by separate allocations for teaching and research. This move was in line with Government Ministers' aims to concentrate research in a small number of major universities and to allow other institutions to pursue research only in specialist fields for which they were well known.

Research in HE institutions

Academic research in Britain has always had a high reputation worldwide. The research carried out in higher education provides the knowledge base for industry and commerce to build upon and is a major source of trained people at all levels. The Government is trying to encourage increased investment by industry in research and development, including research in collaboration with higher education. The 1993 White Paper **Realising our potential: a strategy for science, engineering and technology** (Cabinet Office *et al.* 1993) proposed a new Government strategy to improve the nation's competitiveness and quality of life, with more focused research and better informed decisions about research funding, which take account of the needs of industry.

The University of Wales

The development of higher education in Wales has resulted in a University of Wales, based on a federation of colleges, with 21,000 full- and part-time students. Early HE in Wales was conducted at Lampeter

College, founded in 1828, which provided a widely-based but religious education and was allowed to award degrees from 1852. Lampeter did not develop into a university due to its association with the Church of England. A campaign developed for a national University of Wales based on a number of colleges. In 1872 a residential college was founded at Aberystwyth, which became a university college in 1889. Other colleges were founded in South Wales at Cardiff and at Bangor in the north. The present University of Wales is based on six constituent colleges. Each college receives a grant directly from the HEFC, while the University of Wales itself receives funds for central initiatives such as the development of Welsh language provision. Each college puts forward its five year academic plan in parallel with a university federal plan, which had begun to attempt some subject rationalisation. The Welsh Committee, which advised the Universities Funding Council on the Principality's higher education requirements, was replaced by the Welsh Higher Education Funding Council, based in Cardiff, in 1993.

HE in Scotland and Northern Ireland

Scotland did not have an exercise similar to the PCFC one in England between 1989 and 1993, since the 17 Scottish Central Institutions were already funded through the Scottish Education Department.

Northern Ireland has two universities: Queen's and Ulster. Queen's University of Belfast was founded in 1908 and offers degree and postgraduate courses in a wide range of subjects. The University of Ulster is based on three major sites in Londonderry, Coleraine and Newtonabbey. It was formed from a 1984 merger of the New University of Ulster and Ulster Polytechnic. The Department of Education for Northern Ireland funds the universities, on a basis of parity with institutions in Great Britain. There is no higher education funding council.

HE students

Over the past 20 years, the nature of the student body in the United Kingdom has changed. While male full-time undergraduates increased by 20 per cent between 1970 and 1989 and women by 30 per cent, the percentage of part-time female students at polytechnics and colleges of higher education increased by 758 per cent. In this sector, mature students counted for two-thirds of all students admitted in 1991. The proportion from ethnic minorities starting courses in the former polytechnics was three times higher than their proportion in the population as a whole. Although women and ethnic minority groups have begun to catch up in participation terms, working class students have not. Blue collar workers get less than half of the proportion of degrees that they should if social class made no difference. Before the Second World War, three-quarters of the population came under the Registrar General categorisation of working class – classes III, IV and V – skilled, non-manual, semiskilled and unskilled workers. In the 1990s, these groups represent less than 40 per cent.

In the 1980s the polytechnic sector had accounted for virtually all the increase in the age participation rate for young students (up from 12.4 per cent to 14.6 per cent) and three-quarters of the increase in part-time students. Mature entrant numbers (those aged 21 and over) have grown by 77 per cent in the decade between 1980 and 1990. In the following year alone, 1990/91, there was a further 10 per cent increase according to DES statistics. At the beginning of the 1990s, mature students entering higher education reached the 250,000 level, outnumbering the traditional 18 years olds for the first time. These numbers were made up of 237,000 first year home students entering universities and colleges and a further 38,000 studying at the Open University. Just over a third of these students were full-time. The rise in participation has been helped by a larger proportion of women entering higher education. Women accounted for 49 per cent of the full-time mature students and 45 per cent of the part-time ones.

HE in the 1990s

Government policy for higher education in the 1990s was outlined in the 1987 White Paper **Higher education: meeting the challenge** (DES 1987). This was the first major review of the whole spectrum of United Kingdom HE since the basic philosophy and structure were laid down a quarter of a century earlier in another document, also called **Higher education**, but better known as the Robbins Report (Ministry of Education 1963). The White Paper proposals for England and Wales were given statutory backing by the ERA. The legislation did not alter some of the major planks of post-war higher education policy such as the institutional divide between the university sector and the polytechnics and colleges (the binary divide) and the basis of eligibility of students for higher education (the Robbins principle). The binary line was only removed in 1993.

The most far reaching part of the legislation was the decision to change the funding and planning structure for English polytechnics and major colleges of higher education by abolishing the planning and funding body, the National Advisory Body for Public Sector Higher Education. Polytechnics and major colleges become independent corporate bodies under the umbrella of a new funding body, the Polytechnics and Colleges Funding Council (PCFC). This move brought the English system more into line with Scotland's organisation of non-university HE, since the central institutions in Scotland were already funded on a national basis by the Scottish Education Department.

The Government has reiterated its view of the purpose and aims of higher education as initially set out in the Robbins Report (Ministry of Education 1963). Higher education should, 'provide not only instruction in skills but also the promotion of the general powers of the mind, the advancement of learning and the transmission of a common culture and standards of citizenship'. It was recognised that a high level of scholarship in the arts, humanities and social sciences is an essential feature of a civilised and cultured country. Research of all kinds is to be encouraged even where it has only an indirect relationship with the world of work. The Government has also emphasised its aim to achieve greater commercial and industrial relevance by fostering positive attitudes to enterprise and developing close communication between academic staff and people in business, but has stressed that meeting the needs of the economy is not the sole purpose of higher education. A further theme of the White Paper, which was echoed in all government policy statements on education and training, was the need to increase efficiency and value for money while improving quality.

New funding arrangements for universities and colleges replaced the grant, which carried with it assumptions of entitlement, by a system of contracts which focus on services provided for customers. Universities and colleges were asked to submit bids based on three to five year academic and corporate development plans to provide courses in nine broad subject areas: engineering and technology; science and mathematics; the built environment; information technology and computing; business and management; health and social services; humanities; art, design and the performing arts; and education. Published performance indicators will include assessments of the quality of provision in each category.

The Council for National Academic Awards

The Council for National Academic Awards (CNAA) was set up in 1964 following a recommendation of the Robbins Report. The main function of the Council was to validate higher education courses and award degrees and diplomas to students in higher education institutions outside the university sector. A study of academic validation in public sector higher education (Lindop, 1985) recommended that polytechnics and colleges should accept maximum responsibility for their own standards. CNAA was asked by government to accredit mature institutions for the task of approving their individual courses, to increase delegation to other institutions as far as possible, and to pay more attention to the quality of teaching and learning and to the achievements of students in both academic and employment terms. This process of encouraging greater self-reliance among institutions was expected to lead to a reduction in CNAA's staffing and costs. The CNAA reached agreement with a small number of large companies for training inside the companies to count towards academic qualifications under the Credit Accumulation and Transfer Scheme (CATS). The CNAA was abolished by the 1992 Further and Higher Education Act, when the former polytechnics took over responsibility for validating their own courses. It has been replaced partly by the Higher Education Quality Council (HEQC), which is owned by the universities themselves, and partly by the Open University's validating service, referred to above.

HE and industry

Just as in further education, the Department of Employment has tried to make institutions more responsive to the needs of industry. The Enterprise Initiative was set up as an attempt by the Government via the former Training Agency to embed elements of the enterprise culture into the HE curriculum. The Initiative aimed at ensuring that students acquire key business and management skills partly through projects based in companies. Pilot institutions were given up to £200,000 over a five year period. This had to be matched by an extra quarter of the funding from local industry and commerce. The Department of Employment encouraged all universities and colleges of higher education to introduce an enterprise element into future courses.

Credit transfer

One of the ways of opening up higher education is a system of credit accumulation like that used in most North American universities. A joint Standing Committee for Continuing Education prepared a report on credit transfer and accumulation and qualifications structures to widen access. The report argued for maximising flexibility in course provision and requirements and the recognition of previous learning. HE courses typically require a commitment in advance to one programme of study over several consecutive years. The Standing Committee called for:

- a common system of credit valuations which embraces and integrates general and vocational qualifications;
- a system which ascribes course units to levels in the context of their intended learning outcomes;
- questions of coherence and progression in planning courses should be considered from the student's perspective;
- a guidance system for students on combinations of credits;
- admitting students to course units without requiring an advance commitment to a complete, specified programme of work.

Funding the students

Most higher education students in the United Kingdom are supported by a system of personal grants to cover the fees for the course and also a contribution to the costs of living expenses, accommodation and books. The level of the contribution is determined by parental income for young people or personal income for mature students, so many students do not receive a full maintenance grant. In England, Wales and Northern Ireland local education authorities are obliged to pay the fees and contribute towards the maintenance of students who embark on courses designated by the DFE as degree-equivalent courses. In Scotland the Education Department pays the grants. Designated courses include university degrees, Higher National Diplomas and DipHE courses. Additions to the grants are given to students living away from home and those living in London. Postgraduate students may be given higher grants to cover the increased length of their terms. Students who have reached the age of 25 (classed as mature) receive full grants, as do those who have been employed for three years before becoming a student.

To be eligible for a grant, students admitted to a designated course must ordinarily have been resident in the United Kingdom for the three years immediately preceding the academic year in which the course begins, and have not previously attended a course of advanced further education of more than two years' duration.

The Government has expressed its wish on a number of occasions to move over to a mixed system of grants and loans. The Secretary of State for Education announced in 1988 that the Government would introduce a system of loans to supplement the mandatory grant from 1990. The parental contribution and grant was frozen from 1990. It is intended that the loan will be increased in forthcoming years in line with projected inflation until it amounts to half the total needed to maintain a student. The scheme is administered by the Student Loans Company on behalf of the Government.

The proposals intend to shift the burden of paying for maintenance away from parents towards students. Students can take out loans over three years, with repayment within 10 years at a zero rate of interest in real terms. Anyone whose income after graduation falls below 85 per cent of national average earnings would make no repayment. As the scheme was originally planned, the major banks were to act as agents and the Treasury would act as guarantor, but the banks withdrew from the operation early in 1990. Critics have argued that the combined effects of higher inflation and declining value of the grant in real terms will leave students worse off when loans are introduced. Affluent parents will benefit from the freeze on parental contributions but as the earnings of the lower paid start to rise they will be expected to start contributing towards their child's upkeep at college.

Administrative and other costs now appear to be such that student loans are unlikely to cut costs to the taxpayer.

Loan defaults were running at a worryingly high level in late 1993 and the Student Loan Company had taken over 600 students to court for non-payment, with a total of £500,000 being owed to the Glasgow-based company by the end of August 1993 (**The Times**, October 1993).

Chapter 22
FE and schools

An understanding of further education and training in the United Kingdom requires some knowledge of how the school system is organised, particularly at secondary level. This is important not only because of the considerable overlap between schools and further education, but also because of the crucial nature of the education standards achieved by students and trainees before they start further education or training. For this reason a separate chapter is devoted to the United Kingdom schools systems.

The relationship of secondary schools to colleges of further education is particularly important. It is worth noting that a system of secondary schooling only really developed in the United Kingdom at the beginning of this century. In the public sector, secondary education started on a localised basis because of the government decision to allow the school boards to provide education for children up to the age of 14. It was only after the First World War that the 1918 Education Act introduced a national requirement for the earliest age of leaving school to be at the end of the term in which the pupil reached the age of 14. The national school leaving age was raised to 15 after the Second World War as a consequence of the 1944 Education Act. The present school leaving age of 16 was instituted in 1972. Since then there has been no strong demand to extend compulsory schooling, but the Government has said that it wants all young people to be engaged in some form of further education or training between the ages of 16 and 18. This post-16 education is carried on in a wide range of institutions, including colleges and schools.

There is an overlap between what schools offer to pupils over the age of 16 and the range of courses available in colleges. The main areas of common provision are in academic and foundation subjects rather than in vocational education, although schools are being encouraged to move into this area of work. Both schools and colleges offer the General Certificate of Education Advanced and Advanced Supplementary levels, the Scottish Certificate of Education Higher Grade and the foundation Certificate of Pre-vocational Education (CPVE), which is being replaced by the Diploma in Vocational Education. Schools cannot operate as centres for vocational examinations at craft and technician level, except in special circumstances, because they do not have the required levels of equipment or staff with the necessary vocational background. The UK has no equivalent of the technical and vocational schools which operate in many European countries; United Kingdom technical schools disappeared with the advent of the comprehensive school system. The different kinds of colleges (sixth form, tertiary and further education) offer a wider choice of A level subjects than school sixth forms. The GCSE or the Scottish Certificate of Education Ordinary or Standard Grades can be taken for the first time or retaken in both schools and FE colleges. GCSE subjects are often studied alongside other courses, which could be either pre-vocational or vocational.

Another overlap exists in the pre-vocational area, where modules within CPVE/DVE and units from a Technical and Vocational Education Initiative (TVEI) scheme are catered for in both schools and colleges. Although pupils on the TVEI complete the first two years of their programme in school, some or all of the third and fourth years can be completed in college. The same overlaps occur in Northern Ireland, except that there is no TVEI programme.

Earlier parts of this book discussed the competition between school sixth forms and colleges, and the moves to set up either sixth form colleges or tertiary colleges in place of sixth forms. The competition for students at GCE A level or SCE Highers was documented in Chapter 7. This chapter concentrates on the attributes of the United Kingdom schools system so that the reader can get a better understanding of how schools tie in to the work of colleges.

Most United Kingdom schools are administered and financed by a local education authority in the public sector as part of local government provision; alternatively they can be controlled by governing bodies which have a substantial degree of autonomy but which receive grants from central government sources; or schools can be in the private sector, operated by individuals, companies or charitable institutions.

Education establishments, including schools, are for of historical reasons often called by different names, which is typical of British tradition. This can be confusing, so the information which follows tries to use the most generally recognised terms. In the United Kingdom, within the public sector there are 30,000 schools as compared to 2,500 outside it. In addition there are 1,800 special schools, largely in the public sector.

Attendance at school in the United Kingdom is compulsory for all children between the ages of five and 16. Outside this compulsory 11 years of school attendance, many younger children attend some form of pre-school nursery education and many secondary school children stay on beyond the compulsory school leaving age. Primary education begins at five and usually ends at 11 with transfer to secondary education, except in some local authorities where there are middle schools. Primary schools are usually organised as either infants' schools (5–7) and junior schools (7–11), or infant and junior for both age groups. Secondary schools are normally for pupils aged 11 to 16, with many secondary schools having sixth forms catering for young people up to the age of 18.

State schools

No fees are charged for tuition in schools in the state sector. These schools are classified as maintained schools and most are funded by the local education authority from the council tax (formerly known as local rates, then the community charge) and government grant. About 1,000 schools are funded directly by the DFE after parents had voted to 'opt-out' of the local authority system. These are known as 'grant maintained schools'. Schools outside the state sector are called independent schools. These schools are often referred to as 'public schools', which can be confusing to anyone unfamiliar with the British system of education.

Local authority maintained schools are divided into two main categories. The first type of school is that which is built, maintained and staffed by the local education authority (LEA). These schools are known as county schools. The second type of school covers the ones outside of the remit of the local education authority, which are usually associated with some kind of voluntary body, often a religious denomination, and for this reason they are known as voluntary schools. Voluntary schools are financially supported by the local education authority and the degree of support determines factors such as local authority membership of the governing body and the composition of staff appointment panels. There are three kinds of voluntary school: controlled, aided and special agreement. The LEA pays all costs and appoints the teachers in controlled schools. In aided schools governing bodies are responsible for repairs to the outside of the school buildings (often with help from the national Education Department), but the LEA pays for internal maintenance and other costs and for the appointment of staff. In the third, the special agreement schools, expenditure is divided between the LEA and the governors, with the LEA paying an agreed figure between one-half and three-quarters of the capital costs.

Independent schools

Independent schools receive no direct financial support from national government or local authorities and they raise their funds from fees and donations. Most private schools do, however, have charitable status which gives them tax benefits. Although the parents of any pupil attending an independent school would normally pay fees, in 1980 the government introduced an Assisted Places Scheme for selected public schools to help parents who cannot afford fees for private education. The assistance parents receive toward the cost of tuition fees is related to their ability to pay. In England and Wales, over 30,000 assisted places for academically able children are available at more than 200 independent schools.

Most independent schools are members of one of the independent schools' associations such as the Headmasters' Conference, or the Governing Bodies of Girls' Schools Association. Many independent schools are single sex, with a roughly equal split between the numbers of boys' and girls' schools. An increasing number of single sex schools have mixed sixth forms. All independent schools must conform to national minimum quality standards both for teaching and for buildings, and are open to investigation by Her Majesty's Inspectorate. Schools which do not come up to nationally recommended standards can be forced by the national Education Department to make good any deficiencies in the quality of teaching and teaching staff, and the size and condition of school premises.

Participation

In England and Wales in 1990, the last year for which figures were available, the number of schools in each of the categories mentioned above was:

- county 15,600;
- voluntary 7,458, of which 3,070 are controlled, 4,314 are aided and 74 are special agreement; and
- independent 2,437.

The maintained sector schools cater for over 7,000,000 pupils.

The majority of English and Welsh secondary schools had between 400 and 1,500 pupils. Comprehensive schools, the most common form of secondary provision, admit pupils without any form of selection. In England, 85 per cent of state secondary schools are classed as comprehensive, in Wales they all are. Three per cent of English pupils are still educated in selective grammar schools, which provide academic courses, and four per cent in the more practically based secondary modern schools. Independent schools account for only seven per cent of pupils.

Wales had 200,000 pupils in 230 secondary schools in 1990. Outside of the maintained sector, there were 67 schools with 12,000 pupils, less than three per cent of the total. There were also 65 special schools catering for 3,800 pupils. Another 4,000 pupils were in 58 nursery schools.

Scotland

Scottish education has developed independently of England and Wales so that, while some parts of the education system are similar, Scotland has a number of distinct features. There has been increasing opposition in recent years to what the Scots see as the imposition of English systems by a London-based government. Responsibility for education in Scotland lies with the Secretary of State for Scotland and the Scottish Education Department. The duty to make local provision rests with the nine regional councils and three island councils. In 1990 Scotland had 3,778 education authority and grant-aided schools for 780,000 children: there were 429 secondary and 346 special schools. In addition, 115 independent schools catered for 32,500 pupils. As in England, schooling normally starts at the age of five, but there are seven years of primary education with the age of transfer to secondary at 12, one year later than the rest of the United Kingdom. All secondary schools are comprehensive.

Northern Ireland

The education service in Northern Ireland is administered from the Department of Education for Northern Ireland through the local mechanism of five education and library boards. As in Britain, there are publicly funded controlled schools and voluntary schools which receive grants towards capital costs and running costs. Northern Ireland also has voluntary grammar schools. The voluntary schools largely reflect the divided nature of the Province between the Protestant and Catholic communities. Comprehensive schools were not established in Northern Ireland to the extent that they were in Britain so the public sector secondary schools are more divided, with nearly 62 per cent of pupils going to secondary intermediate schools and over 38 per cent attending grammar schools.

The grammar schools tend to concentrate on a more academic form of education leading up to GCSE and A levels. 27 per cent of children who attend grammar schools are entitled to free places. Entry to a grammar school was usually determined by selection by a test at 11-plus, but children could transfer later between different forms of secondary school. In 1989 the Government announced the replacement of the 11-plus examination system by records of achievement and formal assessment at the ages of eight and 11, although the system of selective education is to be broadly retained. The Education Reform Order, which came into effect in February 1990, abolished the 11-plus and fee paying places in Northern Ireland's grammar schools.

Under the umbrella of the **Education (Northern Ireland) Act** of 1978, the then Labour government attempted to facilitate the establishment in Northern Ireland of schools likely to be attended by pupils of different religious affiliations and cultural traditions. Provision was made for a new type of school, the controlled integrated school, where children from the Protestant and Roman Catholic communities could be educated together. After 10 years of hesitation, the Conservative government announced in October 1988 that it would positively promote integrated schools. The Department of Education for Northern Ireland was given a statutory responsibility to develop and fund new integrated schools, allowing them all the grants and support that are currently available to existing state and Catholic maintained schools. An independent body was set up to disburse funds, and money is available to groups of parents who want to start new schools. Existing schools are encouraged to apply for integrated status, which will carry 100 per cent funding as opposed to the current 75 per cent for denominational schools. The Education Reform (Northern Ireland) Order allows for the creation of integrated schools using similar machinery for opting out as under the Education Reform Act on the mainland. Of the 1,200 schools in the Province, only a small number are integrated. In 1992, an agreement was reached with the Catholic schools to supply 100 per cent of capital costs (instead of 85 per cent) if the schools became the equivalent of the English voluntary schools and lost the church-nominated majority on the governing bodies.

City technology colleges

In England in 1986 the government announced plans for a new system of 11–18 schools, to be called city technology colleges (CTCs), which would be outside local authority control and would be supported by private sector companies. The education provided would be free to pupils. The school curriculum would have a particular bias towards science and technology. The support for CTCs is organised through the City Technology Colleges Trust. The original target was for 20 CTCs in inner city areas by 1990 but this was not achieved and only 13 had been set up by 1991. The delay in implementation was partly due to reluctance on the part of major companies to give large sums of money to schools outside the local authorities in case it jeopardised other ventures they are involved in with the state sector comprehensives. Legislation was amended in one case to widen the definition of CTCs to include art and design, which a particular company wanted to promote. The Department for Education originally promised that all, or a substantial part of, the capital costs would come from private sector companies, but the Government has had to step in to cover a lot of the building costs. The first CTC opened at Solihull in the West Midlands in September 1988 with 180 pupils. In Scotland, provision was made in 1989 for technological academies in areas of urban deprivation.

Grant-maintained schools

The 1988 Education Reform Act provided for the governing body of any maintained secondary school or large primary school in England and Wales to apply to opt out of local authority control and to achieve grant-maintained status. (The 1989 Self-Governing Schools etc. Act in Scotland allows schools in Scotland to opt out although none have expressed a desire to do so.) South of the border the new institutions can become grant-maintained schools in receipt of direct funding from the Secretary of State for Education. The procedure for England is that if the application to opt out is successful, the school will receive an annual maintenance grant which will be determined by the Department for Education on the basis of what the LEA would have spent directly on provision at the school, together with moneys to cover LEA central services and benefits which the school could have drawn on.

The first school to choose to opt out was Skegness Grammar School in Lincolnshire. Of the first 33 schools wanting to opt out, two-thirds were under threat of closure resulting from reorganisation schemes to take out excess school places. They were evenly split between urban and rural areas and just under half are in Conservative-controlled local education authorities. By the end of 1993 there were over 1,000 grant-maintained schools. If schools vote to opt out of local authority control they must maintain their original form of organisation: a comprehensive school will have to remain comprehensive and cannot become selective in its intake. Some local education authorities are finding that if a school opts out, their options for managing the resources for those remaining are considerably reduced. The LEA's ability to plan will be considerably impaired by schools opting out.

In its 1992 White Paper, **Choice and diversity: a new framework for schools** (DFE 1992c), the Government proposed a new funding agency for schools for opted-out schools and an easier transition to grant-maintained status and these were established through the 1993 Schools Act. The Government hopes, and will encourage, more schools to opt out. As the proportion of pupils in an LEA being educated in grant-maintained schools reaches 10 per cent, the funding agency will take on responsibility for the rationalisation of places in GM schools and share with the LEA the responsibility for securing sufficient school places. If the critical figure reaches 75 per cent, the funding agency will take over complete responsibility from the LEA for securing the provision of sufficient places.

Further changes brought about by ERA

There has been considerable discussion over the last decade about how to make schools more open and accountable to parents and the local community. The debate was started by the 1977 **Taylor Report** (Taylor 1977). Since then there has been an emphasis on shifting the balance of power towards the school and away from the local education authority, mainly by reducing the number of LEA-appointed governors. In 1986, the Government laid down new national criteria for the governance of schools. In county and voluntary controlled schools (but not voluntary aided and special agreement schools) governors nominated by the local education authority could no longer be in a majority and the number of elected parent governors was increased.

The Education Reform Act took governor power a stage further in England and Wales. Headteachers and governing bodies had some powers in the past to vary spending between selective headings of the school budget, but there had been a growing demand for a wider range of powers. ERA required LEAs to devise schemes of financial delegation which would make clear the total resources to be spent on all of their maintained primary and secondary schools, with the exception of certain items determined at local authority level. LEAs then allocated the sum between schools in accordance with a formula agreed with the Secretary of State. The formula is based almost entirely on weighted student numbers.

Responsibility for the allocated budget is delegated to the governors of all secondary schools and large primary schools. Governors are then free to spend the budget as they wish so long as they fulfil the statutory duties imposed on the LEA and the school. All these schemes had to be submitted to the Secretary of State for approval in 1989.

A DES Circular (DES 1988d) listed the two main aims of these schemes of financial delegation as: first, to ensure that parents and the community know on what basis the available resources are distributed in their area and how much is being spent on each school; and second, to give the governors of all county and voluntary secondary schools, and of larger primary schools, freedom to take expenditure decisions that match their own priorities, and the guarantee that their own schools will benefit if they achieve efficiency savings.

Scotland

The process of setting up new governing bodies in Scotland – to be called school boards – only became law at the end of 1988 as a result of the **School Boards (Scotland) Act**. At the end of 1989 the Government published the Self-Governing Schools Etc. (Scotland) Act which enables Scottish schools to withdraw from local authority control to become self-governing. It creates two new types of school, self-governing schools and technological academies. Self-governing schools remain in the public sector and charge no fees but are subject to the provisions of a 'parents' charter' with regard to admissions. The schools are funded by direct government grant from the Scottish Education Department at a level matching the resources which the school could reasonably have expected to receive if it had remained within the education authority. These changes to education in Scotland are seen by many as unsuitable English ideas being foisted on the Scots and have aroused a lot of opposition. The main Scottish teaching union (the Educational Institute of Scotland), ran a publicity campaign against the Government's policy of 'Anglicization', which was supported by many other bodies.

Scotland had developed a number of initiatives prior to any pressures from London. For example, curriculum reforms were started in the 1970s by the then Consultative Committee on the Curriculum (now the Scottish Consultative Council on the Curriculum). The guidelines issued indicated the progress pupils should make each year and set out modes of study, which ensures a broad range of subjects. Scotland gave almost unlimited rights to parents over the choice of schools in 1981 and curtailed the admissions controls available to local education authorities. This was seven years before the Education Reform Act.

The National Curriculum

The ERA placed a clear responsibility on English and Welsh local education authorities for the delivery of a National Curriculum. The National Curriculum is followed by all pupils of compulsory school age registered at county, voluntary or special schools maintained by the education authority, or at new grant-maintained schools.

The National Curriculum consists of the three core subjects of English, mathematics and science (and Welsh where appropriate), and seven other foundation subjects: history, geography, technology, a modern foreign language in secondary school, art, music and physical education. Religious education is not part of the National Curriculum, even though it is a legal requirement, because it is locally determined, although the Government has recently specified in some detail its key elements. Each subject of the National Curriculum has attainment targets and programmes of study. It also has assessment arrangements for the purpose of ascertaining what pupils have achieved in relation to the attainment targets for each of the four key stages. Nationally prescribed tests, which are independently moderated, have been devised to assess pupils against that which the attainment targets specify they should have learned and mastered. (In Scotland, pupils will be tested at eight and 12 in English and mathematics only.) The key stages cover the 11 years of compulsory school: years 1–2; years 3–6; years 7–9; and years 10–11.

A National Curriculum Council (NCC) was established in 1988 to keep the whole curriculum under review, to advise the Government on changes and for curriculum development. In the secondary sector the NCC was tasked to establish consistency of standards and content between subject working groups. In 1993 it, along with the Secondary Examinations and Assessment Council, was replaced by a new body, the Schools Curriculum and Assessment Authority (SCAA).

A number of problems have arisen and are continuing to arise in connection with the National Curriculum. There were disagreements between the Government and some subject working groups. The Government has stuck to its plans to test young people at the ages of seven, 11, 14 and 16, but modified arrangements after considerable criticism and a teacher boycott of the tests in 1993. Following a Government review led by Sir Ron Dearing, the arrangements for the National Curriculum and its assessment have been considerably simplified.

A common curriculum in Northern Ireland

In Northern Ireland the Government legislated for a common curriculum in 1989. The curriculum changes are broadly on the lines of the reforms in England and Wales except that religious education would have the same importance as mainstream subjects (but without compulsion) and the Irish language is given an equal place with its own programme of study and assessment. Another major difference is that there will be a requirement for pupils to study cross-curricular themes, including education for mutual understanding and cultural heritage.

Quality assurance in schools

The quality of secondary provision is monitored by the school itself, by local education authority advisers and inspectors, and by the central HM Inspectorate. HMI pay regular visits to schools and publish reports. Major inspections are occasionally carried out to give Ministers and the Education Departments an indication of the way things are changing in schools. The HMI reports for England and Wales (HMI 1988b), found that three-quarters of schools were performing satisfactorily or better, and half had some notably good features. Fewer than one school in 10 was thought to be poor or very poor. One-fifth had some major weakness due to lower standards in parts of the curriculum.

The main changes noted by HMI in the 1980s were that the number and range of options offered in English and Welsh secondary schools had been reduced, showing a clear trend towards a more common curriculum. On discipline, the HMI found that the vast majority of schools were orderly, hardworking and free from serious trouble. Educational standards had shown some evidence of slight improvement but this was difficult to define. The report (HMI 1988b) stated that the majority of schools were adequately staffed, although there was a continuing shortage of qualified teachers in physical science, maths and design technology. The teaching force as a whole was better qualified than in past years but had a higher average age and less chance of promotion opportunities. In post-16, HMI highlighted the disadvantages of schools with small sixth forms; secondary school consortia set up to provide a wide range of A level subjects did not generally solve the problems.

Demographic change

Secondary schools and their local education authorities have a major management problem as falling rolls leave a large number of unfilled school places. For example, for Great Britain, there was a drop of 17 per cent between 1987 and 1993 in the number of young people reaching the statutory school leaving age, and a 33 per cent decrease in the period 1981–93. An Audit Commission Report on England and Wales pointed out that nearly half of all secondary schools were well below the guidelines of 900 pupils and that these schools could be costing as much as £250 million to keep open. The Commission suggested that the number of empty school places would be up to nearly a quarter in the early 1990s. However, the ability of schools to opt out when under threat of closure is causing havoc with LEA attempts to take out surplus places.

The number of secondary schools was decreasing rapidly in the 1980s in England (from 4,728 to 3,976) and Wales (254 to 231), but not in Scotland and Northern Ireland where there has been much more hostility to school closures. Because all closures must be sanctioned by the national Education Departments, local education authorities have not been helped by the fact that decisions are often delayed by up to a year. In many areas, local education authorities were unable to put extra money into expanding further education provision in the 1980s and early 1990s owing to the drain caused by subsidising empty secondary places.

Teachers

In the United Kingdom in 1989/90, 513,000 people were teaching in schools, of whom 464,000 taught in the public sector. There were just over 210,000 primary school teachers, of whom 81 per cent were women. Secondary school teachers numbered 239,000; 48 per cent were women. 52 per cent of all teachers in local authority schools were graduates, representing about 65 per cent of men and 45 per cent of women teachers. The proportion of graduates is increasing each year as more students come from Postgraduate Certificate of Education (PGCE) and Bachelor of Education (BEd) degree courses. Of those successfully completing an initial teacher training course in 1989, 10,400 were graduates as opposed to 7,000 non-graduates.

Those people who wish to teach in English and Welsh maintained schools, or in a special school which is not maintained, will not normally be employed by local education authorities unless they have qualified teacher status (QTS). The 1982 Regulations relating to teachers specify six possible routes to QTS, but two routes account for the vast majority of teachers. The main route followed by over 90 per cent of the teaching force is the successful completion of a course of initial teacher training (often abbreviated to ITT) which has been approved by the Secretary of State for Education. Another four per cent successfully complete courses of initial teacher training outside England and Wales, which are recognised as comparable, two-thirds of this group being from Scotland and Northern Ireland.

Lecturers in further and higher education in any part of the UK are not required to have qualified teacher status.

In the future, trained teachers from other member states of the European Community can be appointed by local authorities or school governing bodies. If the draft Directive on a general system for the recognition of higher education diplomas is agreed, those with teacher training qualifications obtained on the basis of a minimum of three years' higher education in other European Community countries will be eligible for qualified teacher status.

From 1965 the pay of school teachers in England and Wales was determined under statutory arrangements outlined in the Remuneration of Teachers Act. A system of collective bargaining operated through a statutory body known as the Burnham Primary and Secondary Committee. After two years of industrial action by the teachers' trade unions, the Government abolished the Burnham Committee arrangements in 1987 and set up an interim committee to advise the Education Secretary on school teachers' pay and conditions of service. Opposition to the Interim Advisory Committee has come from the main teaching unions. The largest union, the National Union of Teachers (NUT), has urged that negotiating rights should be restored and is supported in this by the findings of the International Labour Organisation. The NUT wanted a national joint council arrangement, with pay disputes being referred to arbitration which would be binding on both the employers and teachers' unions. The other teaching unions are the Association of Teachers and Lecturers (ATL), the National Association of Schoolmasters/Union of Women Teachers (NAS/UWT), the Professional Association of Teachers (PAT), the National Association of Headteachers (NAHT) and the Secondary Heads Association (SHA).

In Northern Ireland the recommendations of England and Wales are usually taken as guidance for establishing pay levels. The three recognised teachers' unions are the Ulster Teachers' Union, the Irish National Teachers' Organisation and the NAS/UWT.

Scottish school teachers have not had their negotiating machinery changed. From 1987 a common single salary scale was created for primary and secondary teachers, with additional payments for qualifications and for posts of special responsibility. The main teachers' union in Scotland is the Educational Institute of Scotland (EIS).

All teachers in public or grant-aided schools in Scotland are required to register with the General Teaching Council for Scotland, an independent body. The General Teaching Council (GTC) is constituted by statute to advise the Secretary of State on a range of matters relating to the teaching profession. Its functions are to review standards of entry to the profession, to consider the supply of teachers, to keep itself informed on training given in colleges of education, to establish a register of teachers, and to exercise disciplinary powers over the register for schools and further education.

Attempts have been made in England by the University Council for the Education of Teachers to start a general teaching council. Discussions have been going on since 1984. In 1988, 16 teachers' associations approached the Secretary of State for Education to hold a conference on the establishment of a general teaching council. Although this request was refused on the basis that the GTC proposal did not include parent and employer representation, further efforts were made in 1989 in conjunction with the College of Preceptors. Each attempt has been deflected by the Government.

Appendices

Appendix 1   *References*

Appendix 2   *Glossary of terms*

Appendix 3   *Abbreviations and acronyms*

Appendix 4   *The United Kingdom and its education system*

Appendix 1
References

Audit Commission (1985) Obtaining better value from further education. HMSO

Audit Commission (1988) Surplus capacity in secondary schools: a progress report. Occasional papers no. 6. HMSO. ISBN:0117013986

Ball, C *et al.* (1991) Governing colleges into the 21st century. Coombe Lodge Report. Volume 22 Number 7. Blagdon, The Staff College

Bees, M and M Swords (Eds.) (1990) National Vocational Qualifications and further education. Kogan Page. ISBN:0749402458

Birch, D W (1988) Managing resources in further education: a handbook for college managers. Blagdon, Further Education Staff College ISBN:0907659551

Bridgwood, A (1989) Staff development and appraisal in FE: an interim report. National Foundation for Educational Research

British Broadcasting Corporation (1984) Your guide to the new exams. Scottish Standard Grade (14–16). BBC Scotland

Cabinet Office/Office of Public Service and Science/Office of Science and Technology (1993) Realising our potential: a strategy for science, engineering and technology. Cm 2250. HMSO

Cantor, L M and I F Roberts (1986) Further education today: a critical review. 3rd edition. Routledge and Kegan Paul ISBN:071021040X

Central Statistical Office (1992) Regional trends number 27. HMSO ISSN:02611783

Chartered Institute of Public Finance and Accountancy (annual) Education statistics (estimates). CIPFA.

City and Guilds of London Institute (1989) Policy and practice schemes, certificate, assessment and syllabuses: the next five years 1992–1997. CGLI

Coles, A J *et al.* (1988) User requirement for computerised management information systems for further education colleges: a report funded by the Department of Education and Science. DES/Welsh Office ISBN:0855223022

Confederation of British Industry (1989) Towards a skills revolution: report of the Vocational Education and Training Task Force. CBI ISBN:0852014759

Confederation of British Industry (1991) World class targets. CBI

Coopers and Lybrand (1988) Local management of schools: a report to the Department of Education and Science.

Coopers and Lybrand Associates (1985) A challenge to complacency: changing attitudes to training. Manpower Services Commission/National Economic Development Council ISBN:0863921345

Cuthbert, R (ed.) (1988) **Going corporate** Blagdon, Further Education Staff College [o/p] ISBN:0907659578

Department for Education (1992a) **Statistical bulletin 14/92.** July

Department for Education (1992b) Latest figures show dramatic increase in 16–18 year olds in education. **DFE News release 243/92.** DFE

Department for Education (1992c) **Choice and diversity: a new framework for schools. Cm 2021.** HMSO ISBN:0101202121.

Department of Economic Development (1988) **The organisation of training in Northern Ireland: proposals for the future.** DED

Department of Education and Science (annual) **Education statistics for the United Kingdom.** HMSO

Department of Education and Science (1966) **A plan for polytechnics and other colleges. Cm 3006.** HMSO

Department of Education and Science (1970) **Government and conduct of establishments of further education. Circular 7/70.** HMSO

Department of Education and Science (1973) **Adult education: a plan for development. Sir L Russell (Chair)** HMSO ISBN:0112703364

Department of Education and Science (1984) **Education for employees: an HMI survey of part-time release for 16–19 year olds.** HMSO ISBN:0112703976

Department of Education and Science (1985a) **Education and training for young people. Cm 9482.** HMSO ISBN:0101948204

Department of Education and Science (1985b) **The Further Education Act 1985: commercial activities in further education. Circular 6/85.** HMSO

Department of Education and Science (1987) **Higher education: meeting the challenge. Cm 114.** HMSO ISBN:0101011423

Department of Education and Science (1988a) **Advancing A levels: report of a committee appointed by the Secretary of State for Education and Science and the Secretary of State for Wales. Chairman: G R Higginson.** HMSO ISBN:0112706525

Department of Education and Science (1988b) **Education Reform Act 1988: governance of maintained further and higher education colleges. Circular 8/88.** HMSO

Department of Education and Science (1988c) **Education Reform Act 1988: local management of further and higher education colleges: planning and delegation schemes and articles of government. Circular 9/88.** HMSO

Department of Education and Science (1988d) **Education Reform Act: local management of schools. Circular 7/88.** HMSO

Department of Education and Science (1988e) **Survey of adult education centres in England 1985–86: enrolments, courses, hours of tuition and subjects of study.** DES Statistical Bulletin 10/88 (August)

Department of Education and Science (1988f) **GCSE: improving examinations at 16+.** DES

Department of Education and Science (1988g) **Qualified teacher status: consultation document.** DES.

Department of Education and Science (1988h) **School teachers' pay and conditions document.** HMSO ISBN:0112706541

Department of Education and Science (1990) **What 1992 means for education.** DES

Department of Education and Science (1992) **Access to FE for adults.** HMSO

Department of Education and Science *et al.* (1991a) **Education and training for the 21st century. Volume I Cm 1536, Volume II Cm 1536.** HMSO ISBN:0101153627

Department of Education and Science *et al.* (1991b) **Higher education: a new framework. Cm 1541.** HMSO ISBN:0101154127

Department of Education and Science/Department of Employment (1986) **Working together: education and training. Cm 9823.** HMSO ISBN:0101982305

Department of Education and Science/Welsh Office (1980) **Examinations 16–18.** A consultation paper. DES/WO

Department of Education and Science/Welsh Office (1982) **17+: a new qualification.** HMSO ISBN:0112703070

Department of Education and Science/Welsh Office (1985) **Better schools. Cm 9469.** HMSO. ISBN:0101946902

Department of Education and Science/Welsh Office (1987) **Managing colleges efficiently: report of a study of efficiency in non-advanced further education for the government and local authority associations.** HMSO ISBN:0112706266

Department of Education for Northern Ireland (1984) **Education in Northern Ireland in 1983.** HMSO. ISBN:0337041474.

Department of Education for Northern Ireland (1988a) **Education in Northern Ireland: proposals for reform.** DENI

Department of Education for Northern Ireland (1988b) **Education reform in Northern Ireland: the way forward.** DENI

Department of Employment (annual) **Training statistics.** HMSO

Department of Employment (1981) **A new training initiative: a programme for action.** HMSO ISBN:0101845502

Department of Employment (1984) **Training for jobs. Cm 9135.** HMSO ISBN:0101913508

Department of Employment (1988a) **Employment for the 1990s. Cm 540**. HMSO. ISBN:0101054025.

Department of Employment (1988b) **Training for employment. Cm 316**. HMSO. ISBN:0101031629.

Department of Employment (1990) **1990s: the skills decade: strategic guidance from the Secretary of State for Employment on training and enterprise.** Employment Department

Department of Employment (1992) **Training credits: a report on the first twelve months.** Employment Department

Employment Gazette (1991) Labour force survey. Reported in several issues throughout 1991.

Employment Gazette (1992a) TEC directors Jan 92 p34

Employment Gazette (1992b) Feb 92 p66

Employment Policy Institute (1994) **Employment Policy Institute economic report. Volume 8 Number 1.** February 1994

European Communities Commission (1990) **Activities of the Commission of the European Communities in the fields of education, training and youth policy during 1989.** EURYDICE

Further Education Funding Council (1992a) **Incorporation matters. Circular 92/09.** FEFC

Further Education Funding Council (1992b) **Students with learning difficulties and disabilities. Circular 92/06.** FEFC

Further Education Funding Council (1992c) **College strategic plans. Circular 92/11.** FEFC

Further Education Funding Council (1992d) **College strategic plans. Circular 92/18.** FEFC

Further Education Funding Council (1992e) **Financial forecasts cash flow profiles. Circular 92/16.** FEFC

Further Education Funding Council (1993a) **Funding learning.** FEFC

Further Education Funding Council (1993b) **Recurrent funding methodology 1994–95. Circular 93/14.** FEFC

Further Education Funding Council (1993c) **Recurrent funding methodology 1994–95: allocation mechanism. Circular 93/16.** FEFC

Further Education Funding Council (1993d) **Recurrent funding methodology: tariff values for 1994–95. Circular 93/32.** FEFC

Further Education Funding Council (1994) **General circular. Circular 94/05.** FEFC

Further Education Funding Council for Wales (1993a) **Institutional plans. Bulletin XIII.** FEFCW

Further Education Funding Council for Wales (1993b) **Institutional plans 1993/94–1995/96. Bulletin B23/93.** FEFCW

Further Education Funding Council Wales (1993c) **Funding further education in Wales.**

Further Education Unit (1979) **A basis for choice.** (1992 – 2nd edition) FEU

Further Education Unit (1981) **ABC in action.** FEU

Further Education Unit (1987) **Provision and participation in adult education.** FEU

Further Education Unit (1988) Development planning in NAFE. **Bulletin no 8.** FEU

Further Education Unit (1989) **Opportunity 1992: college courses and the Single European Market.** FEU

Further Education Unit/The Staff College (1994) **A strategic planning handbook.** FEU/The Staff College

Gow, L and A McPherson (1981) **Tell them from me.** Pergamon ISBN:0080257380 (hardback). 0080257399 (paperback).

Graystone, John (1991) New governing bodies in maintained FE: size and composition. **Mendip Paper MP014.** Blagdon, The Staff College

HM Inspectorate (1985) **Part-time advanced further education: an HMI survey of vocational courses.** HMSO ISBN:0112705820

HM Inspectorate (1987) **NAFE. Non-advanced further education in practice.** HMSO ISBN:0112706096

HM Inspectorate (1988a) **Report by HM Inspectors on the General Certificate of Secondary Education: an interim report of the introduction of the new examination in England and Wales.** HMI Report 129/88

HM Inspectorate (1988b) **Secondary schools: an appraisal by HMI: a report based on inspections in England 1982–1986.** HMSO ISBN:0112706533

HM Inspectorate (1988c) **A survey of courses leading to the CPVE.** Ref. 88/252 DES

HMI Inspectorate (1989a) **GCE AS examinations: the first two years.** DES

HM Inspectorate (1989b) **Further education in practice: tertiary colleges: an HMI survey.** HMSO ISBN:0112706789

HM Inspectorate (1989c) **The initial response of further education to the Education Reform Act.** DES

HM Inspectorate (1991a) **Six years on: teaching, learning and assessment in national certificate programmes in Scottish FE colleges.** HMSO ISBN: 011494184X

HM Inspectorate (1991b) **Education for adults: a review by HMI.** HMSO ISBN:0112707386

HM Inspectorate (1991c) **Technical and Vocational Education Initiative (TVEI) England and Wales 1983–90.** HMSO ISBN: 011270767X

HM Inspectorate (1991d) **The impact of the Education Reform Act on further education.** Ref. 35/91/NS DES

HM Inspectorate (1991e) **Education responses to unemployed adults.** Ref. 91/ 036

HM Inspectorate (1991f) **The effects of governors on further and higher education.** Ref. 293/91/NS DES

HM Inspectorate (1991g) **The responsiveness of further education to the Single European Market: a report by HMI.** DES

HM Inspectorate (1992) **Education in England 1990–91: the annual report of HM Senior Chief Inspector of schools.** DES

Howie (1992) **Upper secondary education in Scotland: report of the committee to review curriculum and examinations in the 5th and 6th years of secondary education in Scotland.** HMSO ISBN: 0114942048

Industry Department for Scotland (1988) **Scottish Enterprise: a new approach to training and enterprise creation. Cm 534.** HMSO. ISBN:0101053428.

Institute of Manpower Studies (1987) The full fact finding study of the NSTO system. **IMS Report No. 147.** IMS

Jessup, G (1991) **Outcomes: national vocational qualifications.** Falmer Press ISBN:1850009732

Lindop, Sir Norman (Chair) (1985) **Academic validation in public sector higher education: the report of the enquiry into the academic validation of degree courses in public sector higher education. Cm 9501.** HMSO ISBN: 0101950101

Manpower Services Commission (1981a) **A framework for the future: a sector by sector review of industrial and commercial training.** MSC

Manpower Services Commission (1981b) **A new training initiative: an agenda for action.** MSC

Manpower Services Commission (1982) **Youth Task Group report.** MSC.

Manpower Services Commission (1983) **Towards an adult training strategy: a discussion paper.** MSC ISBN:0905932846

Manpower Services Commission (1984) **A new training initiative: the modernisation of occupational training: a position statement.** MSC ISBN: 0863920640

Manpower Services Commission (1985a) **Development of the Youth Training Scheme: a report.** MSC ISBN: 0863921116

Manpower Services Commission (1985b) **Working group on training objectives and content: a report.** MSC ISBN:0863921175

Manpower Services Commission/Department of Education and Science (1986) **Review of vocational qualifications in England and Wales: a report by the working group. Chairman: H G De Ville.** HMSO

McAleer, J and G McAleavy (1988) Northern Ireland *in* **National Association of Teachers in Further and Higher Education college administration: a handbook.** 2nd Edition. pp100-11

Ministry of Education (1956) **Technical education. Cmd 9703.** HMSO

Ministry of Education (1963) **Committee on higher education. Higher education. Chair Lord Robbins. Cmd 2154.** HMSO

Murray A (ed) (1991) **Working with Europe: a handbook.** Further Education Unit.

Nash, S (1988) The perks of joining the reform club. **Times Educational Supplement.** 9 September 1988 p18

National Advisory Body for Public Sector Higher Education (1987) **Management for a purpose: the report of the Good Management Practice Group.** NAB

National Association of Teachers in Further and Higher Education (1981) **Further education in Northern Ireland: a policy statement.** NATFHE

National Economic Development Office/Manpower Services Commission (1984) **Competence and competition: training and education in the Federal Republic of Germany, the United States and Japan.** NEDO. ISBN:0729206521

Russell, Russ (1979) **The FE system of England and Wales.** Blagdon, Further Education Staff College [o/p]

Sargant, N (1991) **Learning and leisure: sample survey of participation in adult learning.** National Institute of Adult Continuing Education

Scottish Education Department (1979) **16–18s in Scotland: the first two years of post-compulsory education.** SED

Scottish Education Department (1982) **The Munn and Dunning Reports: framework for decision: a consultative paper on the Government's proposals for implementation.** SED

Scottish Education Department (1983a) **16-18s in Scotland: an action plan.** SED

Scottish Education Department (1983b) **Reform of curriculum and assessment in S3 and S4 in Scotland: implementation of the Government's development programme: a consultative paper.** SED

Scottish Education Department (1984a) **School and further education in scotland: a single examining body?** SED

Scottish Education Department (1984b) **16–18s in Scotland: an action plan: guide to teaching staff**. SED

Scottish Education Department (1984c) **The provision of guidance**. SED

Scottish Education Department (1985) **Future strategy for higher education in Scotland: Report of the Scottish Tertiary Education Advisory Council on its review of higher education in Scotland. Chairman Donald McCallum. Cm 9676.** HMSO ISBN: 0101967608

Scottish Education Department (1986) **Commercial activities in local authority further education colleges in Scotland: a consultative paper**. SED

Scottish Education Department/Curriculum Advice and Support Team [undated] **Fast forward with further education**. Produced by CAST and the Scottish Education Department. (Pamphlet with publication information.)

Scottish Office (1991) **Access and opportunity: a strategy for education and training**. Cm 1530 HMSO

Secondary Examinations Council (1988) **The examining groups for the GCSE.** SEC

Stoney, M S and A Lines (1987) **YTS: The impact on FE**. NFER–Nelson ISBN:0700511512

Taylor, T (Chair) (1977) **A new partnership for our schools**. HMSO ISBN: 0112704573

The Times (1993) 13 October, p5

Trades Union Congress (1989) **Skills 2000.** TUC ISBN:1850061807

Training Agency (1989) **Training in Britain: a study of funding, activity and attitudes** (four reports). HMSO ISBN:011361280X

Training Commission (1988a) **The funding of vocational education and training: funding study research programme: some early research findings. Background Note number 2.** Training Commission

Training Commission (1988b) **A general guide to employment training**. Training Commission

Turner, C (ed) (1991) **Guide to college management**. Longman. ISBN:0582080266

Warnock, W H (Chair) (1978) **Special education needs. Cm 7212.** HMSO ISBN: 010172120X

Welsh Office (1988a) **Education Reform Act 1988: local management of further and higher education institutions in Wales: planning and delegation schemes and articles of government. Circular 38/88.** Welsh Office

Welsh Office (1988b) **Education Reform Act 1988: governance of maintained further and higher education institutions in Wales. Circular 37/88.** Welsh Office

Acts of Parliament/Statutory Instrument in chronological order

Education Act 1918

Education Act 1944 Chapter 31. HMSO.

Industrial Training Act 1964 Chapter 16. HMSO

Remuneration of Teachers Act 1965 Chapter 3. HMSO

Education (number 2) Act 1968 Chapter 37 HMSO. ISBN:0105437689

Education Act 1968 Chapter 17 HMSO. ISBN:0105417688

Education (Scotland) Act 1969 Chapter 49. HMSO. ISBN:0105449695.

Education (Scotland) Act 1973 Chapter 59. HMSO. ISBN:0105459739

Employment and Training Act 1973 Chapter 50. HMSO. ISBN:0105450731

Education (Northern Ireland) Act 1978 Chapter 13. HMSO. ISBN:010541378X

Education (Scotland) Act 1980 Chapter 44. HMSO. ISBN:0105444804

Education Act 1981 Chapter 60. HMSO. ISBN: 0105460818

The Further Education Act 1985 Chapter 47. HMSO. ISBN:0105447854

Employment Act 1988 Chapter 19 HMSO. ISBN:0105419885.

Education Reform Act 1988 Chapter 40 HMSO. ISBN:0105440884

Social Security Act 1988 Chapter 7. HMSO. ISBN:0105407887

School Boards (Scotland) Act 1988 Chapter 47. HMSO. ISBN:0105447889

Self-Governing Schools etc (Scotland) Act 1989 Chapter 39. HMSO. ISBN:0105439894

Education Reform (Northern Ireland) Order (1989) SI 2406 (NI20) HMSO

Further and Higher Education Act 1992 Chapter 13 (1992). HMSO. ISBN:0105413925

Further and Higher Education (Scotland) Act 1992 Chapter 37. HMSO. ISBN:0105437921

Education (government of further education corporations) (former further education colleges) regulation. **Statutory Instrument 1963**. HMSO 1992

Appendix 2
Glossary of terms

ACCREDITATION The issue of formal recognition that bodies or institutions or the procedures used by them meet specific requirements.

ASSESSMENT Appraisal or estimation of an individual's degree of ability by a variety of means which could include written tests, practical tasks, assignments, course work, interviews, etc. Assessment may be internal (carried out by the tutor) or external (carried out by an external agency, usually in the form of written tests).

AWARDS A general term for qualifications issued by examining or validating bodies.

CERTIFYING BODY An organisation which issues a document formally attesting that the document holder has passed in specified assessments and/or fulfilled specified requirements.

COMPETENCE The ability to perform a particular activity to a prescribed standard.

CREDIT ACCUMULATION The arrangements which enable candidates to accumulate a specified number of credits, usually by successful completion of individual modules, to qualify for an award.

CREDIT TRANSFER The acceptance of an award, or credit gained towards an award, as credit towards another award.

CURRICULUM The entire programme of learning experiences which together make up a course. Also the entire range of learning experiences provided by an institution.

EXAMINATION One or more tests or assessments of knowledge or proficiency, involving the use of either written or oral questions and/or exercises.

EXAMINING AND VALIDATING BODIES Examining bodies are organisations which make awards to candidates who pass examinations which the organisation has set and marked to its own syllabuses. A validating body is one which makes awards to candidates who successfully complete an internally or externally assessed course which the organisation has approved and monitored.

EXPERIENTIAL LEARNING Learning through experience rather than through study or formal instruction.

FORMATIVE ASSESSMENT Assessment during a programme of education or training of a student's achievements on topics already covered to confirm progress or identify areas for remedial work.

GREEN PAPER A Green Paper sets out government proposals for future policy in the form of a discussion document, without commitment to action.

MODERATION Procedures to align standards of assessment between different test papers, testing occasions, examiners, centres, etc. For example, the internal assessment may be moderated by an external examiner who ascertains that the

---

assessment standards of a group of internal examiners are consistent from candidate to candidate and comparable with those of such examiners in similar institutions elsewhere.

MODULE A module of accreditation is a discrete unit for awarding credit within a system of qualifications. The module is defined in terms of an area of competence and the standards by which the competence is assessed. A module of learning is a separate and self-standing part of educational or training programmes designed as a series to lead to a certain level of qualification or attainment or as a related group from which programmes may be chosen according to need.

OCCUPATIONAL GROUP A group of jobs centred on the same basic discipline, such as catering, and within which recruitment qualifications overlap. Employees will tend to move up or across the job group by extending or developing their knowledge and skills.

PRE-VOCATIONAL EDUCATION Education designed to give people a broad preparation and requisite knowledge for entry to the world of work generally, normally developed through study and experience of one or more broad groups of occupations.

PROFESSIONAL BODY An organisation set up to represent the interests of a group of people in an occupational area, which may have taken on the role of setting entry standards for the occupational area – including the conducting of examinations and validation.

PROGRESSION The movement, or potential for movement, of a student or trainee from one discrete unit of education or training to another unit at a more advanced level.

STANDARDS Agreed and recognised levels of competence – whether skills, knowledge, understanding or experience – to be achieved through education or training, or required to perform a job.

SUMMATIVE ASSESSMENT Assessment, either during or at the end of a programme of education or training, of a student's achievement on the topics covered to provide evidence for final grading or certification.

SYLLABUS A concise, written description of the subject matter of a course or training programme.

VALIDATION The process of scrutinising a proposed course and of deciding whether or not it should be approved as being of an appropriate nature and standard for the award to which it is intended to lead and, if this proves to be the case, of then specifying the conditions which must be fulfilled if the course is to start. Validation may be internal or external depending on whether it is carried out by the institution which provides the course or by an outside body.

WHITE PAPER A White Paper describes official policy towards an issue and is often a prelude to legislation, e.g. the famous White Paper on educational reconstruction in 1943 which was followed by the 1944 Education Act.

WORK EXPERIENCE Placement of a student or trainee with a company or organisation to give experience of the working environment.

Appendix 3
Abbreviations and acronyms

ABE	Adult basic education
ABRC	Advisory Board for the Research Councils
ACC	Association of County Councils
ACFHE	Association of Colleges of Further and Higher Education (forerunner of AfE)
AfC	Association for Colleges
ALBSU	Adult Literacy and Basic Skills Unit
AMA	Association of Metropolitan Authorities
AMB	Area Manpower Board (existed before TECs/LECs)
AMMA	Assistant Masters and Mistresses Association
AMS	Annual Monitoring Survey
APC	Association of Principals of Colleges
AS	Advanced Supplementary level
ATA	Approved training agent
ATC	Adult training centre
ATM	Approved training manager
ATO	Approved training organisation
AUT	Association of University Teachers
B.Ed	Bachelor of Education
BEC	Business Education Council
BTEC	Business and Technology Education Council
CAST	Curriculum Advice and Support Team (Scotland)
CATS	Credit Accumulation and Transfer Scheme
CBI	Confederation of British Industry
CCC	Central Curriculum Council (Scotland)
CEDEFOP	European Centre for the Development of Vocational Training
CEF	Colleges' Employers' Forum
CEO	Chief education officer
CFE	College of further education
CGLI	City and Guilds of London Institute
CIPFA	Chartered Institute of Public Finance and Accountancy
CITB	Construction Industry Training Board
CMIS	College management information system
CNAA	Council for National Academic Awards
COIC	Careers and occupational information centre
COMETT	Community Action Programme for Education and Training for Technology (EEC)
CPVE	Certificate of Pre-vocational Education
CSE	Certificate of Secondary Education (before GCSE)
CSYS	Certificate of Sixth Year Studies
CTC	City technology college
CVCP	Committee of Vice Chancellors and Principals
DE	Department of Employment

DED	Department of Economic Development (Northern Ireland)
DELTA	Developing European Learning through Technological Advance
DENI	Department of Education, Northern Ireland
DES	Department of Education and Science (forerunner of DfE)
DFE	Department for Education (formerly Department of Education and Science)
DG	Directorate General (EEC)
DoE	Department of the Environment
DTI	Department of Trade and Industry
DVE	Diploma of Vocational Education (CGLI)
EA	Employment Action
EEC	European Economic Community
EFL	English as a foreign language
EIS	Educational Institute of Scotland
EITB	Engineering Industry Training Board (now EnTra)
ELB	Education and Library Board (Northern Ireland)
EnTra	Engineering Training Association
ERA	1988 Education Reform Act
ERASMUS	European Action Scheme for the Mobility of University Students (EEC)
ESF	European Social Fund
ESG	Education Support Grant
ESL	English as a second language
ESOL	English for speakers of other languages
ET	Employment Training
FAST	Forum for Access Studies
FE	Further education
FEFC	Further Education Funding Council
FEFCW	Further Education Funding Council for Wales
FESC	Further Education Staff College (now The Staff College)
FESR	Further Education Statistical Return
FEU	Further Education Unit
GCE	General Certificate of Education (before GCSE)
GCSE	General Certificate of Secondary Education
GNVQ	General National Vocational Qualification
GSVQ	General Scottish Vocational Qualification
GTA	Group training association
GTC	General Teaching Council (Scotland)
HE	Higher education
HEFCE	Higher Education Funding Council – England
HEFCS	Higher Education Funding Council – Scotland
HEFCW	Higher Education Funding Council – Wales
HMI	Her Majesty's Inspectorate
HNC	Higher National Certificate
IB	International Baccalaureate
ILB	Industry lead body
ILEA	Inner London Education Authority (now abolished)
ILTS	Industrial Language Training Service
INTO	Irish National Teachers Organisation

ITB	Industrial training board
ITEC	Information technology centre
ITT	Initial teacher training
LEA	Local education authority
LEC	Local enterprise company (Scotland's version of TECs)
LEN	Local employer network
LIB	Lead industry body
MSC	Manpower Services Commission (before Training, Enterprise and Education Directorate of the Department of the Employment)
NAB	National Advisory Body for Public Sector Higher Education in England and Wales (forerunner of PCFC, now in HEFC)
NAFE	Non-advanced further education
NAHT	National Association of Headteachers
NAS/UWT	National Association of Schoolmasters/Union of Women Teachers.
NATFHE	National Association of Teachers in Further and Higher Education
NBHS	National Bureau for Handicapped Students
NCC	National Curriculum Council
NCITO	National Council of Industrial Training Organisations
NCVQ	National Council for Vocational Qualifications
NEC	National Extension College
NFER	National Foundation for Educational Research
NIACE	National Institute for Adult Continuing Education
NITA	Northern Ireland Training Authority
NROVA	National record of vocational achievement
NSTO	Non-statutory training organisation
NTTF	National Training Task Force
NUS	National Union of Students
NUT	National Union of Teachers
NVQ	National Vocational Qualification
OC	Open College
OLF	Open Learning Federation (was Open Polytechnic)
ONC	Ordinary National Certificate
OU	Open University
PAT	Professional Association of Teachers
PCEF	Polytechnics and Colleges Employers' Forum
PCFC	Polytechnics and Colleges Funding Council (now in HEFC)
PGCE	Postgraduate Certificate of Education
PICKUP	Professional, Industrial and Commercial Updating
QTS	Qualified teacher status
RAC	Regional advisory council for further education
RCB	Regional Curriculum Base
REPLAN	A former DFE programme to promote the development of education opportunities for the adult unemployed
RET	Record of education and training (SCOTVEC)
RSA	Royal Society of Arts Examinations Board
RVQ	Review of vocational qualifications
SAMI	System for accessing modular information (SCOTVEC)
SCCF	Scottish College Councils' Forum
SCDC	Schools Curriculum Development Council

SCE	Scottish Certificate of Education
SCOTBEC	Scottish Business Education Council
SCOTEC	Scottish Technician Education Council
SCOTVEC	Scottish Vocational Education Council
SCRAC	Standing Conference of Regional Advisory Councils
SCRE	Scottish Council for Research in Education
SDA	Scottish Development Agency
SE	Scottish Enterprise
SEAC	School Examinations and Assessment Council
SEB	Scottish Examination Board
SED	Scottish Education Department
SFEU	Scottish Further Education Unit
SHA	Secondary Heads Association
SIACE	Scottish Institute of Adult and Continuing Education
SSFE	Scottish School of Further Education
SSR	Student:staff ratio
STA	Skills Training Agency
SVQ	Scottish Vocational Qualification
SWAP	Scottish Wider Access Programme
TA	Training Agency (now TEED)
TAP	Training access point
TCA	Tertiary Colleges Association
TEC	Technician Education Council (until 1983)
TEC	Training and enterprise council
TEED	Training, Enterprise and Education Directorate of the Department of Employment
TES	Times Educational Supplement
TFW	Training For Work (formerly Employment Training)
TNPU	TECs' and National Providers' Unit
TOC	Training occupation classification
TSAS	Training Standards Advisory Service
TSI	Training Standards Inspector
TUC	Trades Union Congress
TVEI	Technical and Vocational Education Initiative
UDACE	Unit for the Development of Adult Continuing Education (part of FEU from 1992).
UFC	Universities Funding Council (now in HEFC)
UGC	University Grants Committee (the forerunner of UFC, now in HEFC)
UK	United Kingdom
UTU	Ulster Teachers Union
UVP	Unified Vocational Preparation (became part of the Youth Training Scheme, later Youth Training)
VET	Vocational Education and Training
WAB	Wales Advisory Body for Local Authority Higher Education (now HEFC Wales)
WEA	Workers' Education Association
WJEC	Welsh Joint Education Committee
WOED	Welsh Office Education Department

WRFE	Work-related further education
WRNAFE	Work-related non-advanced further education (shortened to WRFE)
YOP	Youth Opportunities Programme (became part of the Youth Training Scheme, later Youth Training)
YT	Youth Training
YTP	Youth Training Programme (Northern Ireland)
YTS	Youth Training Scheme

Appendix 4
The United Kingdom and its education system

The United Kingdom (UK) is the shortened form of the full name, the United Kingdom of Great Britain and Northern Ireland. It consists of four main parts: England, Wales, Scotland (which are parts of the larger island of Great Britain), and Northern Ireland. The people of the United Kingdom are known as the British.

The name Britain is also commonly used to describe the whole of the United Kingdom. It was first used from the year 1800 to describe all the islands in the British Isles, including the whole of Ireland. From 1922, 26 of the 32 counties in Ireland broke away from the United Kingdom to become an independent state, retaining the name of Ireland but officially called Eire. The six remaining counties in Ulster stayed in the United Kingdom to form the province of Northern Ireland.

The constituent parts of the United Kingdom vary greatly both in area and population. England is the largest with a population of more than 47 million people living in an area covering over 130,000 square kilometres situated in the south of Great Britain. The Principality of Wales (Cymru) is situated in the extreme west of the central southern portion of Great Britain in an area of 20,000 square kilometres and has 2.8 million inhabitants, of whom about 18 per cent speak Welsh. Wales was annexed by the English in 1284, and formally united to England by the Acts of Union in 1536 and 1542.

The Kingdom of Scotland forms the northern part of Great Britain and includes the islands of the Inner and Outer Hebrides, Orkney, Shetland and many others. Scotland has just over five million inhabitants dispersed over 78,000 square kilometres. About 82,000 people, mainly in the Highlands and Islands region, speak, read and write Gaelic, the language of the Scottish Celts. Scotland was united with England in 1603 when the king of Scotland, James VI, became James I of Great Britain. The 1707 Act of Union united the Scottish and English Parliaments.

Northern Ireland is made up of six counties and has 1.6 million people in 14,000 square kilometres. It was given its own separate Parliament and executive government in 1921. Since the division of Ireland there has been sectarian conflict between the Protestant majority, most of whom wish to continue links with Great Britain, and the minority Catholic group, many of whom would like to unite with Eire – a Catholic country. (Of those professing a religious denomination in Northern Ireland at the census in 1981, 46 per cent said they were Protestants and 28 per cent Catholic.) The United Kingdom Government abolished the Northern Ireland Parliament in 1973, after continuing conflict between the two communities, but transferred some of its legislative functions to a Northern Ireland Assembly and Executive. The Executive proved unpopular and within a few months direct rule from London was introduced (in 1974). Temporary arrangements were made for Northern Ireland to be governed directly by the Secretary of State for Northern Ireland. These arrangements persisted until 1982, when elections were held for a new, devolved Ulster Assembly. The Assembly lasted only until 1986 before it was disbanded in favour of direct rule again.

Associated with the United Kingdom, but separate from it, are the islands of the British seas which are classed as Crown dependencies. The Isle of Man is in the Irish Sea, equidistant from England, Scotland and Ireland. It has its own legal and administrative arrangements for a population of 65,000 people. The Channel Islands, off the north west coast of France, have their own legislative assemblies and systems of local administration. The official languages used in the Channel Islands are English and French, with English being the language in daily use. The populations of the two main islands are 77,000 in Jersey and 56,000 in Guernsey.

The United Kingdom is a member of the European Community (EC) and, in particular, the European Economic Community (EEC) which it joined in 1973. The Community is currently made up of 12 countries – Belgium, Denmark, Germany, France, Ireland (Eire), Greece, Italy, Luxembourg, the Netherlands, Portugal, Spain and the United Kingdom.

The main objectives of the EEC,, as explained in Article Two of the Treaty of Rome, are to promote throughout the Community a harmonious development of economic activities, a continuous and balanced expansion, an increase in stability, an accelerated raising of the standard of living and closer relations between states belonging to it.

The directly elected European Parliament has limited formal powers but considerable influence. The executive of the EEC is the Commission, which is independent of the constituent national governments. The Commission is responsible for developing policies, for implementing the treaties and decisions of the Council of Ministers and for detailed administration of the Community. Major legislation is enacted by the Council of Ministers. Legislation can be in the form of directly binding Regulations; Directives which bind the member states on the timetable and result but not the means of implementation; and Decisions which are specifically targeted to individuals or member states. In addition there are other devices, which are often used in the areas of education and training, but which are only recommendations to member states. The Commission is made up of 22 Directorates General (DGs) with most education and training coming under Directorate General V – Employment, Social Affairs, Education and Vocational Training.

The United Kingdom does not have a written constitution but relies instead on a combination of statute, common law and convention. The United Kingdom is technically ruled by a constitutional monarch but is effectively governed by Ministers of the Crown in the name of the Queen, who is head of both the state and the Government. The chief minister is the Prime Minister. The key parts of Government are the legislature, the executive and the judiciary. Parliament is the supreme legislature; it can pass laws covering the United Kingdom as a whole or any part of it separately.

Parliament consists of a directly elected House of Commons and an unelected House of Lords, the majority of whom are hereditary but some are life peers. As well as passing legislation, Parliament provides the means of carrying on the work of Government by voting taxation measures and scrutinising Government policy and administration. The executive consists of Her Majesty's Government, which is the Cabinet and other Ministers. The judiciary is independent of the executive and legislature.

Ultimate responsibility for education in the United Kingdom lies with the United Kingdom Government. Different Government Ministers look after education in the four parts of the United Kingdom. Because of its much greater population, England has a separate Secretary of State for Education who is a member of the Prime Minister's Cabinet. The Secretary of State for Education reports to the House of Commons on English (and often Welsh) education matters, or via a delegated structure through a Minister of State or a junior Minister with a range of responsibilities.

For Wales, Scotland and Northern Ireland, there is no separate post of Secretary of State for Education. Instead, each of these parts of the United Kingdom has a single Secretary of State as its chief Minister. The Secretaries of State for Wales, Scotland and Northern Ireland are Cabinet members and have responsibility for the whole range of governmental functions. Education is only one of these functions and is usually part of the responsibility of a junior Minister, who is not of Cabinet rank. The three Secretaries of State report to the House of Commons, themselves, or through junior Ministers.

The four Secretaries of State who are responsible for education in the United Kingdom are supported by Departments of Education, which are mainly concerned with the formulation of policy. In England, the Department for Education (DFE) has few executive functions and has no general remit to administer schools or further education colleges directly. In Wales, Scotland and Northern Ireland the Education Departments are part of the Welsh Office, the Scottish Office and the Northern Ireland Office respectively.

The status of the national Education Departments has grown in the 20th century as the size and esteem of the education service have grown. In

England, a full-scale Ministry of Education was first created by the 1944 Education Act, which also extended secondary education to all children. A Department of Education and Science, headed by a Secretary of State, was established in 1964, when responsibilities were added for scientific research and the universities. The title was changed to the Department for Education in 1992 when the responsibility for science was removed.

The Department for Education in England is responsible for the broad allocation of educational resources, for standards and guidelines on education buildings, for the supply and training of teachers and lecturers and their superannuation arrangements in England and Wales. The Department also controls some grants earmarked for specific purposes. Although a major part of the money spent on education comes from national taxes, which are controlled by central Government, the local authorities are responsible for most of the spending on buildings and running costs of maintained schools. The further and higher education funding councils control spending in the further education colleges sector and the higher education institutions sector.

The Welsh Office Education Department (WOED) has responsibility for schools, further and higher education, youth and community services and adult education. The DfE still holds the overall remit for the research councils, mandatory and postgraduate awards to students, and the pay, superannuation and qualifications of teachers and lecturers. The Welsh Office Education Department is headed by a senior civil servant. The general supervision of the Scottish national system of education, except for the universities, is the responsibility of the Secretary of State for Scotland, acting through the Scottish Education Department (SED).

The Department of Education for Northern Ireland (DENI) is a separate part of the Northern Ireland Office which carries out its functions under the control of the Secretary of State for Northern Ireland. The Department of Education is responsible for central policy coordination, legislation and financial control of the education and library services. Local education and library boards do not raise moneys through local taxes; most of their finance comes through the Department of Education Northern Ireland which plays a greater role at local level than the Education Departments on the mainland. DENI's full range of responsibilities includes the development of primary, secondary, further and higher education, community and adult education, special education, overseeing the five education and library boards, teacher training, teachers' and lecturers' salaries and superannuation, examinations, the arts, libraries, youth services, sport and recreation, community services and facilities, and the improvement of community relations. The Department works closely with other Government departments, particularly the Department of Economic Development (DED) on the Youth Training, and with the Northern Ireland Training Authority (NITA) and the Department of Agriculture for work with colleges providing agricultural education and training. DENI also funds a wide range of community-based activities.

Secretaries of State and their Education Departments have a duty to promote the education of the people of the United Kingdom and the progressive development of institutions devoted to that purpose. They must ensure that local education authorities under their control and direction put into practice the national policy to provide a varied and comprehensive service in every area. In 1988 the Government considerably strengthened its powers over the educational functions of local councils and the process of encouraging schools to opt out of local authority control has continued in the 1990s.

One of the underlying assumptions on which education in the United Kingdom has been based is that of a nationally organised education service which is locally administered. In the past the role of the Government was to enact new laws or issue guidance on the organisation of education, but it traditionally had little to say about the nature of the curriculum. It was only at the end of the 1980s that the Conservative Government decided to establish a national curriculum for the compulsory part of schooling in Great Britain. While much of the responsibility for schools has been given to local education authorities, Secretaries of State have the power to intervene if it can be demonstrated to their satisfaction that an individual local education authority has failed to discharge a duty required by Parliament, or if it has acted unreasonably with regard to the powers given to it or in fulfilling the duties required of it. The removal of, first, the polytechnics and colleges of higher education from local authorities at the end of the 1980s and then the creation of a national further education sector from 1993 continued the weakening of the local education authority system, which had been dominant during the 20th century, and signalled a move to the 19th century model of large numbers of institutions each with its own controlling governing body.

The United Kingdom has national inspectors of education, called Her Majesty's Inspectorate (HMI). The idea of an independent inspection body goes back a long way, the first HM Inspectorate dating back to 1839. The Inspectorate is the professional arm of the four national Education Departments and advises Ministers and their Departments on the quality of educational provision. Its main function is to assess current standards and to monitor trends in schools and colleges based largely on inspection visits. These inspections range from one inspector sampling one institution to large scale visits of groups of inspectors looking at major areas of educational provision on a national basis. The visits are written up in HMI reports which are published and form part of the database from which government policy is developed.

The advisory role of HM Inspectorate is not confined to the Education Departments but also operates with local authorities and their institutions, arising from HMI assessments of standards and trends both locally and nationally. The Inspectorate also has a regulatory role in that it advises Government about good practice, promising developments and observed weaknesses. The Inspectorate has a quality improvement function through its advice and assistance to those in education institutions, its contributions to training, its publications and its assessor role on bodies such as examining and validating boards.

Government dissatisfaction with HMI has meant a move in the early 1990s to privatise some of the functions of HMI and to cut its size. In 1992, the process of setting up privatised teams of people to inspect schools from 1993 was begun, in order to carry out the programme of the statutory four-yearly inspections. The FE funding councils have their own inspectors.

The idea of local government is strongly rooted in the United Kingdom. It has been accepted that while national government has the right to lay down policy guidelines on education matters, it has been the prerogative of local government, in conjunction with education institutions, to say how it should be delivered. Local government is based on the local council, consisting of councillors elected for a fixed renewable period, which determines policy on a range of local issues.

During the 1980s the Government sought to change the balance of power between national and local governments in favour of national government by reducing the powers of local councils and placing restrictions on the way they were governed. This continued into the 1990s with the removal of FE and sixth form colleges from the LEAs in 1993, after institutions of higher education had been detached in 1989. Further plans to promote a larger number of opted-out schools to be funded by a separate body could lead to a vastly reduced LEA role. It is worth reflecting on how local government originally came to be involved in providing education in order to put into context the current debates about the reduced power and influence of local education authorities.

Local level administration was created as part of the growing strength of municipal organisation in British towns and cities in the last half of the 19th century. County councils and county borough councils were established by the Local Government Act of 1888. The idea of a county or county borough council acting as an education authority came from a recommendation of the Royal Commission on Secondary Education in 1895. Prior to this, the national Education Department was responsible for a fragmented system of 2,568 School Boards, together with 14,238 schools which were independent of school board control. Local education authorities came into being at the turn of the century after the passing of the 1902 Education Act which transferred powers from the large number of school boards to a smaller number of education authorities based on local councils.

Local authorities were responsible for building schools and colleges, employing staff and laying down guidelines for what school pupils should be taught and what range of courses should be offered in colleges. Schools and colleges then worked within the local framework to deliver the curriculum. Local authorities have been responsible for up to 85 per cent of the total public spending on education but this is diminishing. Each local authority with educational responsibilities is required by law to appoint an education committee which it must consult before exercising its educational powers. Most education committees contain teachers as co-opted members, as well as industrialists, church representatives and parents, but elected councillors must comprise at least two-thirds of the membership. The day-to-day administration of education in each local education authority is the responsibility of the chief education officer (CEO) (sometimes called the director of education). If the rate at which schools opt out accelerates in the 1990s, the LEAs may be wound up or left with a few residual responsibilities.

As outlined earlier, recent Government legislation has tilted the balance of these arrangements in that it has considerably reduced the influence of local education authorities. The Government now has much greater powers to intervene at local level. There has always been friction between national government policy-making and local implementation, especially when different political parties are in control at national and local levels. The Government has stated that it had to increase its central powers so as to be able to devolve decision-making to local schools and colleges because local authorities could not be trusted to do so. It believed that increased parental choice would allow market forces to operate to the benefit of the more successful institutions. The Government wants educational administration to be more varied and flexible and dependent on individual initiatives from schools.

The number and size of local councils in England were largely determined in 1974 when local government was extensively reorganised. This rationalisation created a two-tier system of counties at the top level and district councils below. Around 1,400 councils in England and Wales were reduced to just over 450. A similar reorganisation in Scotland in 1975 produced nine regional and 53 district authorities, together with three authorities in the Western and Northern Isles. In England there have been further changes with the scrapping of the metropolitan county councils and the Greater London Council. The **Education Reform Act** abolished (in 1990) the Inner London Education Authority (ILEA), a directly elected LEA covering the 12 boroughs in the central area of London.

Not all local councils are education authorities. There are currently 97 LEAs in England, eight Welsh county LEAs, 12 Scottish regional education authorities and five education and library boards in Northern Ireland.

The local education authority must work within the legal framework laid down by the various Education Acts and the Secretary of State's regulations. The LEA is responsible for providing and maintaining the state sector schools in its area. It also recruits and pays the salaries of teachers who work in them and provides educational buildings, materials, equipment and back-up and advisory services.

As public bodies established by statute, local education authorities are bound by a major legal principle – *ultra vires*. In effect this means that LEAs can only act within the powers given them by national legislation. If an LEA cannot show that its actions are derived from statutorily defined powers, it is acting *ultra vires* and a court of law can order it to stop. This is not always easy to prove in practice, but it could result in councillors being surcharged for unauthorised expenditure after an investigation by the Audit Commission – an independent body appointed by national government.

Although some English county councils are large, there is nothing to parallel the American or West German systems of state government. The only regional level of educational organisation is that related to further education through the regional committees of the Further Education Funding Council and the non-statutory regional advisory councils for FE (RACs).

The national network of RACs was set up as a consequence of a report on Higher Technological Education in 1945, but three of the RACs (Yorkshire, West Midlands and Wales) were established before the Second World War. There are nine RACs in England and the Welsh Joint Education Committee acts as an RAC in Wales. The councils used to be financed by contributions from local authorities within the relevant area, but this role was passed to colleges after 1993.

The role of RACs has altered over their lifetimes. With the removal of FE colleges from LEAs, the much-reduced RACs now tend to concentrate on particular aspects of the service. Typical areas of work have been the in-service training of teachers, industrial training and vocational education, collaboration with the TECs and the Department of Employment, agricultural education, regionally-based examinations and curriculum development.

The Welsh Joint Education Committee has more breadth than the English RACs in that it is a statutory body, with powers arising from the executive responsibilities given to joint education committees by the 1944 Education Act. The Welsh body contains representatives of all the eight Welsh LEAs, together with members of the teaching profession, industry and the University of Wales. It is the only RAC which also acts as a GCSE examining body as well as being a regional examining body for technical and commercial examinations.

The 1988 Education Reform Act and the 1992 Further and Higher Education Acts created uncertainty about the future role of the RACs. Higher education course approval was abolished at regional level. The work of co-ordinating the planning of further education, that of higher education which remains in colleges, and some in-service teacher training was removed in 1993 when the LEAs lost responsibility for further education. It remains to be seen if they will survive.

Index

A

academic board 142

academic education 5, 10, 44

academic research 220

academic students 69-70

academic/vocational divide 80-1

access courses 75, 88-91, 156

accountability, in schools 233

accreditation 190

accreditation of prior learning 9, 50, 60

administrative staff 143

adult education 10, 11, 24, 82-94

adult education centres 83

adult education courses 87-8

Adult Literacy and Basic Skills Unit 94

adult training 205-11

age profile, of lecturing staff 148

agricultural colleges 2

Annual Monitoring Survey 128-9

annual planning framework 112

annual review system 108

apprentice training 5, 19, 168

apprenticeships 4, 166

approved training centres 52, 54, 57, 198-9

art & design colleges 2

art & design courses 18

Assisted Places Scheme 229

Associated Examining Board 74

Association for Colleges 138

Association for Principals of Sixth Form Colleges 149

Association of Colleges for Further and Higher Education 138

Association of College Management 150

Association of Principals of Colleges 150

Association of Teachers and Lecturers 238

Astra Training Services 176

attendance modes 34-5

attrition rates 4

auditing 122-3

B

basic skills education 84, 91-2

binary line 220
　abolition 214

boards of management (Scotland) 32

Business & Technology Education Council 38, 52-4
　courses 213

business courses 37, 162

Business Improvement Initiative 191

C

capital funds 127, 128

Career Development Loans 182

careers guidance 194

careers service 163-4

caring courses 18

catering staff 143

Central Training Council 167

Certificate of Pre-Vocational Education 45, 63-4

chambers of commerce 179

charitable status 29

City & Guilds of London Institute 3, 39, 54-6, 80

city technology colleges 232

college boundaries 154, 212

college cultures 86, 140

College of Preceptors 239

colleges of advanced technology 219

Colleges' Employers' Forum 149

colleges of further education see further education colleges

commercial activities 22

community colleges 10, 11, 16, 85, 156

community demand 10-11

Community Education Council 94

community education service 16, 85

Community Industry 203

Community Programme 167

community schools 83

compacts 68

competition 18, 76

Comptroller and Auditor General 122

computing courses 37

Confederation of British Industry 189, 194

construction courses 37, 40

Consultative Committee on the Curriculum 73

core funding 127

core skills 45, 51, 52, 60

corporate status 22

Council for National Academic Awards 20, 214, 223-4

counselling and guidance services 86

county colleges 19

course fees 87

course provision
  BTEC 53
  modular 50
  post-16 62-6

courses
  funding 40-1
  gender stereotyping 36, 67
  subject areas 37-8
  validation 223-4

creche facilities 86

credit accumulation 224

Credit Accumulation and Transfer Scheme 224

credits 9, 49, 55-6, 59, 164, 194-5

cross-college posts 143-4

Crown dependencies 260

Curriculum Advice and Support Team 116

curriculum bodies 45-6
  see also Further Education Unit

curriculum development 114
  in Northern Ireland 236
  in Scotland 235
  see also National Curriculum

D

day continuation schools 19

daytime release courses 4

Dearing Report 236

delegated funding 125

demographic change effects 237

Department of Economic Development (N.I.) 170, 175, 202

Department for Education 205,261,262
    further education planning 106-7
Department of Education (N.I.) 262
Department of Social Security 91
development plans 6, 223
Diploma of Vocational Education 45,
    64
disabled students 95
distance learning 86
diversity
    of students 39
    of vocational provision 10

E

Education Act 1944 6, 19
Education Act 1981 45
Education Reform Act 1988
    6-7, 14,20-1, 98,106-7, 212
Education Support Grant 124
education system 259-67
    comparison with competitors 6
    see also further education colleges;
    schools
Educational Institute of Scotland 150,
    239
educational institutions,maintained 7, 8
educational qualifications, of
    workforce 163
employed status, for YTs 198
employers
    local networks 179
    private training 181-2
    training partnerships 68, 165, 210
Employment Action 208
Employment Department 23, 68, 105,
    163, 168, 183, 191
employment sectors 160-2
employment service 167
Employment Training 5, 86, 91, 169,
    206-9

engineering courses 18, 37, 162, 183
Engineering Industry Training Board
    174
English as a foreign language 17
English for speakers of other
    languages 84, 92, 209
Enterprise Allowance Scheme 177
Enterprise Initiative 168, 224
EnTra 174
equal opportunities policies 9, 95
ethnic origin 36-7
    of lecturing staff 148
European community 260
    trained teachers 238
European Social Fund 86
evening classes 4, 83, 85
examining and validating bodies 3, 9,
    38-9, 45-6, 51, 97
examining boards 71, 74

F

financial management 125-6
    of schools 234
flexible learning 17
formula funding 109, 126
    capital funds 127
formula-based funding process 22
foundation learning targets 190, 193
franchising arrangements 156, 213
French Baccalaureate 76
full-time students 7, 34
funding 7-8, 25, 27-8, 100, 106, 124-8
    growth 113, 120
    higher education 214-15
    see also further education funding
    councils
Funding Council for Scotland 118
funding eligibility criteria 41

Further Education Act 1985 22

Further & Higher Education Act 1992
7-8, 9, 14, 23, 40, 87, 98, 109, 121

further education
definitions 7, 21, 212
diversification 10
division of responsibilities 130
legal basis 18-32
maintained 8
see also students

further education colleges 2-3, 9-15
access for disabled 95-6
adult education 85-91
commercial activities 22
historical development 3-8
income 123-4
independence from LEA 104, 109
relationship with TECs 178

further education corporations 29-31,
121, 131-2
strategic planning 112

further education courses 8, 9-11, 12,
27
adult 84, 87-8
categorisation 212

further education funding councils 8,
25, 87, 104-5, 109-11, 118-21

Further Education Funding Council 2,
25, 98-9, 110, 118-21, 126-7
funding criteria 41

Further Education Funding Council
for Wales 26, 110, 126, 127-8

further education institutions 2
diversity 42-5
stratification 218

Further Education Lecturers National
Section 150

Further Education Statistical Record
128

further education teacher training 145

further education trends 113

Further Education Unit 94, 114-15
post-16 report 62-3

G

gender balance
in further education 36
of lecturing staff 148
of YT schemes 197

General Certificate of Education
Advanced levels 5, 10, 14, 39, 70,
73-5

General Certificate of Education
Advanced Supplementary levels
76-9

General Certificate of Secondary
Education 39, 71

General National Vocational
Qualifications 39, 46, 51

General Scottish Vocational
Qualifications 60

general teaching council 239

General Teaching Council for
Scotland 239

German Abitur 76

governing bodies 31, 43, 108, 126,
130-2, 134
composition 136-7
legal liability 135-6
of schools 234
of sixth form colleges 133-4

government policy 44-5, 195, 222-3
see also White Papers

government training centres 4, 155,
166

governor training 137-8

grading systems 75

grant-maintained schools 229, 232-3

grants 24
higher education 225
to universities 218

group awards 58

Group Training Association 192

guilds 166

H

Her Majesty's Inspectorate 236, 263-4

Higginson Committee 75

higher education 155-6, 212, 213, 214
 funding 214, 218, 225
 funding cutbacks 121
 growth 216-20
 selection devices 74-5, 88-91

higher education courses 44,213-4

Higher Education Funding Council
 for England 22, 118, 155, 214-15

Higher Education Funding Council
 for Scotland 215

Higher Education Quality Council
 224

higher education students 215-6,221-2

Higher National Certificate 4

Home Office 92

hotel & catering courses 37

Howie Committee 60

I

Imperial College of Science and
 Technology 54

income sources 123-4

income support rules 91
 and ET 207
 and YT 200-1

independence 20, 29, 104

independent further education
 institutions 16-17

independent schools 229-30

independent university 218

Industrial Language Training Service
 209

industrial training boards 5,155, 166,
 173-5

industry lead bodies 48, 172, 199

Information Technology Centres 197

information technology courses 40

initial training 200

inspection teams, privatisation 264

inspectors, further education 264

institutes of higher education 83

integration, of special needs students
 96-7, 101

International Baccalaureate 81

Investors in People 182

Irish National Teachers' Organisation
 238

J

job market 160-2

JobCentres 168

Jobplan Workshops 208

job-related training 183-7

L

labour market
 influence on vocational provision
 10-11, 23, 158-9, 162-3
 information dissemination 191

labour market trends 159-61

Lancashire County Council, speech
 therapy case 102

learning difficulties 26, 45, 96
 definitions 98-9

learning targets 190

lecturing staff 96, 147-8
 appraisal 151-2
 conditions of service 146-7
 see also part-time lecturing staff

legal liability 135-6

legislation 18-32, 266
 governing bodies 130-1

special needs provision 98-9
  training 166, 173

leisure-time occupation 21, 88

life skills 96

literacy & numeracy courses 84, 91

loan defaults 226

loan schemes 182, 225-6

local education authorities 104, 264-5
  adult education services 85, 87
  development plans 6
  further education planning 106-8
  loss of control and power 8, 20,
  22-3, 265
  responsibilities 23-4, 228, 265-6
  schools administration 229

local employer networks 104, 179

local enterprise councils 170, 178,
  202

Local Government Management
  Board 149

local government 264
  reorganisation 265

local needs 6, 10-11, 23, 105, 108,
  112

London
  adult education participation 88

M

maintained schools 229, 230

management information systems 129

management information systems co-
  ordinator 143

management spine 143

management team 139

management training 115, 205

Manpower Services Commission 6,
  61,63, 105, 106, 167-8
  training initiatives 188-9, 205-6

manufacturing companies decline 10,
  161

marginal funding 127

market-led structures 11-12, 18

marketing officer 143

maths courses 37

matrix structure 142

mature students 70, 74, 83, 84, 86,
  222
  see also adult education

mechanics institutes 3, 82

mergers 2, 111-12, 140

mission statement 42, 112

mixed economy programme 70

moderators 52

modular courses 39, 58, 67

monitoring 128-9

N

National Advisory Body 220

National Advisory Council for
  Industry and Commerce 218

National Advisory Council for the
  Youth Service in England and
  Wales 204

National Association of Headteachers
  238

National Association of
  Schoolmasters/Union of Women
  Teachers 238

National Association of Teachers in
  Further and Higher Education 149-
  50

National Audit Office 122

National Bureau for Students with
  Disabilities 100

National Council of Industrial
  Training Organisations 173

National Council for Vocational
  Qualifications 9, 46, 47-8, 97

National Curriculum 67, 72, 235-6

National Curriculum Council 67, 235

National Development Prospectus 106

National Economic Development
Office 201

National Education Guidance 94

National Extension College 17

National Foundation for Educational
Research 116-17

National Institute of Adult Continuing
Education 93

National Joint Council for Further
Education 143, 149, 150

National Record of Vocational
Achievement 46, 49-50

National Training Awards 182

National Training Task Force 177,
189

National Union of Teachers 238

National Vocational Qualifications
46, 48-9, 168, 189-90
for special needs students 97

needs analysis 112

new universities 90, 155, 217, 218

non-academic employees 143

non-advanced further education 212

non-statutory training bodies 172-3

Northern Ireland 74, 155, 259-60
education funding 118
education service 231-2, 236
further education colleges 2, 20-1,
109, 112, 159
further education salaries 149
higher education 215, 221
industrial training boards 175
YT programme 202-3

Northern Ireland Further Education
Negotiating Committee 149

Northern Ireland Training Authority
171

O

'Objective 3' 188, 205, 206

occupational competence 199
assessment 199-20

occupational groupings 160

Occupational Standards Councils 172

'one-line' budget 18

Open College 17

open learning 17, 86

Open University 217, 224
students 222

Open University Validating Service
217-18

operating statement 112

Ordinary National Certificate 4

organisational structures 142-3

P

parental choice 265

part-time lecturing staff 86, 147

part-time students 12, 91

participation rates
academic students 69
ethnic origin 36-7
factors influencing 91
gender 36
mode of attendance 35-6
schools 230

pay structures 18, 148-9

performance indicators, in higher
education 220

physically disabled 95-6

planned failure rate 74, 78

planning, of further education 104-13,
266-7

polytechnics 20, 155, 219

Polytechnics & Colleges Funding
Council 7, 22, 118, 220, 222

population, of United Kingdom 259

post-16 provision 5-6, 13-14, 44-5, 62-6, 227
   choices 193

pre-vocational students 61-3

principal 105
   responsibilities 139, 150-1

prison education 92

private colleges 2

private sector training 155, 165, 181-2, 205

Professional, Industrial & Commercial Updating Courses 84, 115, 205, 209-10

Professional Association of Teachers 238

professional associations 150
   examinations 213

public schools 229

Q

qualified teacher status 238

quality 28
   of training 171-2

Quality Assessment Committee 28-9

quality assessment units, higher education funding councils 214

quality assurance systems 52, 149, 236

R

recession effects 5, 7, 37, 45, 61, 160
   on training demand 176

Record of Education & Training 59

REPLAN courses 84, 115, 205, 210-11

regional advisory councils 266

regional planning, in further education 107, 111, 266

research, in higher education 220

residential colleges 84

Revenue Support Grants 124

Robbins Report 219, 222

Royal Society of Arts 3, 39, 56-7

Russell Committee 83

S

safety officer 143

salary scales 143, 238

SAMI 59

school closures 237

school consortia 14

schools 42, 156, 227-33
   special needs provision 100-1
   surplus places 237

Schools Curriculum and Assessment Authority 67, 235

Schools Examinations & Assessment Council 71

Scotland 259
   adult education 94
   education system 230-1, 234-5
   funding methodology 127
   further education colleges 2
   further education programmes of learning 40
   group awards 58
   higher education 21-2, 155, 221
   legislation 23, 31-2
   local enterprise councils 178, 202
   PICKUP 210
   school boards 234
   YTS 196

Scottish Certificate of Education 39, 72-3

Scottish College Councils' Forum 149

Scottish Council for Research in Education 117

Scottish Development Agency 170

Scottish Education Department 7, 24, 32, 221, 222, 261

Scottish Enterprise 170

Scottish Examinations Board 73

Scottish Further and Higher Education Association 150

Scottish Further Education Unit 116

Scottish Higher Grade 13, 14, 79-80, 213

Scottish National Certificate 58-9, 190, 213

Scottish Vocational Education Council 38-9, 46, 57-9

Scottish Vocational Qualifications 59-60

secondary education 227
    quality assurance 236-7

Secondary Heads Association 238

secondary modern schools 3

secondary schools 25, 227

secretarial courses 162

self-employment 161

sensitivity analysis 112

service industries 10, 160-1

sixth form colleges 2, 6, 10, 13, 14-15, 69, 99-100, 112
    governance 133-4

SKILL 100

skill shortages 5, 161, 182-7

Skillcentres 166, 176

skills training 180-92

Skills Training Agency 176

Small Firms Service 177

social security, and YT 200-1

special educational needs provision 8, 45, 95-102, 112, 200

speech therapy 102

sponsorship 24

staff appraisal 151-2

Staff College 115-16

staff development officer 143

staff training 145

staffing 150-1

standards 46
    educational 236
    training programmes 190-1

Standards Programme 189-91, 199

Standing Committee for Continuing Education 224

statementing 99-100, 101

strategic management 140-1

strategic plans 109, 112, 141

student:staff ratios 129, 151

student attendance 2

student liaison officer 143

Student Loans Company 225-6

student recruitment 10, 143

student support services 86, 144

students 12, 34, 43-4
    annual allocations 108
    diversity 39
    ethnic minority 36-7
    statistics 84, 113
    target numbers 18
    see also academic students; full-time students; higher education students; part-time students; pre-vocational students; vocational students

subject-based programme areas 108

surplus school places 237

System for Assessing Modular Information 59

T

target numbers 18

Taylor Report 233

teacher training 237-8

teachers 236, 237-9

teaching standards 148

Teaching English as a Foreign Lanuage 57

Technical & Vocational Education Initiative 6, 23, 65-7, 168, 178, 228
and special needs students 98

technical colleges 4, 5, 11, 166

technical education 3-4, 219

technical schools 3, 227

technicians 143

Technological Baccalaureate 80

technological universities 219

TECs and National Providers Unit 179

tertiary colleges 6, 10, 12, 13, 15-16, 69-70
organisational structure 142

Tertiary Colleges Association 138

textile courses 18

three year plans 43, 106,112

Tomlinson committee 99

trades unions 149-50
criticism of ET 207
teaching 238

Training, Enterprise & Education Directorate 63, 169, 190, 191

training 21, 44, 165-6
costs 182
initiatives 188-91, 206-11
legislation 166
local advisory bodies 176-7
outcomes 199
quality 171-2
standards 190-1
statistics 180

Training Access Point 192

training agencies 155, 166-71

Training Agency 23, 42-3, 169

Training and Development Lead Body 190

training and employment schemes 5, 61

training and enterprise councils 106, 177-8, 202
training credits 194

Training Commission 168-9, 176, 177

training credits see credits

training data 180-1

Training for Work 91, 178, 208

Training Occupation Classification 105

training partnerships 68

training policy 166-81
in Northern Ireland 170-1, 175
in Scotland 170
in Wales 170

Training Standards Advisory Service 171

training targets 49, 190-1

transport 24

U

Ulster Teachers' Union 238

ultra vires 266

unemployment 5, 45, 86, 87, 205
REPLAN scheme 210-11

Unified Vocational Preparation programme 63, 196

Unit for the Development of Adult Continuing Education 93-4, 115

United States of America 68, 76

universities 90
ancient 216
new 217

Northern Ireland 221
technological 219

Universities Funding Council 220

University Council for the Education
of Teachers 239

University Grants Committee 218

university extra-mural studies
departments 83, 92

University Extension Movement 82

University of Wales 220-1

V

vocational A levels 39-40

vocational education 3, 5, 44, 58, 108,
154, 158-9, 167-8
see also Technical and Vocational
Education Initiative

vocational preparation courses 8

vocational qualifications 47

vocational students 47

vocational training 180-92
voluntary organisations, and adult
education 83

W

Wales 259
further education colleges 2, 112
higher education colleges 220-1
school pupils 230
tertiary colleges 12, 14
training policy 170
YTS 196

Warnock Committee 101

Welsh Development Agency 177

Welsh Higher Educational Funding
Council 221

Welsh Joint Education Committee
266

Welsh Office 170, 261
Education Department 262

West Germany 6

White Papers
education 66, 77, 233
employment 171-2, 177
further education 23, 80, 109, 195
higher education 214, 219, 220
training 42-3, 63-4, 66, 105, 193

women
in further education 36, 86, 113
in higher education 222
in workforce 36, 159

Work Experience on Employers'
Premises 196

Workers' Education Association 82,
83, 92-3

workforce 159

work-related further education 23, 52,
105-6, 112, 158, 168, 178
gender participation rates 36

Y

Youth Opportunities Programme 63,
196
in Northern Ireland 202

youth service 203-4

Youth Training 5, 155, 164, 178, 196-
202
placements 198

Youth Training Programme, Northern
Ireland 202

Youth Training Scheme 65,167, 195-6

youth unemployment 61